ENGLISH LITERATURE

OF THE

NINETEENTH CENTURY

ENGLISH LITERATURE

OF THE

NINETEENTH CENTURY

BY

REGINALD C. CHURCHILL

BOOKS FOR LIBRARIES PRESS
FREEPORT, NEW YORK

INTERNATIONAL STANDARD BOOK NUMBER:
0-8369-5594-3

LIBRARY OF CONGRESS CATALOG CARD NUMBER:
75-140351

PRINTED IN THE UNITED STATES OF AMERICA

PREFACE

THE nineteenth century is probably the most voluminous period in English literature, the period when the public for books of all kinds was growing rapidly and when the majority of our great publishing houses were coming into existence. To describe such a crowded period in a small space two methods are possible: the method of literary criticism, dividing the sheep from the goats—the sheep of one critical school being inevitably the goats of another—or the method of literary history, laying less stress on individual authors and more on the various movements of the time. This book comes into the second category, my object being, not so much to add to the existing critical material, as to provide—for the sixth-form and university student and for the general reader—a guide to the complicated literary developments of the century. Some of these developments have social, religious, or scientific associations, and in no period is it more essential than in the nineteenth century to consider literature as a whole, not merely the poetry and the fiction which are its greatest artistic achievements.

No absolute division, of course, exists between literary criticism and literary history. The difference is partly one of stress or interest, partly one of tone. To take an easy example: it is literary criticism that remarks on the relation of Pre-Raphaelite poetry to the poetry of Keats, but it is literary history that points out the fact that it was in one of Keats's letters first printed in Lord Houghton's collection of 1848 that the Pre-Raphaelite Movement found both its name and inspiration. In the matter of tone, it is mainly a difference between the historical "we" and the critical "I"—the "we" trying to keep in mind, as much as possible, that there are varying opinions on most works of literature, the "I" expressing the writer's personal opinion alone.

Literary history is sometimes criticised for being over-burdened with names and dates. But most of these are necessary for reference, and a greater danger may lie in seeing past literature too much through the eyes of modern criticism. It is not unknown for people to have read Mr X on Wordsworth before—or instead of—reading Wordsworth. I myself read the majority of nineteenth-century literature before I had read any criticism at all; and this perhaps is the ideal. I have accordingly kept my main text clear of critical controversy, relegating my list of authorities to a full Bibliography at the back. My indebtedness to previous historians, critics, biographers, and scholars may be seen there. Here I should like to express my particular obligation to the criticism of F. R. Leavis and to the historical works by D. C. Somervell, by A. J. Wyatt and Henry Clay, and by George Sampson.

R. C. C.

ACKNOWLEDGMENTS

For permission to quote from copyright material, the author and publishers are grateful to the following:—

Messrs Constable & Co. Ltd, for extracts from the *Poems of George Meredith*; The Society of Authors and Messrs Jonathan Cape Ltd, for a poem by A. E. Housman; the Trustees of the Hardy Estate and Messrs Macmillan & Co. Ltd, for extracts from the *Collected Poems of Thomas Hardy*; and Messrs A. P. Watt & Son and Messrs Macmillan & Co. Ltd, for a poem from the *Collected Poems of W. B. Yeats*.

CONTENTS

ENGLISH LITERATURE OF THE NINETEENTH CENTURY

CHAPTER I

THE ROMANTIC MOVEMENT IN POETRY

1798-1824

"They who have been accustomed to the gaudiness and inane phraseology of many modern writers, if they persist in reading this book to its conclusion, will, no doubt, frequently have to struggle with feelings of strangeness and awkwardness: they will look round for poetry, and will be induced to inquire by what species of courtesy these attempts can be permitted to assume that title."

WORDSWORTH : Preface to the *Lyrical Ballads.*

Dates and Definitions

Many people now living know from personal experience that the first day of the twentieth century was not so very different from the last day of the nineteenth ; and younger people will observe eventually the lack of sudden change between the last day of the twentieth century and the first day of the twenty-first. Years and centuries are arithmetical conveniences, and it is seldom that the changes in politics and society, the great events by which we divide our history, coincide either with the opening of a year or the opening of a century.

The opening of the nineteenth century is no exception to this rule. Napoleon had been made First Consul, and in June he had defeated the Austrians at Marengo. But who was Napoleon ? He was the child—or perhaps the step-child—of the French Revolution, and it is from 1789, the storming of the Bastille, that we date an epoch in both French and European history, as it is from 1776, the Declaration of Independence, that we date an epoch in the history of

America. There is no similar date in English history, and books on the political thought of England in the nineteenth century often begin with the French event of '89.

These being the common acceptances of social and political history, we should not suppose that literary history is much more convenient for us. What were the literary events of the years 1800-1 ? Maria Edgeworth published her first novel, *Castle Rackrent* ; Wordsworth finished the first two books of the *Prelude*, and had conversations with his friend Coleridge ; Cobbett returned to England from the United States ; Southey published a long poem called *Thalaba* ; and Charles Lamb went to the India House in the mornings and returned in the evenings, and—so the story goes—on being rebuked by one of his chiefs for unpunctuality with the comment, "I notice, Mr Lamb, that you come very late every morning," replied, unabashed, "Yes, but see how early I go . . ."

There seems nothing in these events from which we could date a period, but we can ask a similar question to that asked in the second paragraph. Who were these people ? and, particularly, who were Wordsworth and Coleridge that their private conversations should appear to be so important ! And by answering this question we are relieved for a moment, for "every schoolboy knows" that Wordsworth and Coleridge were the poets who, in September 1798, inaugurated the Romantic Movement in Poetry—or, as it is sometimes called, the Romantic Revival—with the publication of the *Lyrical Ballads*.

The relief, however, is temporary. We are now provided with a date, which anticipates the century by only a few years, but we are saddled with an almost meaningless phrase that seems to demand an immediate definition. What precisely was this Romantic Movement ? in what sense was it "romantic", and in what sense a "revival" ? Such questions cannot be answered precisely, and the terms are better understood by following the development of language and ideas than by learning a plausible definition. In the first place we should try to find out what aspects of eighteenth-century verse were apparently so distasteful to Wordsworth and Coleridge ; what language and what ideas did they dislike, and what did they

attempt to put in their place ? And what was in the general
climate of the age that made their experiments, original
though they were, typical of the younger generation ? Let
us leave definitions to those, like Dickens's Mr Gradgrind, to
whom a horse is a "graminivorous quadruped", and see what
the poets Wordsworth and Coleridge were actually trying to
do in the year 1798.

Importance of the Year 1798

Paradoxically, we are indebted for part of our answer
to those very years 1800-1 which we have dismissed as being
of no great importance. For there is one relevant event which
we omitted : the *Lyrical Ballads* had a second edition, in two
volumes, in January 1801, and to this Wordsworth contributed
a Preface, dated 1800, justifying the poetic revolution that had
startled—and amused—the literary world two years before.
But the theories advanced in the Preface, the fruit of the conversations with Coleridge, did not arise from the poetry. It
was more the other way about : the *Lyrical Ballads* were
experiments (both collaborators use this word) deliberately
made from theoretical discussions. So we can accept the year
of first publication, 1798, as being the year of definite revolution, remembering as minor points that Wordsworth and
Coleridge first discussed the scheme privately in 1797, and
that Wordsworth justified it in public in 1800-1, and again
in 1802, when he added to the Preface an Appendix on Poetic
Diction.

Reaction from Eighteenth-Century Poetic Diction

Like all poetic revolutions, the revolution of Wordsworth
and Coleridge was primarily directed against artificial,
academic verse—"the gaudiness and inane phraseology" that
Wordsworth spoke of, the poetic diction of the eighteenth
century. Wordsworth took examples from Gray, Johnson, and
Cowper, but these were distinguished poets who on several
occasions—the most famous instance is Gray's *Elegy*—managed to make of the current diction really impressive achievements. What Wordsworth and Coleridge were fighting against

can be seen more clearly if we take, not the lesser productions of distinguished poets, but the average production of a minor poet. The Reverend Gilbert White, the celebrated naturalist, is a good example, because his prose was the natural product of a keen observation of life, but his verse the unnatural eighteenth-century habit of finding English equivalents for Latin turns of speech. The Curate who could write plainly of "the copulation of frogs" or "the natural term of a hog's life" was forced, without original poetic genius, to write his verse like this :

> Amusive birds ! — say where your hid retreat
> When the frost rages and the tempests beat ;
> Whence your return, by such nice instinct led,
> When spring, soft season, lifts her bloomy head ?

And the man who could state an observed fact in such a plain and simple manner as to be probably the first of British field-workers was able also to pen the following effusion—which refers, it is not superfluous to note, to a barometer :

> Push'd by the weightier atmosphere, up springs
> The ponderous Mercury, from scale to scale
> Mounting, amidst the Torricellian tube.

Such verse seems to us the very reverse of natural, but it was the normal way of writing poetry at the time ; indeed, Wordsworth himself in his earliest works wrote in that style, as can be seen from his poem *Descriptive Sketches taken during a Pedestrian Tour among the Alps*, which was begun in 1791 and published in 1793. Although it contains some original passages, and is historically important because Coleridge's enthusiasm for it led to the first meeting of the two poets, most of this poem is truly "pedestrian", typical of the eighteenth-century academic verse which they were soon afterwards to challenge. A representative piece in the 1793 edition (the poem was later revised) runs as follows :

> The cloister startles at the gleam of arms,
> And Blasphemy the shuddering fane alarms ;
> Nod the cloud-piercing pines their troubl'd heads,
> Spires, rocks, and lawns, a browner night o'erspreads.
> Strong terror checks the female peasant's sighs.

> And start th' astonish'd shades at female eyes.
> The thundering tube the aged angler hears,
> And swells the groaning torrent with his tears.

We have only to compare that "correct", lifeless poetry
with the truly living, dramatic poetry of the *Lines composed
a few miles above Tintern Abbey*—probably the best of
Wordsworth's contributions to the *Lyrical Ballads*—to realise,
not only what an advance the poet had personally made, but
what was the nature of his challenge to the accepted standards.
Summing it up briefly, we could say that, whereas in the
Descriptive Sketches Wordsworth sits himself down with
the conscious determination to "compose a poem", here, in the
Tintern Abbey, whatever the initial consciousness of "writing
a lyrical ballad", he seems to be speaking to us, we hear the
living voice, as we do in Shakespeare ; he speaks, for instance,
of his boyhood :

> I cannot paint
> What then I was. The sounding cataract
> Haunted me like a passion : the tall rock,
> The mountain, and the deep and gloomy wood,
> Their colours and their forms, were then to me
> An appetite ; a feeling and a love,
> That had no need of a remoter charm,
> By thought supplied, nor any interest
> Unborrowed from the eye.

That time is past, he goes on, but he has compensations for it :

> For I have learned
> To look on nature, not as in the hour
> Of thoughtless youth ; but hearing oftentimes
> The still, sad music of humanity,
> Nor harsh nor grating, though of ample power
> To chasten and subdue. And I have felt
> A presence that disturbs me with the joy
> Of elevated thoughts ; a sense sublime
> Of something far more deeply interfused,
> Whose dwelling is the light of setting suns,
> And the round ocean and the living air,
> And the blue sky, and in the mind of man :
> A motion and a spirit, that impels
> All thinking things, all objects of all thought,
> And rolls through all things.

Nature and Imagination

"The principal object," wrote Wordsworth, "which I proposed to myself in these Poems was to chuse incidents and situations from common life, and to relate or describe them throughout, as far as was possible, in a selection of language really used by men, and, at the same time, to throw over them a certain colouring of imagination, whereby ordinary things should be presented to the mind in an unusual way."

"During the first year that Mr Wordsworth and I were neighbours," wrote Coleridge in *Biographia Literaria* (1817), "our conversations turned frequently on the two cardinal points of poetry, the power of exciting the sympathy of the reader by a faithful adherence to the truth of nature, and the power of giving the interest of novelty by the modifying colours of imagination . . . The thought suggested itself (to which of us I do not recollect) that a series of poems might be composed of two sorts. In the one, the incidents and agents were to be, in part at least, supernatural; and the excellence aimed at was to consist in the interesting of the affections by the dramatic truth of such emotions, as would naturally accompany such situations, supposing them real . . . For the second class, subjects were to be chosen from ordinary life; the characters and incidents were to be such as will be found in every village and its vicinity where there is a meditative and feeling mind to seek after them, or to notice them when they present themselves.

"In this idea originated the plan of the *Lyrical Ballads*; in which it was agreed that my endeavours should be directed to persons and characters supernatural, or at least romantic; yet so as to transfer from our inward nature a human interest and a semblance of truth sufficient to procure for these shadows of imagination that willing suspension of disbelief for the moment, which constitutes poetic faith. Mr Wordsworth, on the other hand, was to propose to himself as his object, to give the charm of novelty to things of every day, and to excite a feeling analogous to the supernatural, by awakening the mind's attention from the lethargy of custom, and directing it to the loveliness and the wonders of the world before us.''

Coleridge goes on to say that his friend's ''industry had proved so much more successful, and the number of his poems so much greater, that my compositions, instead of forming a balance, appeared rather an interpolation of heterogeneous matter.'' But this is not really the case, either in quality or quantity ; for the chief of Coleridge's contributions was the long *Rime of the Ancient Mariner*, generally considered, with the possible exception of Wordsworth's *Tintern Abbey*, the greatest poem in the whole collection. And some of Wordsworth's contributions were far from successful. He took tremendous risks of bathos and, although the contempt of the greater part of the contemporary literary public for the *Lyrical Ballads* was obviously not justified, we can excuse the ribaldry that greeted such things as the opening of *Goody Blake and Harry Gill*, acknowledged by the poet himself to be ''one of the rudest of this collection'' :

> Oh ! what's the matter ? what's the matter ?
> What is't that ails young Harry Gill ?
> That evermore his teeth they chatter,
> Chatter, chatter, chatter still !

Few distinguished poets can have suffered more parodies than Wordsworth, but it is worth noting that probably the best parody of him ever written—Lewis Carroll's in *Through the Looking Glass*—is a skit on a poem *Resolution and Independence, or The Leech-Gatherer* (composed 1802, published 1807) that, while it certainly contains some unconscious humour, is among the greatest poems Wordsworth ever wrote, a remarkable work of genius.

"Nature" in Philosophy, Politics, and Painting

From the vantage point of a century and a half distant, we can fit the *Lyrical Ballads* into the general Romantic Movement in Europe at the end of the eighteenth century. This would not altogether have pleased Wordsworth himself, for part of the Preface is directed against the fashionable aspects of that movement, against ''frantic novels, sickly and stupid

German Tragedies, and deluges of idle and extravagant stories in verse." And for those who connect "romanticism" with "feeling at the expense of thinking", Wordsworth's own diagnosis is salutary: "All good poetry is the spontaneous overflow of powerful feelings: and though this be true, Poems to which any value can be attached were never produced on any variety of subjects but by a man, who, being possessed of more than usual organic sensibility, had also thought long and deeply." This passage is often quoted in its first phrase, without the reader being aware of the author's qualifying remarks; which can be compared with part of Coleridge's famous definition of Imagination: "a more than usual state of emotion, with more than usual order."

The contemporary European romanticism, in its ephemeral aspects, was a more than usual state of emotion, with more than usual disorder. A modern historian has said that the fundamental impulse of the Romantic Movement can be found in the simple phrase, "the Call of the Wild." Rousseau was the first great prophet of the movement, and his books, written in the middle of the eighteenth century, contrast civilisation with "Nature", to the disadvantage of the former. Although he was appreciative of the beauty of wild scenery, the "Nature" of his political writings is a kind of Garden of Eden, out of which Man has mistakenly strayed and to which he must find his way back. The French Revolution, in some of its features, was an expression in political terms of the Romantic Movement, and it is not surprising that most of the young English poets welcomed it enthusiastically: "Bliss was it in that dawn to be alive," wrote Wordsworth, "But to be young was very heaven."

The end of the eighteenth century was also the beginning of the Industrial Revolution in England, and, while most of the earlier poets of the century were fundamentally of the city —Pope and Johnson are obvious examples—we associate most of the later poets with the country. And not only the poets, but the painters. For the years 1770 to 1830 were the period of the first great native school of landscape painting, the superb achievements of such artists as Crome, Constable,

Gainsborough, Turner, Cox. Reaction against "the dark Satanic mills" of Blake's poem resulted in Englishmen becoming aware, more than ever now that it was threatened, of the beauty of their countryside. And the poets and painters shared that feeling, and fed it by their books and canvases. Furthermore, industry before the Industrial Revolution had been widely scattered; with the drawing of the population into vast towns in the north and midlands, large areas of the countryside became lonely and picturesque, suitable haunts for the nostalgic, romantic mind.

Influence of the Ballads

We must now look at three influences upon Wordsworth and Coleridge, connected with what has been said, but deserving a brief mention alone. The first and most important of these influences was that of the old ballads.

The majority of ballads date from the fifteenth century, and Thomas Percy, later Bishop of Dromore, published a selection of them—*Reliques of Ancient English Poetry*—in 1765. Scott followed him in the North with his *Minstrelsy of the Scottish Border* (1802-3), and there were collections of Irish ballads, notably Charlotte Brooke's *Reliques of Irish Poetry* (1789).

The influence of Percy's collection was extraordinary. Wordsworth wrote in 1815 : "For our own country, its poetry has been absolutely redeemed by it. I do not think that there is an able writer in verse of the present day who would not be proud to acknowledge his obligations to the *Reliques*; I know that it is so with my friends; and, for myself, I am happy in this occasion to make a public avowal of my own." And Scott wrote that he had never read a book "half so frequently or with half the enthusiasm."

For a time the fame of Percy's work was overshadowed by the contemporary success of James Macpherson, who in 1760 published *Fragments of Ancient Poetry collected in the Highlands of Scotland*, which was followed by the epics *Fingal* and *Temora*, claimed as translations of the third-century bard Ossian. Challenged by Dr Johnson, Macpherson failed to produce his originals, and it is thought now that most of the writing was spurious. The Ossianic Muse had a European reputation in the eighteenth and early nineteenth centuries, and it is ironic to record the fact that in French schools—at any rate, till quite recently—Macpherson is taught as one of the glories of British literature.*

Since Percy's collection, many poets have written ballads, with varying degrees of success or successful imitation. Some of Wordsworth's own, as we have observed, descend rather frequently into bathos. Few modern poets have really succeeded in equalling or surpassing their original sources. One of the exceptions—besides the *Ancient Mariner*—is Scott's famous short ballad, *Proud Maisie*, which, brief as it is, is perhaps his finest achievement in verse :

> Proud Maisie is in the wood,
>   Walking so early ;
> Sweet Robin sits on the bush,
>   Singing so rarely.
> "Tell me, thou bonny bird,
>   When shall I marry me ? "—
> "When six braw gentlemen
>   Kirkward shall carry ye."
> "Who makes the bridal bed,
>   Birdie, say truly ? "—
> "The gray-headed sexton
>   That delves the grave duly.
> The glow-worm o'er grave and stone
>   Shall light thee steady,
> The owl from the steeple sing,
>   ' Welcome, proud lady.' "

---

* A somewhat similar perverted genius was Thomas Chatterton, to whose memory Keats inscribed *Endymion*. He composed poems which he claimed as the work of Thomas Rowley, an imaginary monk of the fifteenth century. Accepted as genuine for a time and then being realised as forgeries, they did not establish the young poet as he had hoped, and in 1770, at the age of eighteen, he committed suicide. Keats has an early sonnet beginning "O Chatterton ! how very sad thy fate ! ", and it is interesting to observe that Wordsworth, who wrote that "from my very childhood I have felt the falsehood that pervades the volumes imposed upon the world under the name of Ossian", referred in *Resolution and Independence* to "Chatterton, the marvellous Boy, The sleepless Soul that perished in his pride."

Influence of Burns and Blake

Ballads were originally the productions of early centuries and nameless minstrels, and thus the antithesis of most of the poetry of the eighteenth century, which was consciously modern and sophisticated. The "classicism" of Pope and Johnson is that of Greece and Rome seen through contemporary eyes, and the early eighteenth century is known as the Augustan Age because the writers of the day made a consistent attempt to parallel under Queen Anne the achievements of Vergil, Horace, Ovid, and Livy, under the Emperor Augustus. Though Pope admired the Jacobean poet Donne, he "versified" him, as Dryden had Chaucer shortly before : that is, translated him into the verse-form of the age, the heroic couplet. And though Johnson admired Shakespeare, he could "scarcely check his risibility" at the expression "blanket of the dark" that occurs in *Macbeth*. Pope was a great poet, who, like all great poets, rose at his best above his age ; and Johnson, on the lowest estimate, was a distinguished verse-writer. But it became the accepted notion that certain expressions, ideas, rhythms, were "poetic", others not ; and the revival of ballad poetry was a much-needed antidote.

Their influence was combined with the influence of two great poets, one a Scot, the other a Londoner, who were largely self-taught and thus out of the reach of classical prejudice.* Robert Burns, the National Poet of Scotland, belongs to the eighteenth century entirely, and William Blake (1757-1827) did the majority of his best work in that period. So they do not call for more than a brief mention here.

Burns, the son of a small farmer, had a great success with his *Poems, chiefly in the Scottish Dialect* (1786), which made him the lion of the subsequent Edinburgh season. Later he published an enlarged edition, and contributed many songs

---

* The student of Wordsworth will also want to glance through the work of a very interesting minor poet, Mark Akenside, particularly at the lines 31-57 in Book IV of *Pleasures of the Imagination* (1770). These lines, beginning "O ye dales Of Tyne, and ye most ancient woodlands", are included in some modern anthologies.

to popular anthologies—sometimes wholly original, some-
times combining inspiration from different traditional sources.
Only a Scotsman can discuss his poetry adequately, for most
of the best of it is in the West Scots dialect; for example,
Holy Willie's Prayer, *The Twa Herds*, *Death and Doctor
Hornbook*, *Tam o' Shanter*, and *The Jolly Beggars*. Words-
worth was a great admirer of Burns, and refers to him in
Resolution and Independence :

> I thought . . .
> Of Him who walked in glory and in joy
> Following his plough, along the mountain-side.

Blake, the son of a hosier, was born in Soho, and became
an engraver.   One of the most original of English geniuses,
he was also original in his "publication", for his poems
appeared in books designed and printed by himself—and
which remained unknown to the general literary public.   He
was poor and neglected in his own time, but to-day his reputation, both as poet and artist, stands high.   There is a
collection of his paintings in the Tate Gallery.

Between 1789 and 1794 appeared his *Songs of Innocence,
Marriage of Heaven and Hell*, *Visions of the Daughters of
Albion*, and *Songs of Experience*.   His later poems are, in
general, more obscure ; but there are some interesting exceptions, notably parts of *Milton* and *Jerusalem*, both begun
about 1800-3, *The Auguries of Innocence* (*c.* 1801-3), and
The Everlasting Gospel (*c.* 1810).   The *Milton* contains the
famous piece beginning

> And did those feet in ancient time
> Walk upon England's mountains green . . .

which is equally impressive sung as a hymn or read as a poem.
The Auguries of Innocence opens with a stanza that could be
claimed as Blake's poetry and philosophy in miniature :

> To see a World in a grain of sand,
> And a Heaven in a wild flower,
> Hold Infinity in the palm of your hand,
> And Eternity in an hour.

Blake was eccentric* and saw visions ; some say he was mad. But—to paraphrase slightly Wordsworth's compliment —there is something in the madness of this man that interests us more than the sanity of others.

Wordsworth, 1770-1850

We have described the main features of the Romantic Revolution in poetry ; we must now go on to treat separately the chief poets of the period 1798-1824. We begin with the so-called "Lake School"—Wordsworth, Coleridge, Southey— and continue with Byron, Shelley, Keats. Although the former three lived beyond 1824, it is generally considered that their best work falls within the period ; Southey's work, indeed, is mainly of historical interest now, and Wordsworth and Coleridge wrote their finest things in the decade 1798-1807.

William Wordsworth, the son of Lord Lonsdale's agent, was born and educated in Cumberland, and afterwards at Cambridge. Going to France in 1791, he sympathised with the revolutionaries, but fell in love with the daughter of a Royalist family, who bore him a child. Returning to England just before the Terror, he published *The Evening Walk* and *Descriptive Sketches* in 1793. In 1795 two events occurred which decided the course of his future life : he met Coleridge, and, just as his financial prospects seemed hopeless, he received a legacy of £900. In 1797 he settled with his sister Dorothy† in Somerset, in order to be near Coleridge. The outcome of their discussions on the Quantock Hills was the *Lyrical Ballads*. Wordsworth refers to the joint authorship in his long autobiographical poem *The Prelude* :

* A friend once discovered him and his wife sitting naked, reading *Paradise Lost* "in character." Blake called out cheerfully, "Come in ! it's only Adam and Eve."
† Dorothy Wordsworth (1771-1855) is important in connection with her brother and Coleridge rather than in her own literary right ; but her letters and journals are extremely interesting in themselves, and sometimes we are able to compare her prose treatment of a subject or incident with her brother's verse treatment. The most famous example is her description of the daffodils which inspired Wordsworth's "I wandered lonely as a cloud."

That summer, under whose indulgent skies
Upon smooth Quantock's airy ridge we roved
Unchecked, or loitered mid her sylvan combs,
Thou in bewitching words, with happy heart,
Didst chaunt the vision of that Ancient Man,
The bright-eyed Mariner;
And I, associated with such labour, steeped
In soft forgetfulness the livelong hours,
Murmuring of him who, joyous hap, was found,
After the perils of his moonlight ride,
Near the loud waterfall.

After visiting Germany in the winter of 1798-9, Wordsworth
and his sister settled at Grasmere in Westmorland, whence
they removed in 1813 to Rydal Mount, his home until his
death.   In 1802 he married Mary Hutchinson, and in the
same year Lord Lonsdale died and his successor procured
for the poet the sinecure office of Distributor of Stamps for
Westmorland, which placed him in easy circumstances for
the rest of his life.   In 1843 he succeeded Southey as Poet
Laureate.

His early revolutionary ardour gave way, after the rise of
Napoleon, to a patriotic conservatism.   The young Browning
called him "The Lost Leader"; Byron was never weary of
sneering at him and Southey for their change of politics; and
there is a passage in Peacock's satire *Crotchet Castle* (1831)
plainly referring to Wordsworth and Southey as "Mr Wilful
Wontsee, and Mr Rumblesack Shantsee, poets of some note,
who used to see visions of Utopia, and pure republics beyond
the Western deep : but finding that these El Dorados brought
them no revenue, they turned their vision-seeing faculty into
the more profitable channel of espying all sorts of virtues in
the high and the mighty, who were able and willing to pay
for the discovery."

Political considerations had no doubt something to do with
Wordsworth's increasing fame among the "respectable"; but
the story of his reputation is fundamentally one of a poet who
—in the famous phrase—"has created the taste by which he
is to be enjoyed."   The poetic revolution gradually became
the norm: "Every year," wrote Southey truly in 1823,

"shows more and more how strongly Wordsworth's poetry has leavened the rising generation." "Up to 1820," wrote De Quincey, "the name of Wordsworth was trampled under foot; from 1820 to 1830 it was militant; from 1830 to 1835 it has been triumphant." To which we may add that, from 1835 to his death, Wordsworth was a venerated Victorian institution, Rydal Mount becoming a Mecca of pious pilgrimage.

Wordsworth's Best Poems

It is rather ironic that Wordsworth was producing his best poetry when he was most abused, and that when he became accepted his inspiration comparatively failed. His *Poetical Works* make up a big volume: the Oxford edition runs into nearly a thousand pages, in double columns. For the student this is the best edition, though it is unfortunate that the poet should have grouped his poems, not in chronological order (his custom was to improve pieces year by year), but in philosophical: "Poems of the Imagination", "Poems of the Fancy", and so forth. For the general reader, a good selection, roughly in order of composition, is preferable.

Most of his fine things are comparatively short, ranging from sonnets like "The world is too much with us" to poems like *Michael*, of some 500 lines. And most of them were written during the decade from the *Lyrical Ballads* (1798) to the *Poems in Two Volumes* (1807). One of the exceptions is the *Extempore Effusion upon the Death of James Hogg* (1835), in which the veteran poet mourns the death, not only of Hogg, "The Ettrick Shepherd", but of Scott, "the mighty Minstrel", of Coleridge, "the rapt One, of the godlike forehead", of Lamb, "the frolic and the gentle", of Crabbe, and of Felicia Hemans.

His long autobiographical poem, *The Prelude, or Growth of a Poet's Mind*, which contains about 8,000 lines, was begun in 1799 and finished in 1804, but it was not published till 1850, immediately after his death. For such a lengthy work, the interest is remarkably sustained, but the first few books are undoubtedly the best. It was intended, together with *The Excursion*, to form part of a great poem, *The Recluse*—which would certainly have been a great poem in length. The best part of *The Excursion*, which contains about 9,000 lines, is *Margaret, or The Ruined Cottage*, which was composed 1795-7 and later merged into Book One of the long poem, published in 1814. This contains some of the poet's most dramatic language; for instance, the lines admired by Shelley and quoted by him in the Preface to his own poem *Alastor* (1815) :

> The good die first,
> And those whose hearts are dry as summer dust
> Burn to the socket.

Wordsworth's only work in dramatic form, however—*The Borderers* (1796)—is extremely dull. Like a modern poet, T. S. Eliot, who resembles him also in having started a poetic revolution and "creating the taste by which he is enjoyed", Wordsworth is less dramatic in his drama than in his non-dramatic poems. One of his greatest and most dramatic pieces is also one of his shortest, and can be fittingly quoted in conclusion ; it was written in 1799 :

> A slumber did my spirit seal ;
> I had no human fears :
> She seemed a thing that could not feel
> The touch of earthly years.
>
> No motion has she now, no force ;
> She neither hears nor sees ;
> Rolled round in earth's diurnal course,
> With rocks, and stones, and trees.

Coleridge, 1772-1834

The son of a Devonshire clergyman, Samuel Taylor Coleridge was a contemporary of Lamb at Christ's Hospital. While at Cambridge, he was moved to write verse by reading the *Sonnets* of W. L. Bowles, a minor poet who also inspired Southey. In 1795 he and Southey planned a communist colony in America, and as part of the preparations married two sisters. The "Pantisocratic" scheme never came off, and the matrimonial voyage was, in one case, hardly less disastrous ; Coleridge separated from his wife, who with her children found refuge in the Southey household.

In 1798, the year of his fruitful collaboration with Wordsworth, Coleridge was secured a modest income for life, through the generosity of the brothers Wedgwood, sons of the famous potter, who were anxious that he should devote himself to poetry and philosophy. He once said of himself that "the walk of the whole man indicates *indolence capable of energies*"; and Lamb called him "an archangel a little damaged." Both in prose and in poetry, his achievement was disappointing, compared with the great possibilities of his genius. Like De Quincey, he became a slave to opium, and from 1816 to his death resided in the care of the physician Gillman at Highgate, where his remarkable conversational powers attracted many young disciples.*

His poetry alone concerns this chapter, and it is remarkable how little of it is memorable. Almost the whole of his popular fame as a poet rests upon three pieces: *The Ancient Mariner, Christabel, Kubla Khan.* (The student should also know such poems as *Frost at Midnight, This Lime-tree Bower my Prison, Dejection,* and *Work without Hope.*) They are often described as "dream poems", partly because it is difficult to describe in words afterwards the great impression that they immediately make. *Kubla Khan* was literally a dream: Coleridge, in the summer of 1797, had been ill, and slept for three hours in his chair. On waking he discovered that he could remember two or three hundred lines of a poem he had been dreaming. He began to write them down, but was interrupted by a visitor, and when left alone again found that the rest of his vision had escaped him. The fragment begins enticingly:

> In Xanadu did Kubla Khan
> A stately pleasure-dome decree:
> Where Alph, the sacred river, ran
> Through caverns measureless to man
> Down to a sunless sea . . .

---

* His eldest son Hartley Coleridge (1796-1849) published verse and prose. His daughter Sara Coleridge (1802-1852) married her cousin, with whom she edited her father's works.

Not even Coleridge himself could explain the poem, though various interpretations have been offered since.

Christabel is also a fragment, though much longer. Coleridge claimed that it was founded on a new principle, "namely, that of counting in each line, the accents, not the syllables." The manuscript was passed round in literary circles, and in 1801 Scott heard it recited and reproduced much the same rhythm in his *Lay of the Last Minstrel*, whence Byron borrowed it for his *Siege of Corinth*.

Two out of the three "dream poems", then, are only fragments; the third, the famous *Mariner*, is complete and undoubtedly Coleridge's masterpiece in verse, among the greatest achievements in English literature. One reads this poem with the same enjoyment the hundredth time as one did the first. It has the quality of many of the most profound works of art, in that it can be appreciated—like *Hamlet*, the *Pilgrim's Progress*, *Gulliver's Travels*—at various levels and at various ages, from youth up. Quotation, as with Gray's *Elegy*, is really superfluous; but worth noting is the subtle way the suspense is created, and also the dramatic pause in the third line of the twentieth verse:

> "God save thee, ancient Mariner!
> From the fiends that plague thee thus!—
> Why look'st thou so?"—'With my cross-bow
> I shot the Albatross!'"

Southey, 1774-1843

Wordsworth and Coleridge are read now with the same interest as by their contemporaries, and with more admiration. The same can hardly be said of Robert Southey, the other member of "the Lake School." Coleridge denied that any such school existed, but the name, originally applied by the *Edinburgh Review*, was taken up by the satirists, one of whom wrote that

> They lived in the Lakes—an appropriate quarter
> For poems diluted with plenty of water.

Southey's poetry, however, seems dry enough to us now, particularly his long narrative poems, *Thalaba the Destroyer*

(1801), a poem much admired by Cardinal Newman ; *Madoc* (1805) ; *The Curse of Kehama* (1810) ; and *Roderick, the Last of the Goths* (1814). His short poems are more readable, and *The Battle of Blenheim* and a few other simple pieces are still found in school anthologies.

He succeeded Henry James Pye as Poet Laureate in 1813, but his laureate *Vision of Judgment* is only remembered now by Byron's brilliant satire on the same subject. Like Wordsworth and Coleridge, he abandoned his earlier revolutionary views, and from 1808 contributed regularly to the Tory *Quarterly Review*, which he helped to found. His output in all branches of literature was tremendous (he wrote, for instance, the standard life of Nelson), and in later years he became associated with Lord Ashley (afterwards Earl of Shaftesbury) in his campaign for factory legislation. His shrewd *Colloquies on the Progress and Prospects of Society* (1830) is a precursor of the social writing of Ruskin and Morris. This zeal for reform is probably a sufficient answer to his critics, who may have confused the ability to strike revolutionary attitudes with the desire to improve social conditions.

Byron, 1788-1824

There is one interesting exception to the general rule that the younger generation of "romantic" poets in the early nineteenth century looked to Wordsworth and Coleridge as their first inspiration. George Gordon Noel, who succeeded his great-uncle as Lord Byron in the year of the *Lyrical Ballads*, was later regarded by Europe as *the* Romantic Poet of England ; but he insisted that the contemporary age was the age of decline in poetry, looked to Dryden and Pope as his exemplars, and castigated Wordsworth, Coleridge, and Southey, both privately and in public. As he wrote in his chief satire *Don Juan* :

> Thou shalt believe in Milton, Dryden, Pope ;
>   Thou shalt not set up Wordsworth, Coleridge, Southey ;
> Because the first is crazed beyond all hope,
>   The second drunk, the third so quaint and mouthy . . .

He was educated at Harrow and Cambridge, and published the juvenile poems *Hours of Idleness* in 1807. Their harsh criticism by Brougham in the *Edinburgh Review* provoked his satire *English Bards and Scotch Reviewers* (1809). He then toured Portugal, Spain, and the Balkans, which he described in the first two cantos of *Childe Harold's Pilgrimage*. Their publication in 1812 made him famous overnight. The poem reached seven editions in four weeks, and for two or three years the poet was enormously popular and feted by "everyone" in London society. "Byronic" melancholy became a fashionable complaint, and on the strength of the poem Byron was henceforth regarded as eccentric, satirical, unhappy, and wicked. He encouraged this view of himself, and talked freely about his personal affairs. Though the series of Oriental verse romances that succeeded the first part of *Childe Harold*—*The Giaour* (1813), *The Bride of Abydos* (1813), *The Corsair* (1814), *Lara* (1814)—were even more successful, public opinion soon turned against him. His separation from his wife in 1816, only a year after their marriage, caused such a scandal that he was virtually—and self-virtuously—hounded out of England.*

For the rest of his life he lived abroad, mostly in Italy. To this period belong his verse dramas, the continuation of *Childe Harold*, and a number of other works, including *Beppo* (1818), *Don Juan* (1819-24), and *The Vision of Judgment* (1822). He sailed for Greece in 1823, in order to aid the Greek struggle for independence, but died of fever at Missolonghi in 1824.

---

* He was right to feel sardonic over this Pecksniffian dismissal, for Regency high society was notoriously immoral: "To be called black by very dirty vessels," it has been observed, "at once amused and disgusted him." Macaulay's essay on Byron in the *Edinburgh Review* fifteen years later opened its account of the affair with the words: "We know no spectacle so ridiculous as the British public in one of its periodical fits of morality . . . Some unfortunate man, in no respect more depraved than hundreds whose offences have been treated with lenity, is singled out as an expiatory sacrifice . . . a sort of whipping-boy, by whose vicarious agonies all the other transgressors of the same class are, it is supposed, sufficiently chastised."

His writings, his life, and his death combined to make him the patron saint of Romanticism and Revolution in Europe; and even in England his sins were speedily forgiven, so that Victorian novelists often have a satirical portrait of a young poetical lady who goes into a swoon at the mention of Missolonghi, and Ruskin reports that his father wished him to become, among other things, a poet as great as Byron— "only pious."

Byron's Work and Reputation

It is as well to explain at first the difference between Byron's reputation as a poet in Europe and his general reputation in his native country. "The English may think of Byron what they please," said Goethe, "but it is certain that they can point to no poet who is his like. He is different from all the rest, and, in the main, greater." Matthew Arnold coupled him with Wordsworth, and Morris called him "the greatest literary power of this century"; but, in general, English critics and readers have been far less enthusiastic than their counterparts abroad, so that a modern admirer speaks of "Byron, so much under-rated by Englishmen."

Perhaps this should be: "Byron, so much over-rated abroad." For the fact remains that foreigners (including, of course, Englishmen when considering foreign works) are not very good judges of poetry. The foreigner's knowledge of English, however great, seldom allows him to distinguish appropriately one poet from another. The French reputation of Macpherson is a case in point, and when foreigners class, as they often do, Byron with Shakespeare, it is obvious to a native that their critical faculties are not working on the quality of the verse.

Both poets are admired abroad for their "philosophy": that is, for something that can be *abstracted* from their poetry, not for their poetry itself. But, whereas for Shakespeare this is the reverse of a compliment, for Byron it approaches nearer his true worth. For there is nothing very much in Byron that cannot be appreciated in the most obvious terms; compared with Wordsworth, he is shallow, and, compared with Keats, he is a cosmopolitan, not an English poet. It is instructive to observe both his personal contemporary admirations and his practice compared with his theory. Though he was correct in his spirited defence of Dryden and Pope against the contemporary depreciation, he was very much out in his preference for Rogers and Campbell over Wordsworth and Coleridge. With all their minor faults of occasional bathos, etc., Wordsworth and Coleridge represented the living voice in poetry in Byron's time, as Dryden and Pope in their own day, while Rogers and Campbell were the mere relics of an ossified tradition. And Byron could condemn Wordsworth with one hand, while producing this admirable imitation of him with the other :

> I live not in myself, but I become
> Portion of that around me ; and to me
> High mountains are a feeling, but the hum
> Of human cities torture : I can see
> Nothing to loathe in nature, save to be
> A link reluctant in a fleshly chain,
> Class'd among creatures, when the soul can flee
> And with the sky, the peak, the heaving plain
> Of ocean, or the stars, mingle, and not in vain.

Childe Harold, from which this comes, though it remains very interesting in places (such things as the Waterloo stanzas and the lines on the dying Gladiator are still rightly celebrated in anthologies), has not survived in its first overwhelming reputation. Byron's modern repute rests rather on two satires : *Don Juan*, left unfinished at his death, and *The Vision of Judgment*, inspired (if that is the right word) by Southey's absurd eulogy on the death of George III. In his Preface, the Laureate had attacked Byron and Shelley under the name of the "Satanic School" ; and Byron took a notable revenge.

His early satires in the classical manner had been comparative failures; though *English Bards and Scotch Reviewers* is still worth reading for its spirit and sting, it shows clearly enough that the brilliance of Pope was beyond his imitator and that the classical style was outworn. It is in *Beppo*

(1818) that Byron begins to find his own manner in satire, and in the *ottava rima* of *Don Juan* and the *Vision of Judgment* he produced his masterpieces. Some critics have complained of his "carelessness" here ; but this is a misapprehension. Byron probably worked hard in order to be "careless" ; the colloquial, contemptuous style is the whole point and virtue of these poems, which have, indeed, little other quality to commend them. A good example is the satire on Wellington in Canto IX of *Don Juan*, published in 1823 :

> Oh, Wellington ! (or "Villainton")—for Fame
>   Sounds the heroic syllables both ways ;
> France could not even conquer your great name,
>   But punn'd it down to this facetious phrase—
> (Beating or beaten she will laugh the same),
>   You have obtain'd great pensions and much praise :
> Glory like yours should any dare gainsay,
> Humanity would rise, and thunder "Nay !" . . .
>
> You are "the best of cut-throats":—do not start ;
>   The phrase is Shakespeare's, and not misapplied : —
> War's a brain-spattering, windpipe-slitting art,
>   Unless her cause by right be sanctified.
> If you have acted *once* a generous part,
>   The world, not the world's masters, will decide,
> And I shall be delighted to learn who,
> Save you and yours, have gain'd by Waterloo ?
>
> I am no flatterer—you've supp'd full of flattery :
>   They say you like it too—'tis no great wonder.
> He whose whole life has been assault and battery,
>   At last may get a little tired of thunder ;
> And swallowing eulogy much more than satire, he
>   May like being praised for every lucky blunder,
> Call'd "Saviour of the Nations"—not yet saved,
> And "Europe's Liberator"—still enslaved . . .
>
> Never had mortal man such opportunity,
>   Except Napoleon, or abused it more :
> You might have freed fallen Europe from the unity
>   Of tyrants, and been blest from shore to shore :
> And *now*—what *is* your fame ? Shall the muse tune it ye ?
>   *Now*—that the rabble's first vain shouts are o'er ?
> Go ! hear it in your famish'd country's cries !
> Behold the world ! and curse your victories !

Shelley, 1792-1822

Percy Bysshe Shelley was the son of a wealthy baronet, and, like other sons of wealthy men in more modern days, opposed almost from birth every tradition, sentiment, and creed of his class. At Eton and at University College, Oxford, he was in constant rebellion against established authority, till in 1811 his share in the pamphlet *The Necessity of Atheism* led to his expulsion from the University. In the same year he married Harriet Westbrook, a girl of sixteen, by whom he had two children, and whom he deserted in 1814 for Mary Godwin, daughter of William Godwin, the novelist and political writer. When Harriet drowned herself in the Serpentine two years later, Mary became Mrs Shelley, and the Court of Chancery deprived the poet of the custody of his children.

In 1818 Shelley left England, and spent the rest of his short life in Italy, where he saw much of Byron, as the interesting poem *Julian and Maddalo* makes evident. In 1822 he and a friend were drowned in the bay of Spezia, and his body was cremated in the presence of Byron, Leigh Hunt, and Edward Trelawny,* the ashes being buried in Rome, near the body of Keats. Shelley was an impulsive, but sincere and generous man, frequently practising the social gospel that he preached. His virtues and his faults can perhaps be summed up fairly by saying that he nearly always *meant well*—which sometimes was extremely unfortunate for his intimates.

Shelley's Best Period

Shelley wrote most of his best poems during the last four or five years of his life, that is in Italy. After he had visited Ireland and Wales, writing pamphlets defending vegetarianism and political freedom, he had published privately the revolutionary poem *Queen Mab* (1813). *Alastor* and *The Revolt of Islam* had followed between 1815 and 1818. In Italy he produced the tragedy *The Cenci*, the satire on

---

* Trelawny was a noted traveller, who fought in the Greek war of independence and wrote *Recollections of a Younger Son* (1835) and *Recollections of Shelley and Byron* (1858).

Wordsworth *Peter Bell the Third*, the lyric drama *Prometheus Unbound* (1820), the elegy on the death of Keats *Adonais* (1821), *Hellas* (1822), as well as the prose essay *A Defence of Poetry* and many short poems, perhaps the best of which is the famous *Ode to the West Wind*. The last verse of this poem is particularly touching, when we remember that the writer had only a few more years to live :

> Make me thy lyre, even as the forest is :
> What if my leaves are falling like its own !
> The tumult of thy mighty harmonies
>
> Will take from both a deep, autumnal tone,
> Sweet thou in sadness. Be thou, Spirit fierce,
> My spirit ! Be thou me, impetuous one !
>
> Drive my dead thoughts over the universe
> Like withered leaves to quicken a new birth !
> And, by the incantation of this verse,
>
> Scatter, as from an unextinguished hearth
> Ashes and sparks, my words among mankind !
> Be through my lips to unawakened earth
>
> The trumpet of a prophecy ! O, Wind,
> If Winter comes, can Spring be far behind ?

Shelley is the patron saint of modern Socialism, partly because Socialists and Communists are often as conservative in their literary tastes as they are revolutionary in their politics. It is common for Communists to talk about "the heights of Parnassus", and Karl Marx's daughter and son-in-law, in their lectures on Shelley, speak of "an army of poesy." Such Victorian academic language, coupled with Marxist technical slang, makes a combination as unlike as possible to the vigour of Shelley's poetry at its best. A good example of this vigorous approach is the sonnet *England in 1819*, which opens :

> An old, mad, blind, despised, and dying king,—
> Princes, the dregs of their dull race, who flow
> Through public scorn,—mud from a muddy spring,—
> Rulers who neither see, nor feel, nor know,
> But leech-like to their fainting country cling,
> Till they drop, blind in blood, without a blow,—
> A people starved and stabbed in the untilled field . . .

This last line refers to ''Peterloo'', a name given, in parody of Waterloo and the Duke of Wellington, to the episode in St Peter's Fields, Manchester, when a peaceful open-air meeting in support of Parliamentary reform was charged by cavalry. Eleven people were killed, and many wounded. Shelley returned to this theme in his greatest satire *The Mask of Anarchy*, in which he puts the blame for this and other repressive acts on to the Tory minister Castlereagh :

> I met Murder on the way—
> He had a mask like Castlereagh—
> Very smooth he looked, yet grim ;
> Seven blood-hounds followed him :
>
> All were fat ; and well they might
> Be in admirable plight,
> For one by one, and two by two,
> He tossed them human hearts to chew
> Which from his wide cloak he drew . . .

This satire, of course, must be read in the context of political vituperation normal in the eighteenth and early nineteenth centuries ; such a mild poet as Gray, for instance, could write political verse almost as blistering as Byron's or Shelley's.

Prometheus Unbound, whose typically Shelleyan hero is the champion of Man against the Gods, and *Hellas*, inspired by the uprising of the Greeks against the Turks, are ''lyric dramas'', modelled roughly on the Greek and intended in their philosophy to form a Christian-Hellenic synthesis. While each contains some interesting passages and a good deal of vivid lyrical verse—everyone knows some famous choruses from them—only the poet's most fervent admirers can now read them without an occasional yawn. As for *Adonais*— Shelley meant well. Which was extremely unfortunate for Keats. Shelley seriously supposed that Keats's death from consumption was aggravated by the savage review of his *Endymion* in the *Quarterly Review*. Byron also was converted to this idea, though he did find it peculiar, as he notes in *Don Juan* :

> 'Tis strange the mind, that very fiery particle,
> Should let itself be snuffed out by an article.

Actually, Keats wrote to his publisher : "Praise or blame has but a momentary effect on the man whose love of beauty in the abstract makes him a severe critic of his own works. My own domestic criticism has given me pain without comparison beyond what *Blackwood* or the *Quarterly* could inflict."

There is more of Shelley than of Keats in *Adonais*, and some of its moving passages became applicable to the poet as well as his subject only a year later :

> From the contagion of the world's slow stain
> He is secure, and now can never mourn
> A heart grown cold, a head grown grey in vain ;
> Nor, when the spirit's self has ceased to burn,
> With sparkless ashes load an unlamented urn . . .
>
> He is a portion of the loveliness
> Which once he made more lovely.

Keats, 1795-1821

Like Blake, John Keats came of lower-class "cockney" stock, his father being employed in livery stables in London. He was apprenticed to a surgeon, and became a student at Guy's Hospital from 1815 to 1817. Partly through ill health, he then abandoned medicine for literature, though his first volume of *Poems* (1817) achieved little recognition. *Endymion*, a long poem of Greek mythology, which followed in 1818, was harshly reviewed in *Blackwood's Magazine* and the *Quarterly Review*, these Tory journals being strongly prejudiced by the poet's friendship with Leigh Hunt, editor of the radical *Examiner*. The tone of these notices was deplorable, but *Endymion* cannot be said to be one of Keats's most successful poems. Probably the best parts of it are the songs in Book IV, particularly the song out of which Hardy quoted a stanza for the epigraph of his novel *The Return of the Native* :

> To Sorrow
> I bade good morrow,
> And thought to leave her far away behind ;
> But cheerly, cheerly,
> She loves me dearly ;

> She is so constant to me, and so kind :
>   I would deceive her,
>   And so leave her,
> But ah ! she is so constant and so kind.

In the same year, 1818, Keats wrote the first version of *Hyperion*, which he revised the following year, and first met Fanny Brawne, to whom he became engaged.   To the period 1818-20 belong most of his best-known poems, including the famous Odes.   The 1820 volume, *Hyperion and Other Poems*, includes the romances *Lamia, Isabella*, and *The Eve of St Agnes* ; short pieces, such as *The Mermaid Tavern* ; and the odes, *To a Nightingale, On a Grecian Urn, To Psyche, To Autumn*, and *On Melancholy*.   The celebrated ballad *La Belle Dame sans Merci* was first printed in the *Indicator*, May 1820, and was not republished till 1848, when Richard Monckton Milnes, Lord Houghton, produced *The Life, Letters and Literary Remains of John Keats*.   These volumes also contained the first publication of the unfinished romance *The Eve of St Mark* and a number of sonnets.

In September 1820, Keats's tubercular condition became very much worse, and, on Shelley's invitation, he sailed for Italy in a vain effort to regain his health.   He died in Rome in February 1821, having lived for only twenty-five years and four months.   His last sonnet, printed by Houghton in the 1848 collection, is often quoted as a symbolic conclusion to his personal history :

> Bright star ! would I were steadfast as thou art—
>   Not in lone splendour hung aloft the night
> And watching, with eternal lids apart,
>   Like Nature's patient, sleepless Eremite,
> The moving waters at their priestlike task
>   Of pure ablution round earth's human shores,
> Or gazing on the new soft fallen mask
>   Of snow upon the mountains and the moors—
> No—yet still steadfast, still unchangeable,
>   Pillow'd upon my fair love's ripening breast,
> To feel for ever its soft fall and swell,
>   Awake for ever in a sweet unrest,
> Still, still to hear her tender-taken breath,
> And so live ever—or else swoon to death.

Keats's Poems and Letters

Keats was formerly credited with being merely "the apostle of beauty, the founder of the Tennysonian school of flawless workmanship." But his valuable letters show his passion for Shakespeare, for the dramatic strength of the English idiom, for the resources of the English language. (In *contrast*, as has been observed, to Tennyson, who wished to make English "as like the Italian as possible.") In expressing his reaction from Milton, in three of his letters of 1818-19, Keats wrote that "*Paradise Lost*, though fine in itself, is a corruption of our language . . . a northern dialect accommodating itself to Greek and Latin inversions and intonations." "I have but lately stood on my guard against Milton. Life to him would be death to me." "Miltonic verse cannot be written but in an artful, or rather, artist's humour. I wish to give myself up to other sensations. English ought to be kept up."

So Keats may be said to have succeeded Wordsworth in the reaction against eighteenth-century poetic diction, which was usually Miltonic, "a northern dialect accommodating itself to Greek and Latin inversions and intonations", but, unlike the best of Milton, not often "fine in itself." Whether Keats could have realised his personal ambition, to write "a few good plays", may be doubted, in view of the almost complete failure of Wordsworth, Coleridge, Southey, Shelley, Byron, in the drama proper; but in the revised fragment of *Hyperion* and in the *Odes*, he does succeed to a remarkable extent in realising the Shakespearean, dramatic potentialities of the native language, in "keeping English up." (And at his best he is often impersonal where Shelley is self-absorbed.) It was mainly the lesser side of Keats—the fairy-tale world most charmingly invoked in *The Eve of St Agnes*—that influenced Tennyson and the Pre-Raphaelites. The *Hyperion* fragment and the *Ode to a Nightingale* (from which the following verses come) belong to a more impressive side of Keats's genius:

I cannot see what flowers are at my feet,
  Nor what soft incense hangs upon the boughs,
But, in embalmed darkness, guess each sweet
  Wherewith the seasonable month endows
The grass, the thicket, and the fruit-tree wild ;
  White hawthorn, and the pastoral eglantine ;
    Fast-fading violets covered up in leaves ;
      And mid-May's eldest child
The coming musk-rose, full of dewy wine,
  The murmurous haunt of flies on summer eves

Darkling I listen ; and, for many a time
I have been half in love with easeful death,
Called him soft names in many a mused rhyme,
  To take into the air my quiet breath ;
Now more than ever seems it rich to die,
  To cease upon the midnight with no pain,
    While thou art pouring forth thy soul abroad
      In such an ecstasy.
Still wouldst thou sing, and I have ears in vain,
  To thy high requiem become a sod.

A Great Period of Poetry, 1786-1824

Few periods in English, or British, poetry can equal that covered by the genius of Burns, Blake, Wordsworth, Coleridge, Byron, Shelley, Keats. It was peculiarly unfortunate that of these seven poets, the last three died so young. What needs to be stressed is the vacancy, the gap caused by the passing, one after the other in the space of a few years, of the three finest poets of the younger generation. If Dickens and George Eliot, as well as Emily Brontë, had died young, we should rightly expect that triple tragedy to have seriously affected the later development of the Victorian novel. So with Byron, Shelley, Keats, in regard to the development of poetry. Victorian verse has its own charm, its limited virtues and interest, but who can deny that it would have taken a different course had one or more of these three poets lived to about 1850 ? It is true that many poets, however long they have lived, have had only the one brief period of impressive genius ; but others, including Shakespeare and Yeats, have developed strongly throughout a long working life. It is at least a possibility that either Byron or Shelley or Keats would have belonged to the latter class rather than the former, and so have extended this great period of poetry up to mid-Victorian times.

Minor Poets and Scott

In every period of literature there are minor figures, of varying degrees of minority, who have to be dismissed in literary history, for reasons of space, in a very few words. Of the minor poets of the Wordsworthian period who are not considered in later chapters, we can mention here Mrs Hemans, who produced many volumes of sentimental verse, including the celebrated *Casabianca*, which had great popularity in her own day and in the Victorian age; Henry Francis Cary, who translated Dante; Charles Wolfe, the author of the well-known *Burial of Sir John Moore*; James Montgomery, a prolific poet, remembered to-day mostly for his hymns; and three poets of humble origin, Robert Bloomfield, who wrote the popular *Farmer's Boy*, John Clare, the author of *Poems of Rural Life* (1820) and *The Village Minstrel* (1821), and Ebenezer Elliott, best known for his *Corn Law Rhymes*, which are said to have materially assisted in that revolt against the Corn Laws which ended in their repeal in 1846.

We have quoted one fine ballad of Sir Walter Scott's. The reasons for considering his poetry as a mere preliminary to his novels will be considered in the next chapter. Scott is as central to the Romantic Movement in Prose as Wordsworth to the Romantic Movement in Poetry, and he said himself that his poems were a temporary deviation from the main purpose of his life.

CHAPTER II

THE ROMANTIC MOVEMENT IN PROSE
1800-1832

> "It is from the great book of Nature . . . that I have
> adventurously essayed to read a chapter to the public."
> SCOTT : Introduction to *Waverley*.

The Gothic Background

"Gothic Romance" is the name usually given to that
series of popular novels in the latter half of the eighteenth
century, and the first few years of the nineteenth, which are,
in some ways, the precursors of Scott, but also of the "penny
bloods" of Victorian youth. It was Horace Walpole, son of
the Whig prime minister, who inaugurated this "reign of
terror" in fiction by the publication of his *Castle of Otranto*
in 1764. This was rather a stupid novel, whose strictly
literary merit did not surpass the architectural worth of its
author's "Gothic castle" at Strawberry Hill. But it was a
great success, and undoubtedly Walpole—like his twentieth-
century namesake—must have had a keen eye for the fashionable demand. Probably he perceived that the time was ripe
for a double reaction : against the realism of the English
novel—Defoe, Fielding, Smollett—and against the classical
manner of the French. By this first attempt he fixed the
romantic scenery of the popular novel for more than a century,
and thus was the original cause of the broken sleep of
generations of Victorian housemaids.

Clara Reeve was the first to follow in Walpole's ghostly
footsteps with her *Old English Baron*, "a Gothic history."
Further causes assisted the progress of the new popular school.
The French Revolution and the birth of sentimental German
literature combined to form a state of mind in English novelists
and novel-readers in which to put the imagination to school in
Germany and to compose or read Gothic romances was to

collaborate with the anti-Gallican, anti-Jacobin movement. (We have seen that the early, revolutionary Wordsworth protested against the romantic extravagance of "frantic novels" and "sickly German tragedies.") Mrs Radcliffe published what may be called the "masterpieces" of the school: *A Sicilian Romance, The Romance of the Forest,* and *The Mysteries of Udolpho* (1794). In his *Ambrosio, or The Monk* (1795) Matthew Lewis combined terror with pornography; while Mrs Roche's *Children of the Abbey* enjoyed a success almost equal to that of *Udolpho*.

These novels were read at first mainly by the upper classes. "During my confinement," wrote Lady Holland in 1800, "I have been reading (among other things) multitudes of novels, most of them sad trash, abounding with the general taste for spectres, hobgoblins, castles, etc." But the fashion did not last for many years among the more intelligent of the upper and upper-middle classes.* It is amusing to read a letter on this subject from Gifford, the editor of the *Quarterly Review*, to John Murray, the publisher: praising Jane Austen's *Pride and Prejudice* in 1815, Gifford wrote: "No dark passages; no secret chambers; no wind-howlings in dark galleries; no drops of blood upon a rusty dagger—things that should now be left to ladies' maids and sentimental washerwomen."

The "now" gives the game away: the fashion had changed. *Before* the fashion had changed, there was little wrong with dark passages, secret chambers, and drops of blood upon rusty daggers!

Maria Edgeworth and Jane Porter

Speaking of his immediate predecessors in fiction, Scott says: "The imitators of Mrs Radcliffe and Mr Lewis were before us; personages who, to all the faults and extravagances of their originals, added that of dullness, with which they can seldom be charged. We strolled through a variety of castles, each of which was regularly called Il Castello; met

---

* Mary Shelley's *Frankenstein* (1817) is probably the last novel of the "terror" school of any literary merit at all.

with as many captains of condottieri; heard various ejacu-
lations of S. Maria and Diabolo; read by a decaying lamp
and in a tapestried chamber dozens of legends as stupid as the
main history; examined such suites of deserted apartments
as might fit up a reasonable barrack; and saw as many
glimmering lights as would make a respectable illumination."

But, besides these mediocre novelists, there were two others
in the early years of the century who pointed out to Scott
the main lines on which his fiction was to be drawn, those of
history and Scottish character. Maria Edgeworth (1767-
1849), daughter of the Irish writer, inventor, and educationist,
Richard Lovell Edgeworth, published her first novel, *Castle
Rackrent*, in 1800. Dealing with Anglo-Irish country society,
it was followed by the similar *Absentee* (1812) and *Ormond*
(1817) and the English novel *Belinda* (1801). Scott praised
her "rich humour, pathetic tenderness, and admirable tact",
and in the General Preface to the *Waverley Novels* (1829)
wrote that his object was to do for Scotland what she had
done for Ireland.

Jane Porter (1776-1850) and her sister Anne, who also
wrote many novels, were daughters of the surgeon to the
E niskillen Dragoons, and seem to have inherited a passion
for the romance of war—or what seems romance at a suitable
distance in space or time. Jane's *Thaddeus of Warsaw*
(1803) and *The Scottish Chiefs* (1810)—both of which
achieved European fame—pointed out roughly the road which
the historical novel was to follow, and it is said that Scott
admitted to George IV that *The Scottish Chiefs* was the parent
of the *Waverley Novels*.

Scott, 1771-1832

Born in Edinburgh, the son of a lawyer, Walter Scott was
educated at the high school and university, and in 1792 qualified as an advocate. His *Minstrelsy of the Scottish Border*
appeared, as we have seen, in 1802, and henceforth he combined the practice of literature with legal work. *The Lay
of the Last Minstrel* (1805) was an immediate success; and
so, too, were *Marmion* (1808), *The Lady of the Lake*

(1810), *Rokeby* (1812), and *Lord of the Isles* (1815). Out
of the proceeds of his verse he purchased and rebuilt the
mansion of Abbotsford on the Tweed.*

According to his own account, he had been led to write
his early romances in verse, instead of prose, by a series of
accidents. As early as 1800, he had written a chapter of a
tale of chivalry in the manner of Walpole; and after the
publication of the *Last Minstrel* in 1805, he wrote the first few
chapters of *Waverley*, which was actually announced by the
publisher Ballantyne as about to appear. But a candid friend,
to whom he submitted these opening chapters, deemed them
unworthy of the author's reputation; so the novel was put
aside, thought of as lost, and the manuscript was not found
again till 1814, when Scott completed the story in a month.

All this proves conclusively that he did not take to prose
fiction because (as he put it) Byron had "bet him" in verse.
This well-known saying is simply another instance of his good-
humoured approach to other people's work and his candid
criticism of his own. He took some of his work seriously, but
by no means all. He told his daughter not to read *The
Lady of the Lake*, as it was "bad poetry", and he admitted that
some of the young heroines of his novels bored him to tears.
The best of his shorter ballads is probably the one we quoted in
the last chapter; the best of his long narrative poems is
perhaps *The Lay of the Last Minstrel*, the nostalgic charm
of which is sufficient reason for its contemporary popularity

* Scott wrote at a fortunate time, in the financial sense. Up to
about the middle of the eighteenth century, the Court and nobility
had been the great patrons of literature, though there were exceptions
to the rule. From about Dr Johnson's time onwards, the publisher
took over the role of patron, and, at the beginning of the nineteenth
century, with an ever-growing reading public, publishers began to
make the fortunes of fashionable authors. Scott received £500 for
the copyright of the *Last Minstrel*, and for *Marmion* 1,000
guineas payable in advance. "It was a price," he said, "that made
men's hair stand on end." He received 1,500 guineas for half the
copyright of *Lord of the Isles*, the other half remaining his property.
In 1814 Moore was paid £3,000 for a poem, unwritten at the time,
to be at least equal in length to *Rokeby*. It is necessary to bear in
mind that we have to multiply by at least three times to get a
comparison in modern currency. The average salary of an English
clergyman *c.* 1815 was about £100 a year.

and the affectionate place it still holds in a corner of our esteem.

The Waverley Novels, 1814-32

Waverley, introduced to the applauding world anonymously, later gave its name to the astonishing series of twenty-nine works produced in the next seventeen years.* The authorship remained a secret—though an increasingly open one—until 1827, when it was divulged at the Theatrical Fund Dinner. Scott went to strange lengths in order to keep his anonymity, quoting from his own poetry and apparently reviewing his own novels in the *Quarterly*, on the appearance of *Tales of My Landlord* in 1816. In reality the latter was a doubled-dyed deception, as he merely copied out an article written by his friend Erskine!

The flood of "the Scotch novels", as they were then called, issued from the Ballantyne press without a pause, and soon their appearance was awaited as eagerly in Paris and Wiemar as in London. Scott's poems had thrown the English-speaking world into a passing excitement—an excitement, in fact, which passed to Byron in 1812. But the novels by "the Great Unknown" were at least "a nine years' wonder" in all the principal countries of Europe. Scott himself later became one of the most popular figures in London. Among his admirers was the Prince Regent, who, on his accession as

* It will be convenient to have a full dated list here:—*Waverley, or 'Tis Sixty Years Since* (1814) ; *Guy Mannering, or The Astrologer* (1815) ; *The Antiquary* (1816) ; *Tales of My Landlord* (*The Black Dwarf* and *Old Mortality*, 1816) ; *Tales of My Landlord*, Second Series (*The Heart of Midlothian*, 1818) ; *Rob Roy* (1818) ; *Tales of My Landlord*, Third Series (*The Bride of Lammermoor* and *The Legend of Montrose*, 1819) ; *Ivanhoe, A Romance* (1820) ; *The Monastery, A Romance* (1820) ; *The Abbot* (1820) ; *Kenilworth, A Romance* (1821) ; *The Pirate* (1822) ; *The Fortunes of Nigel* (1822) ; *Peveril of the Peak* (1822) ; *Quentin Durward* (1823) ; *St Ronan's Well* (1824); *Redgauntlet* (1824); *Tales of the Crusades* (*The Betrothed* and *The Talisman*, 1825) ; *Woodstock, or The Cavalier* (1826) ; *Chronicles of the Canongate* (*The Highland Widow, The Two Drovers, The Surgeon's Daughter*, 1827); *Chronicles of the Canongate*, Second Series (*St Valentine's Day, or The Fair Maid of Perth*, 1828) ; *Anne of Geierstein, or The Maiden of the Mist* (1829) ; *Tales of My Landlord*, Fourth Series (*Count Robert of Paris* and *Castle Dangerous*, 1832).

George IV, lost no time in conferring a baronetcy on his friend.

Scott's life was prosperous and happy till 1826, when he was involved in financial ruin through the bankruptcy of Constable, his chief publisher, with whom fell Ballantyne and Co., the firm of printers and publishers in which Scott had been for many years a sleeping partner. Refusing to accept bankruptcy, he set himself to pay off the combined debts of over £120,000. *Woodstock*, a life of Napoleon, and *Tales of a Grandfather*, are among the chief products of these last painful years.

It was an heroic effort: within five years he had repaid £63,000. But the task killed him. When in 1831 he went for a rest cruise in a vessel placed at his disposal by the King, Wordsworth wrote:

> The might
> Of the whole world's good wishes with him goes;
> Blessings and prayers, in nobler retinue
> Than sceptred king or laurelled conqueror knows,
> Follow this wondrous Potentate.

But he returned to die at Abbotsford in 1832.

Scott as Tory Propagandist

A modern political writer has said that "all art is propaganda", and, while this is extremely debatable, nobody has ever denied the political aspects of the Romantic Movement. In poetry, as we have seen, the politics were mostly "Left", partly as a natural result of the repercussions of the American and French revolutions, partly—and perhaps more fundamentally—as a reaction against the clumsy efforts of Tory governments to solve the admittedly difficult problems of the Industrial Revolution. We have noted how Wordsworth, Coleridge, and Southey lost their early revolutionary opinions, being swept into the current of patriotic conservatism that was the inevitable result of the Terror and Napoleon; but that Byron and Shelley were as enthusiastic for the new spirit in Italy and Greece as Wordsworth had been for that of France twenty years before.

Scott was a great influence on the other side. The
Victorian critic Leslie Stephen noticed the strong relation
between Scott and the great philosopher of the old Toryism,
Edmund Burke, who died in 1797, but whose thought dominated the rulers of England for a generation after. Burke
believed that a traditional order and belief were essential to
the well-being of human society. What Scott did later was
to show, by concrete instances, the value and interest of a
natural body of traditions. Burke's *Reflections on the French
Revolution* had been remarkably widely-read for a book of
that nature, but thousands of ordinary people who hadn't
read Burke read the *Waverley Novels*. Scott's biographer,
Lockhart, had no doubts about their political influence:
"Scott's services, direct and indirect, towards repressing the
revolutionary propensities of his age were vast," he wrote.
It wasn't so much that ordinary people believed Scott's
doctrine of inequality, as that they learnt from him and
Cobbett to respect some of the old order, while still desiring
to reform it. In the long run, Scott was probably a big
influence, not on the side of pure conservatism, as he would
have wished, but on that of constitutional reform.

Scott-land

1814 has claims to a place in the history of Anglo-Scottish
relations almost as powerful as 1603, the union of the two
thrones, or 1707, the union of the two parliaments. The
dislike of many Scotsmen for the English connection found
expression in the Jacobite rebellions of the '15 and the '45;
while it is a well-known fact of English history that many
Englishmen disliked the Scots. The most unpopular prime
minister of the eighteenth century had been Lord Bute—the
target of Wilkes and the poet Churchill in the satirical paper,
the *North Briton*—and the fact that he was a Scot was one of
the charges against him. But no one—as an historian wittily
remarks—disliked Ramsay MacDonald because he was born
at Lossiemouth.

Among the reasons for this change in attitude were the
Waverley Novels. Scott, the Borderer, was well placed to

interpret his country to the English, and his descriptions, in particular, of pre-Reformation Scotland appealed to the romanticism of the age. It is safe to say that, for most English people in the nineteenth century, Scotland meant Boswell, the songs of Burns, the ballads of Scott, and the *Waverley Novels* —and the *Waverley Novels* most of all.

What is more surprising is that, for Scotsmen themselves, Scott created a large part of the modern conception of their country's past. He was the first Scotsman to take all Scotland as his province : Highland Jacobites and Lowlanders were all fellow-countrymen to him. And this united Scotland he presented to Scotsmen and Englishmen alike.

Scott's Novels as History, Entertainment, and Literature

One of the most celebrated of modern historical novelists has recently written that Scott's novels are not "for mature minds." She goes on : "Save for the native ' characters ' he so lovingly described, the population of the Scott country are puppets, whether they have historic names or not. His supernatural effects are failures, save in *Wandering Willie's Tale* [in *Redgauntlet*], one of the great short stories of the world . . . Scott could be very kind to James Hogg without noticing that the befriended man had utterly surpassed Scott himself in *Confessions of a Justified Sinner*."

This is a somewhat severe view ; but it is generally recognised, at any rate, that if we divide the *Waverley Novels* into two groups—the purely historical or pseudo-historical ones, like *Ivanhoe*, where the novelist is trying to re-create a past that has altogether disappeared, and the others, such as *Old Mortality*, where he is reconstructing the recent past of his own country from surviving traditions—it is generally recognised that the latter group is far superior to the former. Such novels as *Quentin Durward* and *The Talisman* are "medieval" in much the same way as the architecture of the "Gothic mansion" at Abbotsford—in other words, they bear to the house the same relation as Walpole's *Castle of Otranto* to his "castle" at Strawberry Hill. (Though Scott was well justified in stressing the "nature" of his novels, in comparison with the romances of the Terror School.)   The historical *Waver-leys* are entertainment literature of high quality, however, and in the Victorian age, when children had few compensations in school, boys and girls were delighted at the idea of learning history while reading novels.   "The psychology of Scott's heroes," says an historian, "is adapted exactly to the intelligence of the schoolroom, and it was, in fact, among children of fifteen that the novels found faithful readers for an entire century."   Scott's blend of history and romance, while not being history itself, is no bad introduction to it; and we owe to him, not merely his own *Waverley* series, but the similar novels of Kingsley, Blackmore, Henty, Conan Doyle, Quiller-Couch, probably not one of whom would have written as he did without Scott's example.

His literary value is best sought for in such novels as *Old Mortality* (probably his masterpiece), *Rob Roy*, *The Heart of Midlothian*, *The Two Drovers*, *Redgauntlet*, and the two novels of contemporary life, *The Antiquary* and *Guy Mannering*.   Historical romances on post-medieval subjects include *Kenilworth* (reign of Elizabeth), *Fortunes of Nigel* (James I), *Legend of Montrose* and *Woodstock* (the Civil War), and *Peveril of the Peak* (Charles II).

Galt, Susan Ferrier, and James Hogg

John Galt (1779-1839), Susan Ferrier (1782-1854), and James Hogg (1770-1835) are the most distinguished successors of Scott in the novel of Scottish life and character.   Galt is mainly known for his *Annals of the Parish* (1821), in which he portrays the life of a Lowlands village, using the local dialect; Susan Ferrier, a very interesting minor novelist who owes something to Smollett and Maria Edgeworth, as well as to her friend Scott, wrote at least two novels which are still worth reading: *The Inheritance* (1824) and *Destiny* (1831); Hogg's only novel is the extraordinary masterpiece *The Private Memoirs and Confessions of a Justified Sinner* (1824).

. Hogg was born in Ettrick Forest, Selkirkshire, and worked as a shepherd at Yarrow; hence his subsequent name in literary circles, "The Ettrick Shepherd."   Though illiterate till the age of thirty, he published *Scottish Pastorals* (1801), which gained him the kindly patronage of Scott, while the latter was "raiding" in the interests of his Border Minstrelsy collection. Hogg published several other volumes of verse, also *The Domestic Manners and Private Life of Walter Scott.* He was among the projectors of *Blackwood's Edinburgh Magazine*, and later figured in its pages, in the character of the Shepherd, as one of the interlocutors in Wilson's *Noctes Ambrosianae.*

His novel was curiously neglected for many years, and it is only comparatively recently that its true stature has been recognised. It is a terrible indictment of the worst, the excessive side of Calvinism, the story of a man, perverted by the doctrine of predestination, who commits crimes with the conviction that, being already "saved", no evil deed can debar him from Heaven.* It can be considered a masterly variation on the Faustus theme, and, in fact, the Devil is one of the chief characters. It has been compared with Bunyan, Poe, and Hawthorne, but its dry, matter-of-fact treatment of the supernatural is quite unique. It is as original in Scottish fiction as Emily Brontë's novel is in English.

"Romantic" and "Regency" Complications

No absolute distinction can be made between the "romantics" and those writers of the Regency period who were more in touch with eighteenth-century taste. It is partly for convenience that this chapter is devoted to writers like Scott, Coleridge, Hazlitt, most of whose work can be considered aspects of the Romantic Movement; and the next to their Regency contemporaries, such as Jane Austen and

---

* It is a common mistake to suppose that this doctrine of predestination is exclusively post-Reformation. As a matter of fact, it was common in the Middle Ages. The *Chronicle* of the Franciscan friar Salimbene in the thirteenth century gives many examples of its evil influence; for instance, a certain Lord Guido, murderer of his wife and others, used to say that "If I am predestined to eternal life, then shall I come thereto, whatsoever may be my sins; and if I am predestined to eternal damnation, so shall it be likewise, in spite of all good deeds."

"the Great Reviewers", who were more the representatives
of the older tradition.   We have just seen that Hogg was
connected with *Blackwood's*, and the romantic critic Hazlitt
wrote for the *Edinburgh*.   Such complications are natural
enough, when we are dealing with contemporaries, and we
shall attempt to discover in the next chapter how the Romantic
Movement subsequently combined with some of the Regency
tradition to form the literary background of the early Victorian
age.   At the moment we have to glance briefly at some of the
principal critics and journalists of the first third of the century
who, in general, supported the Romantic Movement in poetry
and prose.   We begin, naturally, with Coleridge, some of
whose ideas have already been considered in conjunction with
Wordsworth's and part of whose chief critical work, the
Biographia Literaria, has already been quoted.

Coleridge as Critic

It has been said that "Coleridge alone among English
writers is in the front rank at once as poet, as critic, and as
philosopher."   Philosophy proper—that is, in its technical
sense—hardly enters into the scope of this book, but we can
remark in passing that professional philosophers usually consider Coleridge less important as a creative thinker than as
the introducer into England of German idealistic philosophy.
Nevertheless, a good deal of Victorian thought can be traced
back to Coleridge's observations.

It is in criticism that his prose importance mainly consists ;
but here again we have to make a qualification, for it is
probable that the majority of it has gone unrecorded.   We
have mentioned his constitutional indolence, and he was not
so much a writer as a talker.   His conversational powers are
said to have been extraordinary.   "I never was so bethumped
with words," said Carlyle irritably, after a Coleridge session.
In the amusing essay, *My First Acquaintance with Poets*,
Hazlitt writes of his first meeting with Coleridge, who "did
not cease [talking] while he staid ; nor has he since, that I
know of."   And the following anecdote is related of Lamb,
whom Coleridge (who had once studied for the Unitarian

ministry) asked, "Did you ever hear me preach, Charles?"
"I never heard you do anything else," replied Lamb.

This conversational ability must have made Coleridge
rather trying in private life, but it stood him in good stead
when he mounted the lecture platform. He rarely bothered
to prepare a lecture properly; he would come in, with a
marked volume of Shakespeare, for instance, and begin to
talk about it. And the result was often far more stimulating
than a properly prepared lecture. He thought aloud, somewhat in the manner of Dr Johnson, and luckily there was a
Boswell or two to take him down; these fragmentary reports,
together with his own rough notes and marking of passages,
constitute the majority of his criticism that has been preserved.
Lectures and Notes on Shakespeare and *Table Talk* are among
the best. What is, in some respects, his critical masterpiece,
Biographia Literaria (1817), is readable only in parts by those
without philosophical training. The strictly literary criticism
is confined to the famous Chapter XIV—from which we
quoted earlier—and a few other chapters.

In social and religious criticism, Coleridge's influence was
felt on such diverse Victorian movements as the Oxford, the
Broad-Church, the Christian-Socialist, and the "reformed"
Utilitarianism of J. S. Mill. In politics, he moved from
theoretical Communism to an idealistic sort of Toryism that
had little connection with the contemporary Tory party, which
he described as "a cyclops with one eye, and that in the back
of the head." In literature, he may be said to have initiated
Romantic Criticism in England—that is, he tried to judge a
work of art in the light of the principles on which it was
constructed, not according to previous critical authority. Such
a critical revolution had its own dangers, but eighteenth-
century, "classical" criticism was on its last legs, and it is
easy to see how Coleridge's respect for liberty of treatment
and ideas found favour with the younger generation and was
considered akin to political liberty.

Coleridge wrote a good deal for the *Morning Post* from
1799, and edited two unsuccessful periodicals, the *Watchman*
(1796) and the *Friend* (1809). In later years he spoke of

himself as the heir of Burke, and wrote *The Constitution of Church and State* (1830). *Aids to Reflection* (1825) and the posthumous *Confessions of an Inquiring Spirit* (1840) were the most influential of his philosophical works.

The Romantic Essay

There are two principal periods of the English essay : at the opening of the eighteenth century, with Addison, Steele, Swift, and lesser Augustans ; and at the opening of the nineteenth, with Hazlitt, Lamb, Leigh Hunt, De Quincey, etc. Modern essays are often imitations of Hazlitt, with his rather superfluous allusiveness, while the affected language of Lamb has been an unfortunate influence on modern advertisements.

The chief difference between the two periods is a loss of seriousness and an increase in whimsicality. (To be observed, for instance, in the feminine profusion of exclamation-marks and dashes in the essays of Lamb and Hazlitt.) The Augustan essay was a public affair, an affair of the coffee-house ; Addison and Swift wrote as they talked, and conversation then was a highly polite and serious art. The early nineteenth-century essay is much more private ; it has a habit of digging you intimately in the ribs. Lamb's essays and private letters are written in exactly the same style ; indeed, the celebrated essay *Distant Correspondents* is a development of a private letter to a friend in Australia. If the weakness of the one period is dullness, the weakness of the other is affectation. However many yawns we may now be forced to, as we struggle through some of the more boring contributions to the *Spectator*, we need never doubt that the essayist is writing as clearly as possible in the language of his time. But the language of Lamb is sometimes not contemporary at all ; it was influenced by the idiosyncratic style of the seventeenth-century writer Sir Thomas Browne, and thus was "romantic" in much the same way as Walpole's Gothic castle or Scott's Gothic mansion. He could never, for instance, have spoken like this in real life, even as a joke :—"Him shouldst thou haply encounter, with his dim visage pendent

over the grateful stream, regale him with a sumptuous basin
(it will cost thee but three half-pennies) and a slice of delicate
bread and butter (an added half-penny)—so may thy culinary
fires, eased of the o'ercharged secretions from thy worse-placed
hospitalities, curl up a lighter volume to the welkin—so may
the descending soot never taint thy costly well-ingredienced
soups—nor the odious cry, quick-reaching from street to
street, of the fired chimney, invite the rattling engines from
ten adjacent parishes, to disturb for a casual scintillation thy
peace and pocket!''

Hazlitt, even at his most precious, is much more sober than
Lamb, but his style is affected compared with the plain style
of Cobbett, who modelled himself on Swift. Among his
characteristic essays are *On the Conversation of Authors, Of
Persons One would Wish to have Seen, On Actors and Acting,
On the Pleasure of Painting*, and *On Going a Journey*.
Lamb's essays include the famous *Roast Pig, On Some of
the Old Actors, Imperfect Sympathies* ("I have been trying all
my life to like Scotchmen . . ."), and *Mrs Battle's Opinions
on Whist*. The last-named is one of the most amusing.

Hazlitt, 1788-1830

Born at Maidstone, the son of a Nonconformist minister,
William Hazlitt entered journalism in 1812 as a parliamentary
reporter and dramatic critic. He wrote on a great number of
topics for a great number of periodicals, including ite *Morning
Chronicle*, the *Examiner*, the *Champion*, the *London Maga-
zine*, the *Edinburgh Review*, the *Atlas*, and the *New Monthly
Magazine*. His essays and articles were later collected in
books, such as *The Round Table* (1817), *Characters of
Shakespeare's Plays* (1817), *A View of the English Stage*
(1818), *Political Essays* (1819), *Table-Talk* (1821-2), and
The Plain Speaker (1826). He became celebrated also as a
lecturer, his lectures being subsequently published as *The
English Poets* (1818), *The English Comic Writers* (1819), and
Dramatic Literature of the Age of Elizabeth (1820). His
criticism of his contemporaries appeared in *The Spirit of the
Age* (1825).

The collected edition of his works runs to twenty large volumes, but he was not, curiously enough, "a born writer." He frequently spoke in later years of his early difficulties; for a short time during his youth he studied painting in Paris, and returned to England as a portrait-painter (his portrait of Lamb in the dress of a Venetian senator is in the National Portrait Gallery). But he abandoned painting, struggled into authorship, and survived both by merit and determination.

His early revolutionary opinions also survived. He was a great admirer of Napoleon, and insisted that Trafalgar was a tragedy. His *Life of Napoleon*, begun in 1826 and published 1828-30, is his longest and most careful work, but his least read. Perhaps his sense of the contrast between the Emperor and early democratic hopes—a contrast which he denied in print with more eloquence than logic—was partly the reason for his indignation at the Wordsworths and the Southeys; though it should be remembered that it was more accurate even to lump in Napoleon with the Revolution than to dismiss the latter as the Reign of Terror and nothing else.

He was an extreme partisan, and his excessive contempt, in literary criticism, for some of the older writers can be compared with his excessive contempt, in politics, for his opponents. Thus he is a stimulating journalist, but often an unreliable critic, his celebrated "creed of a Tory", for instance —"He has no principles himself, nor does he profess to have any . . ." (etc.)—not being a very good judgment on, say, Sir Walter Scott (whose novels, nevertheless, he greatly admired). A modern critic compares him with Cobbett, and there are some points of resemblance; but Cobbett was probably the more intelligent man and the greater writer on political and social affairs.

In literary criticism, Hazlitt's historical importance is two-fold: he was the interpreter of the Romantic Movement (he said himself that "I am sometimes, I suspect, a better reporter of the ideas of other people than expounder of my own"), and he was associated with Coleridge, Lamb, and De Quincey in the new approach to Shakespeare. If we add to this the facts that he was the best professional dramatic critic of his

time and one of the first to realise the importance of Turner
and other contemporary painters, his general critical and
journalistic achievement can be fairly seen.

Lamb, 1775-1834

Charles Lamb has been mentioned in this book several
times already, and for a perfectly good reason : he was the
friend of many of the distinguished writers of his time,
including Coleridge, Wordsworth, Keats, Hazlitt, and many
anecdotes suggest that he was among the wittiest men of the
witty Regency period. He was a clerk at the India House
for thirty-three years, retiring in 1825. His private life was
tragic : in 1796 his sister Mary (later his collaborator in
Tales from Shakespeare) killed their invalid mother in a fit
of madness, brought on by overwork. Thenceforth Lamb
devoted his life to caring for his sister, in the intervals of the
recurrent fits of insanity which placed her in an asylum. In
1808 he published *Specimens of English Dramatic Poets who
lived About the Time of Shakespeare*, the comments on whom
remain his chief contribution to criticism. In 1820 he began
contributing to the *London Magazine* the famous series of
essays under the pseudonym "Elia", collected in book form
in 1823 and 1833. He also wrote poems, plays, and romances,
but these are generally considered inferior to the essays and the
posthumous collection of letters.

The fact that Lamb was a noted wit, amid all the tragedy
of his private life, suggests a toughness of character not
immediately apparent from the more affected of his essays.
He was a "character", too, in the eccentric sense : seated in
the front row of the pit, he was one of the loudest in hissing
his own farce *Mr H.* off the stage. Some of his recorded
jests (though it is not known for certain which are authentic,
which inventions) are naïveties, like the one mentioned in the
third paragraph of this book. A somewhat similar instance—
though here Lamb himself is the sufferer—is this passage from
the essay *Imperfect Sympathies*:—"I was present not long
since at a party of North Britons, where a son of Burns was
expected, and happened to drop a silly expression (in my

South British way) that I wished it were the father instead of
the son—when four of them started up at once to inform me
that 'that was impossible, because he was dead.' "

Haydon, Leigh Hunt, and Crabb Robinson

Among the Lamb circle were Benjamin Robert Haydon
(1786-1846), Leigh Hunt (1784-1859), and Henry Crabb
Robinson (1775-1867). Haydon, a painter whose large canvases were once esteemed, is now chiefly remembered for his
Autobiography, posthumously edited in 1853. This contains
some extremely interesting passages, also many amusing ones,
notably the scene in Haydon's house where a stranger, "a comp-
troller of stamps", was introduced to Wordsworth, and asked
so many idiotic questions ("Don't you think, sir, *Milton* was
a great genius ?" etc.) that Lamb had to be forcibly prevented
by Haydon and Keats from taking a candle and examining
his "phrenological development." "All the while," concludes
Haydon, "we could hear Lamb struggling in the painting-
room, and calling at intervals, 'Who is that fellow ?   Allow
me to see his organs once more.' "

Hunt began to help his brother John in editing the
Examiner in 1808, and in 1813 was sentenced to two years'
imprisonment for an attack therein on the Prince Regent.   In
prison he wrote his narrative poem *The Story of Rimini*, which
was published in 1816.   In 1821 he was invited to Italy by
Shelley, in order to help him and Byron in writing a new
review called the *Liberal*.   But Shelley was drowned a week
after Hunt's arrival, the *Liberal* perished after four numbers,
Byron and Hunt—to put it mildly—did not get on very well
together, and Hunt returned to London.   He lived for many
years after the death of most of his early friends, and produced
a vast quantity of literary and journalistic work.   Dickens knew
him well during the last ten years of his life, and there is a
caricature of the worst side of him in the Mr Skimpole of
Bleak House.

His poetry, like Haydon's painting, is largely forgotten.
He lives, like Haydon, for his biographical work : *Lord Byron
and Some of his Contemporaries* (1828) and *Autobiography*

(1850). Crabb Robinson wrote diaries, journals, and letters, which are a valuable source of information on his friends Blake, Wordsworth, Coleridge, Lamb, and Southey.

Landor and De Quincey

Walter Savage Landor (1775-1864) and Thomas De Quincey (1785-1859) were two other contemporaries of Scott, Byron, and Lamb who lived, like Wordsworth, well into Victorian times. Landor, like Hunt, was caricatured in *Bleak House*, while the opium-addict, who was born plain Quincey, lived to the ripe old age of seventy-four.

"Poetry was always my amusement, prose my study and business," wrote Landor ; and critical (and uncritical) opinion about his voluminous work has taken the lead from his other famous declaration : "I shall dine late, but the room will be well-lighted, and the guests few but select."

A modern advertising expert would have told Landor that "few but select" is the best recipe for popular success ; but we can acquit a nineteenth-century writer of any such perverted subtlety, especially as the invitation has not been at all widely accepted. The sad fact about Landor's prose and poetry alike is that most of it is boring ; his prose has been admired chiefly by those who confuse material things with spiritual, to whom a nicely-rounded sentence is a thing to be tasted, like a glass of old wine, with one eye fixed in ecstasy on the ceiling. In other words, Landor appeals, not to people who are fond of literature, but to connoisseurs who are fond of books. (He has a distinct relation to the *Yellow Book* of the 'nineties.) With this limited interest, his *Imaginary Conversations* (1824-46) can be skipped through with profit ; every so often we come upon a phrase that lingers in the palate —such as the famous "Laodameia died ; Helen died ; Leda, the beloved of Jupiter, went before . . ."—but even his admirers have admitted that in this vast work "a sense of monotony is inescapable." He is usually read in a brief selection, which contains a few poems, the best parts of the *Imaginary Conversations*, a few dreams from *The Pentameron* (1847), and some other pieces. (He also wrote poetic dramas, of which the best-known was *Count Julian*, 1812.) Coleridge's criticism of his poetry is applicable to most of his prose as well : "The truth is that Landor does not possess imagination in its highest form . . . You have eminences excessively bright, and all the ground around and between them is darkness. Besides which he has never learned with all his energy how to write simple and lucid English."

Thomas De Quincey took to opium at Oxford in 1803, and after a brief period in the Middle Temple settled with the Wordsworths and Coleridge in the Lake District in 1809. In 1820 he moved back to London, and a year later there appeared in the *London Magazine* his famous *Confessions of an English Opium-Eater*, published in book form in 1822. He devoted the rest of his life to miscellaneous writing, living in the neighbourhood of Edinburgh from 1828 to his death.

His later life was that of an eccentric nomadic genius ; he lived in one set of rooms till he was nearly "snowed up" with manuscript, and then moved to another. He published only two books, *Klosterheim* (1832) and *Logic of Political Economy* (1844); the whole of the remainder of his literary activity took the form of articles in various magazines. A demand for a collected edition came in the first place from the United States, where he was much esteemed. The first volume appeared in 1853. He is chiefly remembered to-day for his *Confessions*, for his *Reminiscences of the Lake Poets*, for his "fantasia" *On Murder considered as one of the Fine Arts*, and for his essay *On the Knocking at the Gate in "Macbeth"*. The most divergent estimates of his writings have been made. One of his modern admirers was D. H. Lawrence.

CHAPTER III

JANE AUSTEN, THE REGENCY, AND AFTER
1811-1837

> " ' Oh,' cried Marianne, ' with what transporting
> sensations have I formerly seen them fall ! How have
> I delighted, as I walked, to see them driven in showers
> about me by the wind ! What feelings have they, the
> season, the air altogether inspired ! Now there is no
> one to regard them. They are seen only as a nuisance,
> swept hastily off, and driven as much as possible from
> the sight.'
>
> ' It is not every one,' said Elinor, ' who has your
> passion for dead leaves.' "
>
> JANE AUSTEN : *Sense and Sensibility*.

Dates of the Regency Period

It is rather curious that the short Regency period—that
is, from 1811 to 1820, when the Prince of Wales, afterwards
George IV, acted as Regent during his father's insanity—has
given its name to a much longer period, in popular and also
literary estimation. For instance, the Great Reviews of the
early nineteenth century are often known as "the Regency
Reviews", despite the fact that the *Edinburgh* was founded
as early as 1802, and the *Quarterly* in 1809. And a modern
anthology of Regency Verse takes in early nineteenth-century
poetry in general, in fact from the start of the Romantic
Movement to the age of Victoria.

This last example is curious in another sense, for
"Romantic" and "Regency" are usually used—partly for
convenience of grouping, as has been noted—to indicate
opposing states of mind, the one more visionary, the other
more matter-of-fact, the one more fanciful, the other more
worldly, the one laying stress on the heart, the other on the
head. The most celebrated instance of this contemporary
divergence is, of course, the "war" between the Romantic
Movement and the Regency Reviews—in which, at this

distance of time, it is possible to see some good points in either side. Certainly we cannot accept to-day the common Victorian and Edwardian view that all the good was on the side of the Romantics and all the bad on the side of the Reviews.

Since Jane Austen's first publication, *Sense and Sensibility*—itself an obvious example of the two contemporary attitudes—came out the same year as the Prince Regent took over his father's functions, this chapter begins with 1811, discusses the chief writers of the Regency school, and then goes on to consider briefly the combination of Romantic and Regency ideas which determined the background of the early Victorian literary age. For convenience, we shall treat both Jane Austen and "the Regency Reviews" from their pre-Regency beginnings, and also discuss those minor poets of the early nineteenth century whom the Regency reviewers highly esteemed and sometimes held up as examples for Wordsworth and Keats to follow.

Jane Austen, 1775-1817

Jane Austen was born at Steventon, in Hampshire, where her father was rector. In 1801 the family moved to Bath, and after the death of her father in 1805, to Southampton, finally settling in Chawton, with her brother Edward. She started with burlesque of eighteenth-century romantic novels. *Northanger Abbey* and *Sense and Sensibility* are the developed versions of this burlesque ; the former, published posthumously in 1818 together with *Persuasion*, still contains a good deal of private family joking, but the latter, published 1811, is a highly successful novel on a limited theme. We have only to compare it with one of Fanny Burney's novels—good though these are in some respects—to see how much more life-like are Jane Austen's characters, particularly her male characters. Fanny Burney's heroes are simply too noble for words, and their words are too noble for anything ; whereas Edward Ferrars and Colonel Brandon act and speak like ordinary mortals.*

---

* Frances (Fanny) Burney lived from 1752 to 1840, but the majority of her writing belongs to the eighteenth century. Her best qualities are seen in *Evelina* (1778). *Cecilia* (1782) and *Camilla* (1796) are comparatively stiff and unnatural. In 1793 she married

Pride and Prejudice (1813), *Mansfield Park* (1814), and *Emma* (1815) have more complicated themes. The first-named is easily the most popular of the novels, and it has been observed that Elizabeth and Jane Bennet are subtler versions of Elinor and Marianne. The Bennet parents make a nice contrast, as the author somewhat caustically notes : "Mr Bennet was so odd a mixture of quick parts, sarcastic humour, reserve, and caprice, that the experience of three-and-twenty years had been insufficient to make his wife understand his character. *Her* mind was less difficult to develop. She was a woman of mean understanding, little information, and uncertain temper."

There is possibly a personal reminiscence in Elizabeth's thoughts upon her friend Charlotte's acceptance of the solemn buffoon Mr Collins—whose earlier proposal to Elizabeth herself, and the consequent difference of opinion between Mr and Mrs Bennet, is one of the novel's high comic spots. We know that Jane Austen spent a night of psychological crisis before deciding to revoke in the morning the previous evening's acceptance of a proposal that was, apparently, very suitable in the financial sense ; so there may be some urge to justify her own action when she makes Elizabeth reflect : "She had always felt that Charlotte's opinion of matrimony was not exactly like her own, but she could not have supposed it possible that, when called into action, she would have sacrificed every better feeling to worldly advantage." *

General d'Arblay and from 1802 to 1812 lived in France, returning to publish her last novel, *The Wanderer*, in 1814. Her diaries and letters, first published in 1842, are possibly more valuable than her novels. She spanned a very long period, being the friend of Dr Johnson in youth and of Lamb and Hazlitt in old age.

* That Jane Austen's moral conscience was not the "mode" can be seen from this passage in a recent biography of Caroline Norton, née Sheridan : "One of the most striking features of the English upper classes at this time was their passionate pre-occupation with money. Their lives were spent in an alteration between schemes to acquire it and a startling speed in getting rid of it again. For money a man of fashion would do almost anything. He would cheat his friends, mortgage his estates, impoverish his near relations, marry a hideous heiress. Women also were expected to unite themselves with odious old men or with heartless libertines in the interests of this quest. Their complacency was taken for granted."

Mansfield Park is generally considered to be very interesting rather than highly successful. It is not nearly so neat as *Pride and Prejudice*, and has even been accused of priggishness. Her last completely-revised work was *Emma*, often regarded as her masterpiece. Most of her previous heroines had been more or less static, but Emma develops throughout the novel and is a different kind of person at the end from what she was at the beginning. Here Jane Austen succeeds triumphantly with a difficult theme, where she had only partly succeeded with *Mansfield Park*. *Emma* is probably her most distinguished psychological novel, and *Sense and Sensibility* and *Pride and Prejudice* her best comedies.

Her Achievement and Influence

Jane Austen can be considered the precursor of such careful Victorian novelists as George Eliot and Henry James. George Eliot, in fact, wrote one of the earliest appreciations of her work in Victorian times ; another Victorian novelist, however, was vigorously depreciative: "Anything like warmth or enthusiasm," wrote Charlotte Brontë (whose opinions on novel-writing were as distinct from Jane Austen's as Charlotte's views on matrimony from Elizabeth Bennet's), "anything like warmth or enthusiasm, anything energetic, poignant, heart-felt, is utterly out of place in commending these works : all such demonstration the authoress would have met with a well-bred sneer, would have calmly scorned as outré and extravagant. . . The passions are perfectly unknown to her ; she rejects even a speaking acquaintance with that stormy sisterhood . . . What sees keenly, speaks aptly, moves flexibly, it suits her to study ; but what throbs fast and full, though hidden, what the blood rushes through, what is the unseen seal of life and the sentient target of death— this Miss Austen ignores."

It is not necessary to take sides here ; it is better simply to notice the rather loose, romantic way Charlotte Brontë puts her criticism, while recognising that Jane Austen could not possibly have written, say, *Wuthering Heights*. There are no "rules" in literature, and there are valuable traditions in the English novel other than that represented by the line Richardson-Austen-Eliot-James. There are not only such eccentric masterpieces as *Wuthering Heights* and *Confessions of a Justified Sinner*; there is also the comic tradition in English fiction (connected with the drama), whose eighteenth-century examples were written by Fielding and Smollett, and which reached its highest, almost Shakespearean level in Dickens. Jane Austen could no more have written *Martin Chuzzlewit* than *Confessions of a Justified Sinner* or *Wuthering Heights*.

Peacock, 1785-1866

Thomas Love Peacock's short satirical novels, a passage from one of which we quoted in our discussion of Wordsworth, are more adequate, more adult examples of the kind of bur-lesque which Jane Austen favoured at the start of her career. But, whereas she developed slowly throughout a working life of about twenty-eight years, Peacock in a longer working life never developed at all, *Gryll Grange* (1861) being a tale of exactly the same kind as *Headlong Hall* (1816). His works include poems, plays, and essays, but he is remembered almost entirely for these short satirical novels, often reprinted in one volume, making up about as much space in their entirety as an average-length novel by Dickens. They number seven, and we have mentioned the first and the last; the others are *Nightmare Abbey* (1818), *Maid Marian* (1822), *The Misfortunes of Elphin* (1829), *Crotchet Castle* (1831), and—longer than the rest— *Melincourt* (1817). In all these novels there are scattered songs, some of them satiric, reminding us of the mingled prose and verse of the *Alice* books. Perhaps in some respects Peacock is Lewis Carroll for adult readers; in others, he has been compared with George Meredith, who married his daughter.

Though the intimate friend of the ultra-romantic Shelley, Peacock was a typical man of the Regency. He takes his stand on eighteenth-century common sense, and satirises late-eighteenth-century romantic fiction and the contemporary Romantic Movement with impartial prejudice. He is rather like his own Reverend Doctor Folliot in *Crotchet Castle* : "He is of an admirable temper, and says rude things in a pleasant half-earnest manner, that nobody can take offence with." But his best satire, like Pope's, is always serious enough : the skit on the Malthusian doctrine of population in *Melincourt*, for instance, is extremely funny, but has a serious, human purpose behind it, like many of Dickens's thrusts at Victorian society later on. *Melincourt* also affords us an example, from the first chapter, of the Peacock style where it is most like Jane Austen's : "It was seldom that the presence of a visitor dispelled the solitude of Melincourt ; and the few specimens of the living world with whom its inmates held occasional intercourse were of the usual character of country acquaintance, not calculated to leave behind them any very lively regret, except for the loss of time during the period of their stay."

The Great Reviews

It is time now to look a little more closely at those reviews of the Regency period which were the arbiters of public taste and which we have mentioned from time to time during the last two chapters. Of the *Edinburgh* Scott said that "No genteel family can pretend to be without it", and Carlyle that it was "a kind of Delphic oracle and voice of the inspired for the great majority of what is called ' the intelligent public.' " About 1820, in a population of some fifteen millions, *Blackwood's Magazine* and the *Quarterly* had between them a circulation of 31,000, and the *Edinburgh* 7,000. We must allow for there being about three readers to each copy, and the small provincial papers used to quote the articles. Their power was therefore very great, and it was said of the *Edinburgh* that "to have the entry of its columns was to command the most direct channel for the spread of opinions and the shortest road to influence and celebrity." *

---

* Both the *Edinburgh* and the *Quarterly* were able by their wide sale to pay contributors very highly, at the average rate of 20 guineas a page. At least £60 would be the comparable sum in modern currency, and some of the articles were over ten pages in length. Southey once wrote to Coleridge : "The most profitable line of

The *Edinburgh* was founded in 1802 by three young men, almost entirely unknown at the time : Francis Jeffrey (1773-1850), a Scottish advocate, later Lord Jeffrey ; Sydney Smith (1771-1845), a distinguished scholar from Oxford, who, while waiting for an English living, was in Edinburgh as a private tutor ; and Henry Brougham (1778-1868), the future Lord Chancellor, who had just been called to the Scottish bar. Jeffrey became editor in chief and held that position till 1829.

The first number was a great success. From the start the *Edinburgh* was clearly on the side of what used to be called Whiggery and was beginning to be called Liberalism ; it held reasonable opinions on the French Revolution. Scott contributed several articles, but his romantic Toryism was at variance with the general spirit of the Review. Of the early contributors probably the best was Sydney Smith, famous throughout his life as a brilliant humorist, but also zealous as the advocate for social reform. Later, in August 1825, an interesting event was the appearance of a long article on Milton by an unknown young man named Macaulay, who afterwards became one of the chief props of the Review and contributed to it that long series of articles which were considered by many Victorians as classics in their field.*

The success of the liberal *Edinburgh* made the Tories anxious to have their own review. Scott was more than willing to help, but refused to take on the editorship. The publisher Murray then appealed to the Foreign Secretary,

composition is reviewing . . . I have not yet received so much for the *History of the Brazils* [in three volumes] as for a single article in the *Quarterly.*"

*Thomas Babington, Lord Macaulay (1800-59) will be mentioned in later chapters. He is important in the early Victorian age both as an historian and as a politician. He entered Parliament in 1830, and advocated parliamentary reform and the abolition of slavery. In his *Essays* and in his great unfinished *History of England* (1848-61) he did more than any Victorian to popularise the study of history—particularly social history, in which he was a pioneer. "His *Essays*," wrote Morley in 1881, "have done more than any other writings of this generation to settle the direction of men's historical interest and curiosity. From Eton and Harrow down to an elementary school in St Giles's or Bethnal Green, Macaulay's *Essays* are a text-book. At home and in the colonies they are on every shelf between Shakespeare and the Bible."

George Canning, and after some delay the editorship was pressed on the ex-cabin-boy and shoemaker's apprentice William Gifford (1756-1826), formerly Canning's associate in the political magazine *The Anti-Jacobin*. Thus the *Quarterly*, unlike the *Edinburgh*, was founded by party politicians of high standing; Gifford was editor from its foundation in 1809 to 1824, when he was succeeded by Scott's son-in-law and biographer, John Gibson Lockhart (1794-1854). The *Quarterly* still exists, though, like *Blackwood's Magazine*, it has gone through many changes and no longer has the old influence; the *Edinburgh* ceased publication in 1929.

Blackwood's, started in 1817, was designed to be a Tory rival to the *Edinburgh* in Edinburgh itself. (The *Quarterly*, though with strong Scots connections, was published in London.) Its first few numbers were failures, but then it made a sensation by the so-called "Chaldee MS", which, in language parodied from the Bible, satirised the leading figures of the Scots metropolis. This was the work of three men: Lockhart, the poet and novelist James Hogg, and John Wilson (1785-1854), who wrote under the pseudonym "Christopher North." A later frequent contributor was the Irishman William Maginn, who in 1830 founded *Fraser's Magazine*. It is said that Maginn first suggested the famous *Blackwood* series, the *Noctes Ambrosianae*, so named from Ambrose's Tavern. These "dialogues of the day", which began in 1822 and lasted to 1835, were mostly written by North, Hogg appearing in them in the character of the Shepherd. An example can be quoted, as illustrating not only their style but Wilson's justified pride in the periodical literature of the time :

> NORTH : Now all our philosophical criticism—or nearly all—is periodical ; and fortunate that it is so both for taste and genius. It is poured daily, weekly, monthly, quarterly, into the veins of the people, mixing with their heart and blood. Nay, it is like the very air they breathe . . . The whole surface of society, James, is thus irrigated by a thousand streams ; some deep—some shallow.

SHEPHERD : And the shallow are sufficient for the purpose o' irrigation.

Their Literary Attitude

The Regency reviews became infamous in mid-Victorian times for their generally contemptuous treatment of the Romantic poets. Apart from some snobbish, political, or merely frivolous jibes, though, these criticisms are worth considering on their own merits, because some of the reviewers at least were quite sincere.

The *Edinburgh* was as conservative in literature as it was liberal in politics. Jeffrey attacked Southey's *Thalaba* in the first number ; and, what was more serious, continued for years to see no great difference between Southey's pedestrian romanticism and the living poetry of Wordsworth. Jeffrey was earnest enough, and made a few good points. His review of Wordsworth's *Excursion* opened with the celebrated phrase: "This will never do." He treated Wordsworth as a "case", for which there was now, alas ! no hope—a perfectly fair judgment had Wordsworth been simply the poetaster of *Goody Blake and Harry Gill*, but betraying a lack of genuine feeling for poetry when applied to the Wordsworth of *Tintern Abbey*, *Resolution and Independence*, or, indeed, the best parts of the admittedly rather boring *Excursion*. A small part of this long review can be quoted, as showing the style and procedure:

> The case of Mr Wordsworth, we perceive, is now manifestly hopeless ; and we give him up as altogether incurable, and beyond the power of criticism. We cannot indeed altogether omit taking precautions now and then against the spreading of the malady ;—but for himself, though we shall watch the progress of his symptoms as a matter of professional curiosity and instruction, we really think it right not to harass him any longer with nauseous remedies,—but rather to throw in cordials and lenitives, and wait in patience for the natural termination of the disorder.*

---

* The Reviewers were fond of this malady metaphor. Jeffrey later wrote of Keats in *Blackwood's* : "To witness the disease of any human understanding, however feeble, is distressing ; but the spectacle of an able mind reduced to a state of insanity is of course ten

Jeffrey put part of the reason for Wordsworth's eccentricity, as he saw it, to the account of the poet's country retreat:·

> If Mr Wordsworth, instead of confining himself almost
> entirely to the society of dalesmen and cottagers and little
> children, who form the subjects of his book, had conde-
> scended to mingle a little more with the people who were
> to read and judge of it, we cannot help thinking that its
> texture might have been considerably improved: at least
> it appears to us to be absolutely impossible, that anyone
> who has lived or mixed familiarly with men of literature
> and ordinary judgment of poetry (of course we exclude the
> coadjutors and disciples of his own school) could ever have
> fallen into such gross faults, or so long mistaken them for
> beauties.

That reference to "gross faults" gives us a clue to Jeffrey's poetic faith: he sincerely believed that the "rules" of poetry had been settled and that deviation from them could only be due to ignorance or affectation. He starts his review of Southey's *Thalaba* with the observation that the standards of poetry "were fixed long ago by certain inspired writers whose authority it is no longer lawful to question."

This is a typically academic view, for we find that, when the Romantic Movement finally triumphed in the mid-Victorian age, critics fundamentally similar to Jeffrey—who would, nevertheless, have liked to burn him alive—were as sincerely convinced of the infallibility of their own "rules" and despised all poetry, old or new, which couldn't be fitted in. The *Globe* editor of Pope in 1869, for instance, wrote that some acknowledgment was due to the poet for his noble devotion to his art, "even by those who perceive his short-comings and lament his faults."

times more afflicting. It is with such sorrow as this that we have contemplated the case of Mr John Keats . . . For some time we were in hopes that he might get off with a violent fit or two ; but of late the symptoms are terrible. The phrenzy of the *Poems* was bad enough in its way ; but it did not alarm us half so seriously as the calm, settled, imperturbable drivelling idiocy of *Endymion*. We hope, however, that in so young a person, and with a constitution originally so good, even now the disease is not utterly incurable . . ." (etc.) The review in *Blackwood's* of Hazlitt's *Table Talk* is similar in tone.

The Romantic-Regency War

Sentimental critics of the mid-Victorian age, partly misled by Shelley's honest blunder about the death of Keats, were inclined to deplore altogether the tone of Regency reviewing. But three things have to be borne in mind: (1) that some of these reviewers made good points and were by no means contemptuous of the whole of their subject's work ; (2) that some of the Romantics, particularly Shelley and Hazlitt, gave as good as they got; and (3) that, prejudiced as the Reviews were, Leigh Hunt was invited to write for the *Quarterly*, which counted Lamb among its reviewers, while both Hunt and Hazlitt were welcome contributors to the *Edinburgh*.

It was against what they called "the Cockney School" that the Reviews were most violent. This was partly due to political, not literary, prejudice ; and, in some cases, to social snobbery. The *Edinburgh* was polite compared with *Blackwood's* and the *Quarterly*. The latter damned Hunt's *Rimini* with exceedingly faint praise : "Amidst all his vanity, ignorance and coarseness, there are here and there some well-executed descriptions, and occasionally a line of which the sense and expression are good."

The most virulent attacks on Keats came from *Blackwood's*. The *Quarterly* reviewer, John Wilson Croker (later Secretary to the Admiralty, founder of the Athenaeum Club, who was himself maligned in Disraeli's *Coningsby*), was very severe also, but he did mix with his abuse some recognition of talent. There was a touch of Northern prejudice about these attacks. Edinburgh in the time of the Regency was known as "the Athens of the North", and anything produced by London was regarded as an opportunity to point out the "vulgarity" existing in that less favoured spot. This was certainly a hefty blow in return for the earlier contempt of Scotsmen indulged in by the *North Briton* and by some of the Johnson circle.

The Reviews were best on the negative side ; the objects of their enthusiasm, as Shelley shrewdly noted in the Preface to *Adonais*, were significant in their mediocrity. There are naturally a few exceptions : Scott's and Archbishop Whately's praise of Jane Austen, for instance, in the *Quarterly*. But, as a general rule, the Reviews were far more valuable as a kind of "His Majesty's Opposition" to the Romantic Movement than as advocates for the elegant sentimentality of minor poets such as Rogers.

Crabbe, Moore, Campbell, Rogers

The four poets of whom the Reviews spoke most warmly, and whom they sometimes compared with the Romantics to the latter's disadvantage, were Crabbe, Moore, Campbell, and Rogers. (Jeffrey declared that of all the poets of his day only Campbell and Rogers were secure of immortality.) Of these four writers, only Crabbe is now considered a distinguished, if minor, poet.

George Crabbe (1754-1832) had a very long working career, having produced his first poem in 1775. The best of his early work is *The Village* (1783). A long period of poetic inactivity—or non-publication—was followed by *The Parish Register* (1807), *The Borough* (1810), *Tales* (1812), and *Tales of the Hall* (1819). His outlook in these latter poems has been compared with Jane Austen's; Byron called him "Nature's sternest poet, yet the best"; and, although *Blackwood's* once spoke of his "cynicism", he was usually treated by the Reviews as an established classic. He reacted against the idealised conception of country life, and dealt realistically, especially in his two volumes of *Tales*, with country people, high and low. He owes much to Pope, but at his best his wit is highly original.

Thomas Moore (1779-1852) was an admirable song-writer, singer, and celebrated wit, whose more ambitious work is largely forgotten. He was born in Dublin, and came to England to study law in 1779. Among his many works are the verse romance *Lalla Rookh* (1817), the amusing satire *The Fudge Family in Paris* (1818), *Loves of the Angels* (1823), the *Irish Melodies* (1807-35), and biographies of Sheridan and Byron. Byron included him among the poets whom posterity would certainly prefer to Wordsworth and Coleridge; and the Reviews were generally favourable, although once *Blackwood's* spoke of the "schoolboy key on which Moore's love and heroism is always set." It could be claimed, of course, that he is one of the best-known poets who have ever lived, for many people who have not read a word of Keats or Wordsworth know the "lyrics" of songs like *The Minstrel Boy, Believe me if all those endearing young charms, Oft in the stilly night, She is far from the land,* and *The harp that once through Tara's halls.* Unless the succession of charming Irish tenors dies out altogether, Tom Moore's future popularity is far more certain than Shakespeare's.

Thomas Campbell (1777-1844) is mainly known to-day for his patriotic and battle pieces, which turn up regularly in school anthologies. They are among the finest in their kind, particularly *Hohenlinden* and *The Battle of the Baltic.* His long poems, for instance *The Pleasures of Hope* (1799), which ran through four editions in one year, and *Gertrude of Wyoming* (1819), express sentimental ideas in exceedingly dull eighteenth-century versification. Jeffrey, writing of *Gertrude* in the *Edinburgh,* rejoiced "to see once more a polished and pathetic poem in the old English style of pathos and poetry." If anyone reads these poems to-day, they are likely to find them "pathetic" in a somewhat different sense.

Crabbe—a distinguished minor poet ; Moore—still famous for his melodies ; Campbell—found in school anthologies. Now we descend the last step and come to Samuel Rogers (1763-1855), whom it is safe to say nobody, young or old, reads to-day. Yet he was famous in his time, both as a poet and as a host. He was the son of a banker and became head of the firm, retiring from business in 1803 and devoting the rest of his life to conversation, poetry, and hospitality. His house was the resort of famous beauties, who came to meet well-known authors, and of well-known authors, who came to be introduced to possible patrons. He established his poetical reputation with *The Pleasures of Memory* (1792), which was followed, among others, by a long poem in blank verse *Italy* (1822-8). He was another of the poets whom Byron thought would outlive Wordsworth, and the *Edinburgh* spoke of him

as "already a classic." But he is a dull, "faultless" poet—
which only goes to show how idiotic the latter designation is.

The Regency and the Victorian Age

We have talked of the "war" between the Regency writers
and the Romantics ; it is now time to see who won. This is
not so easy to estimate exactly, in spite of the romantic tendencies of the Victorian age. One of the most obvious things
about Victorian literature is its sentimentality, and it is also
a fact that soon after the Regency period the Great Reviews—
which were always fond of a little pathos, providing it be
elegantly expressed—succumbed altogether to the damp spirit
of the age. When we reach the year 1858, we find the entire
collection of elderly gentlemen at an Edinburgh club—in
the former "Athens of the North" !—weeping in unison over
Adam Bede ; and we have noted that Victorian criticism
regarded with horror the critical tone of the Regency.

So if the Victorian age can be said to have been in general
deeply influenced by the Romantic Movement, it wasn't quite
in the original Wordsworthian sense of "thinking long and
deeply", nor of that "more than usual order" which Coleridge
spoke of. The Victorian sentimentality has an obvious connection with the side of the Regency tradition that we have
just glanced at, with the sentimental elegancies of Campbell,
Moore, and Rogers, and also with the lesser side of the
"Regency-Romantic" Byron. There was sentimentality in
the Era of Enlightenment, the eighteenth century, but in
that period, as in the Regency, it was counteracted to some
extent by the common sense of such people as Johnson,
Jane Austen, Peacock, Cobbett ; and there must have been
plenty of such people, for these writers were popular.
Whereas in the Victorian age—great as it was in many
respects—even the best writers were very sentimental indeed.

It is better, though, to be sentimental than callous. A
glance through *The Creevey Papers* is instructive for anyone
inclined to flatter the Regency period at the total expense
of the Victorian. (*The Croker Papers*, Lord Cockburn's
Memorials of His Time, and *The Greville Memoirs* are also

useful.) Thomas Creevey, M.P. was not a very important person in himself, but he knew most of the Court, gentry, and politicians of the Regency and after, and his lively letters and journals are an eye-opener in regard to the absence of responsibility in public affairs, the way in which serious matters could be decided by personal whim, much-needed reform put off by private squabbles or party intrigue. The Court had power in the early years of the nineteenth century, but it was mostly used to squeeze money out of the Government. The loss of Court power under Victoria, coupled with the decency—one might also say the notorious decency—of that sovereign, resulted in the regaining of royal popularity which had been almost completely lost since Farmer George.

The social troubles of the Regency period, and the subsequent reforms, will be the part concern of the next chapter, where we shall be considering the critics of English society, from Cobbett to Carlyle.

CHAPTER IV

THE MACHINE AGE: CRITICS AND REFORMERS
1815-1859

> "Were we required to characterise this age of ours by a single epithet, we should be tempted to call it, not an Heroical, Devotional, Philosophic or Moral Age, but the Mechanical Age . . . Not the external and physical alone is now managed by machinery but the internal and spiritual also . . . Men are grown mechanical in head and heart, as well as in hand."
>
> CARLYLE: "Signs of the Times" in the *Edinburgh Review*, June 1829.

The Industrial Revolution

It is impossible to give exact dates for the Industrial Revolution, which in a sense is still taking place; but from about 1760 to about 1830 is the period usually indicated for the first big change-over from a largely agricultural Britain to a largely industrial. It was only during the early nineteenth century, however, that the change became strikingly manifest, because till then the revolution in industry had grown up gradually in rural areas. With the emergence of the large factory in the new towns of the north, it is possible to speak of a "revolution" in an entirely accurate sense. For the northern towns were drawing into factory and slum men and women of village tradition who had passed through a revolution themselves. As a personal experience in individual and family lives, the Industrial Revolution was as sudden as its name suggests, however inaccurate the term may be in abstract economics.

The period, of course, was one of rapid change in other matters, and it is important that, while recognising their link with the Industrial Revolution, we should not confuse them with it. The population of this country increased rapidly *at the same time* as the Industrial Revolution—from seven-and-a-half to fourteen millions during the reign of George III—and some writers have taken this as cause and effect; one of them refers to "the fact that machinery, by increasing production, has permitted an increase in population"! This, of course, is not a fact at all, the rapid increase of population being largely due to the improvement in medical skill and sanitation. But it is a fact that the Industrial Revolution and the improvement in medicine and sanitation were both aspects of the scientific advance of 1760-1830.

The increasing numbers had to be fed, and there was as yet little importation of foodstuffs from abroad. The problem was not completely solved, and was complicated by the Napoleonic wars, but it led to a reorganisation of agriculture. Scientific principles were applied to the tilling of the soil, those open fields and commons which had escaped the enclosing movement of previous centuries were now hedged in in their turn, and, while a new class of large tenant farmers grew up and prospered, the old peasantry almost disappeared, either becoming hired labourers of the farmers (as some of them, indeed, had been before) or else drifting to the new towns to work in the factories.

Thus we have an Industrial Revolution on the one hand, and a vast increase in population, leading to an Agricultural Revolution, on the other. The social problems of the period are probably the most complicated in English history. Take, for instance, the contrast between statistical happiness and actual misery—a contrast that Dickens vividly expressed in *Hard Times* later on. The birth-rate increased and the death-rate decreased every census ; terrible diseases, such as smallpox, were at last being checked ; but probably the discontent of the lower classes was greater than at any period since the fourteenth century. Both in town and country competition for jobs kept wages low, and Trade Unions were illegal until 1824, when the Combination Laws were repealed. Many men were unable to earn enough to provide for their families ; women and children went to work in the mills and the mines. Some of the evils which we connect with the Industrial Revolution had, it is true, existed before ; but never, until now, had the misery of the poor been concentrated in a few large towns, to become a disgrace to the nation, and never before had social critics been so zealous in the cry for parliamentary reform to check the new abuses. The cry became more insistent still in the lean years following Waterloo, and now that the danger from outside had passed, men of good will in various spheres of life could turn their full attention to internal problems. That they did so to some effect can be seen, for instance, from the record of the Factory Acts passed —admittedly against strong opposition—by the reformed Parliament.

For some time, though, it was thought that England might follow the example of the French in 1789. The fears of the ruling classes—still largely, until the Reform Bill of 1832, the old landed gentry—resulted in savage repression whenever the poor tried in various ways to better their condition, even when they only met to talk about it. But there were many reasons—some apparently conflicting with others—why the English people preferred reform to revolution. These reasons, of course, concern social history rather than literary, but they are connected with literature in the writings of those critics and reformers of the period whose influence was not only great upon their contemporaries and immediate successors but who are still worth listening to to-day. We can begin with the greatest, William Cobbett, of whom it has been said that there might have been an English Revolution after 1815 if the one Englishman who could have led it had not thrown the whole weight of his influence into the alternative scale of reform.

Cobbett, 1762-1835

"All that I can boast of in my birth," wrote William Cobbett, "is that I was born in old England. With respect to my ancestors, I shall go no further back than my grandfather, and for this very plain reason, that I never heard talk of any prior to him. He was a day-labourer, and I have heard my father say, that he worked for one farmer from the day of his marriage to that of his death, upwards of forty years."

Cobbett himself worked on his father's small farm as a boy, and later in a lawyer's office. In 1784 he enlisted in the army, saw service in Canada, and rose to the rank of Sergeant-Major. Having obtained his discharge, primarily in order to expose financial corruption among his superior officers, he went to France and thence emigrated to the United States, where he became a teacher and also a writer of Tory pamphlets under the pseudonym of Peter Porcupine. He was ruined by libel cases, and was forced to return to England in 1800. Welcomed by the Tory party as a forceful pamphleteer who could show up the Jacobins and the Radicals, he launched with Government backing *Cobbett's Weekly Political Register*, which ran from 1802 till his death in 1835. (He also began, from 1803, the *Parliamentary Debates*, which nine years later passed into the hands of Hansard.) The great majority of this weekly, during its entire existence, was written by Cobbett himself ;* his leading articles were enormous, sometimes taking up most of the paper. They were read by poor men in taverns, and by rich men in the clubs around Westminster. No journalist ever had such influence ; when he turned against them, the Government offered him a bribe of £10,000 to keep his pen dry.

But Cobbett was no more to be bribed than he was to be kept to any Party line. Founded as an extremely orthodox, patriotic journal, in support of Pitt and the French-war policy, the *Register*, as early as 1804, began to change its tune. Cobbett had come to see that the most formidable enemy was within, not outside, and he was soon shouting as loudly for Radical Reform as he had formerly shouted against it. For the next thirty years he argued that the people of England were letting themselves be made the victims of a combination of politicians, stock-jobbers, canting clergymen, and profiteers. In 1810 he was imprisoned for having criticised in the *Register* the flogging of English troops by German mercenaries, and for two years he edited his newspaper from Newgate Gaol.

It was after 1815 that he rose to his full stature, as the voice of the industrial as well as the rural workers. He began to

---

* Another contributor, in its post-Tory period, was the famous old Radical, Major Cartwright, one of the historical figures in Mark Rutherford's novel *The Revolution in Tanner's Lane* (1887).

speak directly to the mill-hands and the miners in the north, by producing off-prints from the *Register*, containing no news that would subject them to the Newspaper Tax,* for sale at a penny and twopence a time. This soon turned into a regular twopenny edition—called "Tuppenny Trash" by its enemies (and later, proudly, by its editor)—which, at the height of its popularity, was selling sixty thousand copies a week.

In 1817, after the suspension of the Habeas Corpus Act, Cobbett beat a temporary retreat to America and did not return till two years had passed. While there he wrote, among other things, *A Grammar of the English Language* (1817), which, apart from its main purpose, is amusing to read because the author, like Dr Johnson in his dictionary, sometimes gets political allusions into his examples: "The nominative is frequently a noun of multitude ; as *mob, parliament, gang.*"—"The gang of borough-tyrants *is* cruel, and *are* also notoriously as ignorant as brutes."

In 1821 he began the series of *Rural Rides* in the *Register*, afterwards collected in book form (1830). Other later works are his *History of the Protestant "Reformation" in England* (1827)—a popular and exaggerated version of the history by the Catholic historian Lingard—and *Advice to Young Men* (1829). In the Reformed Parliament of 1832 he sat as member for Oldham.

Cobbett and Popular Culture

When Cobbett died in 1835, a correspondent in *The Times* —"the bloody old *Times*", as he used to call it—wrote that he was only an "episode" and that he would have no successors. The criticism is partly true, in respect of his status as the last spokesman of the old peasantry, but it is not true of the man as a whole. For his influence was very great on later political and social developments, in particular on the original, reformist Chartist Movement. In point of fact, Cobbett was the link—the highly necessary link—between

---

* Newspapers had been taxed since 1712, and in 1815 the tax stood at fourpence a copy, the normal price of a newspaper being sevenpence. In 1836 the duty was reduced to a penny, and in 1855 it was abolished.

the old English popular culture and the more conscious, more literary cultural developments that followed the Industrial Revolution.

"As to politics," he wrote of his youth, "we were like the rest of the country people in England; that is to say, we neither knew nor thought anything about the matter . . . I do not remember ever having seen a newspaper in the house, and most certainly that privation did not render us less free, happy or industrious."

But observe Cobbett's realisation that the changed conditions rendered necessary a change in popular culture. Of the period 1805 to 1815 he subsequently wrote: "During all this time, the people were reading, and especially the labouring classes. So that England presented to the world this singular spectacle. The Government, the rich, the pretended learned, ignorant of the causes which were shaking society to its base, while a considerable part of the middle class and a large part of the very poorest class of all, understood these causes perfectly well." Of Cobbett's own part in the enlightenment of his countrymen, Samuel Bamford wrote: "At this time [about 1816] the writings of William Cobbett suddenly became of great authority; they were read on nearly every cottage hearth in the manufacturing districts . . . He directed his readers to the true cause of their sufferings—misgovernment; and to the proper corrective—parliamentary reform."

None knew better than Cobbett what a hard, but on the whole happy, life was available to the farm worker in the eighteenth century, certain conditions of freedom and due wages being granted, as they sometimes weren't. And none knew better how the revolution in industry and agriculture was altering that comparatively contented state. But he realised—if not in theory, certainly by his actions—that the change in society must mean a change in popular culture. Labourers in the old rural order could remain illiterate, while still drawing the essentials of culture from their environment and craft traditions; but citizens in the new industrial era, workers in the industries of the big towns, must be able to read, must have cheap, tax-free newspapers and public libraries, must have a vote in both local and national affairs, must understand—and eventually co-operate in—the working of industrial society. This is what connects Cobbett and his predecessor Paine* with later movements like the Co-operative, the Trade Union, the Chartist, all intimately connected also with that Methodist and Nonconformist piety which Cobbett himself so despised.

The details of this revolution in popular culture—so much more impressive than any violent political revolution—are the concern rather of social than of literary history. But we can mention a few names here. Samuel Bamford was imprisoned for his part in the "Peterloo" demonstration; a weaver by trade, he wrote verse, *Passages in the Life of a Radical* (1844), and *Early Days* (1849). Richard Carlile founded the *Republican* in 1813, and for publishing editions of Tom Paine's *Age of Reason* was imprisoned for three years. Francis Place— "the Radical tailor of Charing Cross"—was instrumental in securing the repeal of the Combination Acts in 1824; in 1838 he drafted the People's Charter, with the help of the cabinet-maker William Lovett, Secretary of the London Working Men's Association. Lovett became leader of the "moral-force" Chartists which opposed the "physical-force" school led by the Irish barrister Feargus O'Connor, editor of the *Northern Star*; he was associated with Dr Birkbeck and Henry Brougham in the promotion of Mechanics' Institutes, and in 1876 published *The Life and Struggles of William Lovett in his Pursuit of Bread, Knowledge, and Freedom.*

---

* Thomas Paine (1737-1809) was born of poor Quaker stock and went to America in 1774, where he published *Common-Sense*, an influential republican pamphlet, and fought for the colonists in the War of Independence. Returning to England in 1787, he published in 1791 *The Rights of Man*, an answer to Burke's *Reflections on the French Revolution*. The next year he was indicted for treason but escaped to France, where he represented Calais in the Convention. He supported the abolition of the monarchy, but, opposing the execution of Louis on chivalrous grounds, narrowly escaped the guillotine himself. In 1793 he published *The Age of Reason*, a defence of Deism against both Christianity and atheism, returned to America in 1802, and died in New York. Probably no book was more influential than *The Rights of Man* on the development of English democracy in the nineteenth century.

Other prominent literary Chartists were Henry Hetherington, publisher of the *Poor Man's Guardian*, who suffered several periods of imprisonment for his protests against the stamp duty ; the ex-sailor John Cleave, editor of the popular journal *Cleave's Gazette* ; Thomas Cooper, poet, novelist, scholar, lecturer, preacher, who wrote a very interesting autobiography (1871) ; and George Jacob Holyoake, later associated with the co-operative and secularist movements, who was largely responsible for the abolition of the newspaper tax in 1855. His *Sixty Years of an Agitator's Life* and Collet Dobson Collet's *History of the Taxes on Knowledge* are valuable books for the student of the period.

Less well known is Alexander Somerville of the Scots Greys, who published *The Autobiography of a Working Man* (1848), perhaps the best work of literature in this extensive field. It is probably only bettered by the autobiography which Cobbett intended to write, and didn't, but which has been admirably done for him, out of his varied writings, by a modern editor under the title (Cobbett's own choice) *The Progress of a Ploughboy to a Seat in Parliament.*

Owen and the Evangelicals

Contemporary with Cobbett, and with the popular culture we have glanced at, was a good deal of varied work on social problems, all more or less connected with the physical and mental disturbances that followed the Industrial Revolution. The men and women who did this work are very important in social history, but in a history of literature they have to be dismissed—with one or two exceptions—in a few paragraphs. We can begin with the philanthropists, and first of all mention that rather peculiar genius Robert Owen (1771-1858), whom Leslie Stephen called "one of those bores who are the salt of the earth" and who lives in history as the eccentric pioneer of a number of varied movements, including the Chartist, the Trade Union, the Co-operative, and the infant-school. The story of Owen's Grand National Consolidated Trades Union, and of the Tolpuddle martyrs, is one of the most interesting in the history of early nineteenth-century struggle.

Some of the philanthropists were at the other extreme from Owen, so far as religious and political principles are concerned. (Though the actual reforms seem to have been mostly carried out by a curious combination of aristocratic Christians and radical Agnostics.) A good deal of credit for betterment of social conditions must go to the Evangelicals, the Low-Church party in the Church of England, who had been deeply influenced by Wesley. Their leaders included William Wilberforce, Sir James Stephen (father of Leslie and James Fitzjames Stephen), Hannah More, Charles Simeon, Zachary Macaulay (editor of the *Christian Observer* and father of the great historian), and Lord Shaftesbury. The Evangelicals were often narrow and bigoted ; their merit lay chiefly in their philanthropy, in their zeal to overcome slavery, both at home and abroad.

William Wilberforce (1759-1833) was a wealthy man who lived in a mansion on the edge of Clapham Common ; one of his neighbours was Sir James Stephen. Hence Sydney Smith's nickname for the Evangelicals—"the Clapham Sect." They were also called the "Saints"—"by way of insult," Leslie Stephen explains. Wilberforce entered Parliament in 1780, and in 1833, largely due to his efforts, slavery was finally abolished throughout the British Empire. He wrote religious books, promoted religious education and foreign missions, and was one of the founders of an association for the Better Observance of Sunday.

Associated with him in many of his activities was Hannah More (1745-1833), who had been one of the most brilliant "blue-stockings" in the Johnson-Garrick circle but had retired to the country to work among the poor. She wrote enormous quantities of religious tales and tracts, which had a great success and were found so well-suited to the purpose that the Religious Tract Society was formed to continue the work. The most famous is *Coelebs in Search of a Wife* (1809). Cobbett called her "an old Bishop in petticoats" and offered as a sample of the Evangelical tracts, which he detested,

"Hannah More's account of the celestial death of an Evangelical mouse who, *though starving*, would not touch the master's cheese and bacon."

The Evangelicals were connected with Cambridge, as the other Tractarians, the High-Church movement, with Oxford. An important figure was Charles Simeon, Fellow of King's College (1759-1836), who made the university a nursing mother for the coming Evangelical generation. For years after Simeon's death, undergraduates of extra piety were known in Cambridge as "Sims." (See, for example, Butler's *Way of All Flesh*.) Another prominent Evangelical was Thomas Bowdler, whose expurgated versions of Shakespeare and other authors—"for family reading"—gave rise to the verb "bowdlerise."

With Anthony Ashley Cooper (1801-85), who succeeded to the title of Earl of Shaftesbury, we reach an Evangelical "saint" who has no need of the qualifying inverted commas. He entered Parliament as a Tory in 1826, and was responsible, with Richard Oastler and Joseph Rayner Stephens, for the Act of 1842 forbidding the employment of women and children underground in mines. His famous report on this subject— one of the leading documents in nineteenth-century social history—shocked both the conscience and the morality of the nation. His work at home, coupled with Wilberforce's work for the abolition of negro slavery, and with such things as the founding of the British and Foreign Bible Society, may fairly be said to outweigh the less savoury aspects of the Evangelical movement.*

Philosophers and Economists

More abstract, but not without great influence on practical affairs, was the work of a number of philosophers and economists of the period, the most important of whom were Godwin, Malthus, Bentham, Ricardo, and James and J. S. Mill. Since the younger Mill is by far the most significant as regards

* In Scotland, one of the most interesting Evangelicals was the geologist Hugh Miller (1802-56). He edited the *Witness* from 1840 and wrote *The Old Red Sandstone* (1841) and *Footprints of the Creator* (1847).

literature, and since he is connected with the Utilitarian philosophy of his father and Bentham, and with the economics of Ricardo, we can treat the Utilitarians in a separate section and briefly consider here the work of Godwin and Malthus.

William Godwin (1756-1836) was a political philosopher and didactic novelist most of whose writing belongs to the eighteenth century ; he is chiefly remembered to-day as the husband of the first feminist, Mary Wollstonecraft, and the father-in-law and inspirer of Shelley. In 1793 he achieved fame and notoriety through his *Enquiry concerning Political Justice*, an uncompromising statement of the case for an anarchist and communist society, which had great influence on the younger generation but whose published price of three guineas was the only reason for its not being banned, like the works of Paine, by the Government. He gained a larger audience for his novels, one of which, *The Adventures of Caleb Williams* (1794), a study of social injustice, is a classic in its kind. Hazlitt compared him favourably with Burke, and wrote that "No one was more talked of, more looked up to, more sought after, and wherever liberty, truth, justice was the theme, his name was not far off."

His *Political Justice* provoked a rejoinder with the lengthy title *An Essay on the Principle of Population as it affects the future improvements of society*. The author was Thomas Robert Malthus (1766-1834), a young clergyman who had suffered from the exuberant Godwinian radicalism of his father. The first edition (1798) was followed by a storm of controversy ; Malthus studied the matter further, and produced a second edition, replying to his critics, in 1803. He maintained that every species, including man, tends to increase in geometrical ratio, but that the production of food increases only in arithmetical ratio. Therefore population is kept in check by "famine, disease and war." In the second edition, Malthus added that population could also be restricted by voluntary "moral restraint."

The *Essay* was intended to act as a mere counterblast to the more extravagant notions of the Godwinian "perfectionists." ("Perfectibility," Godwin had written, "is one of the most unequivocal characteristics of the human species.") But inevitably the name of Malthus became either an abomination or a joke to those who were trying to raise the standard of life of the poorer classes, for his doctrine seemed to prove that "the poor will be always with us." * Hazlitt published a *Reply to Malthus* (1807); Shelley wrote "I had rather be damned with Plato and Lord Bacon, than go to Heaven with Paley and Malthus"; and Cobbett wrote an anti-Malthusian play, which can be compared with Peacock's famous skit in the "Rustic Wedding" chapter of *Melincourt*. The following fragment of dialogue from the Cobbett play is worth quoting :

THIMBLE : So, young woman, you are going to be married, I understand.

BETSY : Yes, sir.

THIMBLE : How old are you ?

BETSY : Eighteen, sir.

THIMBLE : Eighteen ! No wonder the country is ruined. How many children had your mother ?

BETSY : Seventeen, sir.

THIMBLE : Monstrous. Nothing can save the country but plague, pestilence, and famine, and sudden death.

The Utilitarians

Jeremy Bentham (1748-1832) is famous as the prophet of a school of thought and practice, known sometimes by the name J. S. Mill gave it, "Utilitarianism", sometimes as Philosophical Radicalism, which had its heyday about 1820-50. It maintained that utility—"The greatest happiness of the greatest number", as Bentham put it, quoting the scientist Priestley—should be the guiding principle in legislation. Bentham set himself the task of devising improvements in the clumsy machine of English law—then regarded as sacrosanct. He was not primarily a philosopher ; he was an exponent of practical reforms, and in the field of legislative practice the

* In Henry Mayhew's *London Labour and the London Poor* (1851) the following piece of Coster wit is reported : "We're not like Methusalem, or some such swell's name, as wanted to murder children afore they was born, as I once heerd lectured about—we're nothing like that."

dogma of "happiness" was, at any rate, a good rough-and-ready test. He held that every man was the best judge of his own happiness, as Adam Smith had held in his *Wealth of Nations* that every trader was the best judge of his own profit. He attacked all laws interfering with the free expression of religious belief or political opinion ; he advocated the legalising of trade unions, the abolition of savage punishments, the reform of the Parliamentary franchise. Nearly all the legislative reforms of the early Victorian age can be traced to his influence. But his doctrine of *laissez-faire* was also responsible for the opposition to other reforms, notably the Factory Acts, and behind the detested new Poor Law of 1834 lurked that "deficiency of Imagination" which J. S. Mill criticised in him, and which Mill in *Dissertations and Discussions*, no less than Dickens in *Oliver Twist* and *Hard Times*, saw as the rough reverse side of the Utilitarian medal.

His chief works are *An Introduction to the Principles of Morals and Legislation* (1789), *A Manual of Political Economy* (1798), and *A Catechism of Parliamentary Reform* (1817). In 1824 he founded, as an organ for his theories, the *Westminster Review*—a journal that was later to have as assistant editor Mary Ann Evans, afterwards famous as George Eliot.

He worked for many years without much recognition, and it was only late in life that his disciples began to gather round him. The chief of these was James Mill (1773-1836), the son of a Scots shoemaker, who became a successful man of affairs and rose to high office in the East India Company, where one of his colleagues was the novelist Peacock. He wrote *Political Economy* (1821) and *An Analysis of the Phenomena of the Human Mind* '1829). Another prominent Benthamite was Henry Brougham, whom we have already noticed as one of the founders of the *Edinburgh Review* ; and associated with the economic doctrines of the Utilitarians, though not actually one of them, was David Ricardo (1772-1823), a prosperous Jewish business man who, encouraged by James Mill, wrote the authoritative work *The Principles of Political Economy and Taxation* (1817).

J. S. Mill, 1806-73

It is with James Mill's son, John Stuart Mill, that we approach at once nearer literature and nearer a criticism of the Benthamite doctrine. (Later there was much academic criticism of both Bentham and Mill by professional philosophers at Oxford and Cambridge, notably by T. H. Green.) Dickens criticised certain tendencies of Utilitarianism in his brief masterpiece *Hard Times*, and it is remarkable how closely the education which Mr Gradgrind gave his unfortunate children resembles that which James Mill gave his son. The story is told in the younger Mill's intensely interesting *Autobiography*, posthumously published in 1873. If this book were not an obviously conscientious record of fact, one might take it as an allegory designed to illustrate the mingled strength and weakness of the Utilitarian scheme of life. The elder Mill deliberately set himself the task of forming the perfect Benthamite. John Mill began the study of Greek at three years old; by the age of seven he had read most of the standard Greek and English historians. Soon he was introduced to Latin, algebra, chemistry, philosophy, economics. At the age of sixteen his education was considered complete; he joined his father in the East India Company and became a regular contributor to the *Westminster* and other Radical periodicals.

Thus his education was extraordinary in its thoroughness on the purely intellectual side, and no less extraordinary for its neglect and repression of his emotional or human character. In 1826, he records, he passed through a mental and spiritual crisis; he found his father's bleakly intellectual Utilitarianism emotionally unsatisfying, and abandoned it in favour of a more human philosophy inspired by Coleridge and the poetry of Wordsworth. In a celebrated essay, printed somewhat ironically in the *Westminster Review*, he speaks of Bentham and Coleridge as "the two seminal minds of the age", and, though he professes himself still a Benthamite, it is plain that he now regarded Coleridge as the necessary complement. He began to understand, as he records in the *Autobiography*, that "among the prime necessities of human well-being" is "the internal culture of the individual." *

In his social philosophy, he gradually abandoned (as did the economist Nassau Senior) the extreme individualism of the older Utilitarians for an outlook more akin to liberal socialism, while still laying great emphasis on the liberty of the individual. This change can be traced in the later editions of *Principles of Political Economy*, first published in 1848. He sat in Parliament as a Radical from 1865 to 1868, and introduced a motion for women's suffrage. His feminist views inspired his essay *On the Subjection of Women* (1869). His philosophical and political writings include *A System of Logic* (1843), the celebrated essay *On Liberty* (1859), and *Considerations on Representative Government* (1861).

He was an influential writer, and very widely read. He published a cheap edition of his *Political Economy*, without author's royalties, in order to bring it within the reach of working-class purses. That so dry a philosopher should have been so popular has often been recognised as a testimony to the seriousness of the age.

Carlyle, 1795-1881

We have noticed the relation of *Hard Times* to Mill's criticism of the human inadequacies of Utilitarianism. Dickens's novel was "inscribed to Thomas Carlyle." This was not simply the compliment of one writer to another; it was an expression of gratitude by the master of imaginative fiction to the man whom he regarded as the strongest moral force in the literature of his time. Carlyle's criticism of what he

---

* A somewhat similar experience to Mill's is described in the *Autobiography* of Charles Darwin, though to Darwin the love of poetry, painting, and music came early, and it was in later life that he found, to his deep regret, that he was losing "the higher aesthetic tastes." "My mind," he wrote, "seems to have become a kind of machine for grinding general laws out of large collections of facts, but why this should have caused the atrophy of that part of the brain alone, on which the higher tastes depend, I cannot conceive . . . The loss of these tastes is a loss of happiness, and may possibly be injurious to the intellect, and more probably to the moral character, by enfeebling the emotional part of our nature."

called "the Mechanical Age" plainly forms part of the background to Dickens's Bumbledom and Gradgrindery, as well as to the work of Ruskin, Morris, and the Pre-Raphaelites.

Carlyle came from the part of Scotland and the kind of humble stock that had formerly produced Burns. His family were members of one of the little religious sects that had broken away from the Scottish Kirk in the eighteenth century. He early lost his faith in Christian doctrine, but he never lost the Puritan's contempt for the standards of Vanity Fair; he never ceased to maintain that moral values were the only values. "The essential Puritan," wrote Leslie Stephen, "may survive, as the case of Carlyle sufficiently showed, when all his dogmas have evaporated; and I confess that, rightly or wrongly, he is a person for whom I have profound respect and much sympathy."

In the early nineteenth century, Scottish education was the most democratic in the world. Carlyle proceeded from the local parish school to the nearest grammar school, and thence to Edinburgh University.

After periods as a teacher, law student, and tutor, he arrived on the literary scene as the interpreter of the German Renaissance. An essay on Goethe's *Faust* appeared in the *Edinburgh Review* in 1822, and this was followed by a *Life of Schiller*, a translation of Goethe's *Wilhelm Meister*, and essays on German literature. In 1826 he married,* and in 1832 wrote his first major work, *Sartor Resartus*. This, after appearing in *Fraser's Magazine*, was published in New York in 1836 (through the enthusiasm of Emerson) and in London two years later. While *Sartor Resartus* is, on the surface, a pedantic discussion of a Philosophy of Clothes by an imaginary German professor Teufelsdrochk (Devilsdung); actually it is a kind of spiritual autobiography, combined with

---

* Mrs Carlyle, née Jane Welsh, lived from 1801 to 1866. Her *Letters* appeared in 1883. The publication of these, and of Carlyle's self-reproaching *Reminiscences* (probably taken too literally by his biographer J. A. Froude), caused a temporary slump in the husband's reputation, and a conviction, equally temporary, that the wife had been a neglected genius. Samuel Butler observed characteristically that "It was very good of God to let Carlyle and Mrs Carlyle marry one another and so make only two people miserable instead of four."

a satire upon things in general—or (which is almost the same) things which Carlyle particularly disliked. Contemporary readers can hardly be blamed for not catching its import, and it did not begin to be widely appreciated till its author had made a reputation in other fields. Like Swift's *Tale of a Tub*, to which it owes something, it is still eminently readable in parts. It is one of those books which can be skipped through with profit several times.

The French Revolution: A History (1837) was his first big success. "It delivered the English mind," wrote Lord Acton, "from the thraldom of Burke." Though as much a commentary on post-revolutionary conditions in England as a history of the then greatest of social upheavals, Carlyle laid the stress on the personalities involved. This was his normal method, both in history and in literary criticism; and, while the results are sometimes impressive, the method has its obvious dangers. His celebrated criticism of Boswell in *Fraser's Magazine* (1832) is a good example of the virtues and vices of this biographical approach.

The years from 1837 to 1840 were occupied by lectures, the fourth and last series of which, *On Heroes, Hero-Worship, and the Heroic in History,* was the most successful; it was published in 1841. The book *Chartism* (1840) attacked the Utilitarian doctrine of *laissez-faire*, and sought to find a remedy for contemporary evils, not in universal suffrage, but in submission to leadership. (The later biographies of Oliver Cromwell and Frederick the Great advocate a similar return to authoritarian government.) *Chartism* was followed by two other excursions into social and political criticism : *Past and Present* (1843) and *Latter-Day Pamphlets* (1850). The first, a comparison between a medieval monastery and a modern factory, has a place in that revival of respect for the Middle Ages which we noticed in the Romantic Movement and which we shall observe again in the Oxford Movement and the Pre-Raphaelites. The second, which contains a denunciation of philanthropy, shocked many of Carlyle's personal friends, including Mill, and had a cool reception in public.

Carlyle's Characteristics and Influence

"A country," remarked Samuel Butler, "is not without honour save in its own prophets." There seems to be something in human nature that delights in the spectacle of an iconoclast tearing down, in theory, one fashionable belief after another. Popular editions of Carlyle's works were absorbed in vast quantities, and he was admired by many people to whom his constructive proposals—so far as he had any—were extremely distasteful. For instance, he was accepted by the artisans and the clerks for his bitterness against the industrial system, and for his doctrine (somewhat similar to the "self-help" creed of Samuel Smiles) of Salvation by Work, not for his foolish worship of those Great Men whom Fielding had classed with pimps and robbers.

He had few positive ideas to give to his generation. He was chiefly concerned to break through its self-complacency and to show it that it was not in a healthy state. He complained that he was born at a time when there was no faith, no religion ; until we get a faith, a religion, he wrote, nothing else is worth striving for.

His style in prose is sometimes rather like Browning's in verse : full of inversions, newly-coined words, strange and archaic forms, it tries to dispense with pronouns, conjunctions, and such small matters. Many pages in the *French Revolution* might seem to be written in a foreign language, were we not reminded of the style of Mrs Carlyle's ancestor John Knox.

We have noticed Carlyle's general influence on Dickens, and we shall see, in later chapters, how great was his influence on Ruskin and Morris. "Carlyle was the revered Master," said Emerson : "Ruskin the beloved disciple." (On Emerson and the New England ethos Carlyle's influence was almost as great.) He made the first major protest against the materialism of Victorian England, and, while his constructive proposals would seem to lead towards some Bismarckian State, the value of his protest remains.

CHAPTER V

THE DRAMA AND DICKENS
1816-1865

> " ' It was all Mrs Bumble. She *would* do it,' urged Mr Bumble, first looking round to ascertain that his partner had left the room.
>
> ' That is no excuse,' replied Mr Brownlow . . . ' The law supposes that your wife acts under your direction.'
>
> ' If the law supposes that,' said Mr Bumble, squeezing his hat emphatically in both hands, ' the law is a ass, a idiot. If that's the eye of the law, the law is a bachelor ; and the worst I wish the law is, that his eye may be opened by experience—by experience.' "
>
> <div align="right">DICKENS : <i>Oliver Twist.</i></div>

Dearth of Dubliners

Richard Brinsley Sheridan was born in Dublin in 1751. He wrote three witty plays : *The Rivals* (1775), *The School for Scandal* (1777), and *The Critic* (1779). He died in 1816.

Oscar Wilde was born in Dublin in 1856. He wrote four witty plays : *Lady Windermere's Fan* (1892), *A Woman of No Importance* (1893), *An Ideal Husband* (1894), and *The Importance of Being Earnest* (1895). He died in 1900.

George Bernard Shaw was born in Dublin in the same year as Oscar Wilde. He wrote many witty plays. The first one to be produced was *Widowers' Houses* (1892).

Between 1779 and 1892—more than a century—there was not a single really distinguished play written and produced in any English theatre. There was not a single dramatist of real distinction, though many of some talent, between the death of Sheridan in 1816 and the emergence of Wilde and Shaw in 1892. There was a dearth of Dubliners,* and no other city in England, Ireland, Scotland, or Wales took Dublin's place as exporter of dramatists to the London stage.

* Such minor dramatists and Dubliners as O'Keefe, Boucicault, and Maturin cannot be considered any real exception.

This is an extraordinary fact: more than a century of stagnation in the drama in the country or the language of Shakespeare and Ben Jonson! It is true that every country which has produced great drama has had just the one short period of genius: for instance, the Elizabethan-Jacobean in England and what has been called "the classical moment" under Louis XIV. But it is not the lack of Shakespeares that is so saddening about the period 1779-1892, it is "the dearth of Dubliners"—that is, the absence between Sheridan and Wilde and Shaw, not simply of supreme genius, which happens only once in a country's dramatic history, but of genuine, though lesser, distinction. Nobody but Shaw believed that Shaw is equal or superior to Shakespeare,* but the stage history of 1779-1892 would have been much brighter had there been a few Shaws or Sheridans or Wildes to offset the slender dramatic talents of Lord Byron in one field and Henry James Byron in another.

Some Reasons for Dramatic Mediocrity

No one has satisfactorily explained this long period of marking time in the history of the English drama. We should distinguish first between the history of the drama and the history of the theatre. Although the great actor Macready, when urging his young friend Browning to try his hand at writing for the stage, spoke of "our degraded drama" and of "the miseries, the humiliations, the heart-sickening disgusts that I have endured in my profession", the history of the nineteenth-century theatre is not wholly one of gloom. Admittedly much of the work done belongs to the region of the penny novelette, and people interested in either literature or acting cannot be expected to share the delight of many Victorians at real waterfalls on the stage in the gigantic spectacles at Drury Lane. (That gigantic spectacles can co-exist with great drama will be known to students of the career of

* His remark in his criticism of Irving's production of *Cymbeline* in the 'nineties is justly notorious: "With the single exception of Homer, there is no eminent writer, not even Sir Walter Scott, whom I can despise so entirely as I despise Shakespeare, when I measure my mind against his."

Molière, who turned from one to the other with the utmost ease.)

But there is more than spectacular triumph in the history of the nineteenth-century theatre : there were no really distinguished original dramatists till the 'nineties, as we have observed, but the nineteenth century is one of the great periods in the history of Shakespearean acting. The talents of such interpreters as Mrs Siddons, Edmund Kean, W. C. Macready, Samuel Phelps, Henry Irving, Ellen Terry, are rightly regarded as an important footnote to the writings of the Shakespearean critics. If the interpretation of Shakespeare reached its lowest level with Bowdler's family edition and Mrs Cowden Clarke's *Girlhood of Shakespeare's Heroines*, the acting of Kean, praised by Lamb and Keats, was evidently on the same high level of achievement in its different sphere as the comments of Coleridge, as later on the critical genius of Arnold was paralleled in the theatre by the career of Phelps, who produced at Sadler's Wells over thirty of Shakespeare's plays. And, though it was pre-eminently, like the late eighteenth century, a period of the actor-manager, no great actor of the nineteenth century took Garrick's liberties with the text of Shakespeare. The plays were acted more as they were intended to be acted, and this gain in stage interpretation went along with the work of the Shakespearean critics and scholars—work that can be criticised itself on several fundamental points but which was nevertheless a genuine achievement—to give to our greatest dramatist a public more sympathetic than any since the Jacobean.

What happened immediately after the Jacobean period has some connection with the decline of the English drama. Although Puritanism has been of immense service to English culture and democracy, as it has been to American, and although an impressive case could be made out for deeming the Puritan Bunyan the most Shakespearean writer of the late seventeenth century, the influence of the Puritan spirit upon the theatre must be judged an extremely bad one. The theatres were closed altogether during the Commonwealth, and when they re-opened after the Restoration, the natural reaction was towards a kind of comedy, witty enough at its best but at its worst boringly obscene, that poked fun, not merely at the most narrow and hypocritical ideas, as Shakespeare and Ben Jonson had done, but at all responsibility and all "bourgeois" morality. One extreme led to the other, and when in 1737 the Licensing Act was passed by the Walpole government to silence the political criticism in the plays of Fielding, there was little scope for dramatists—now that the reaction to Puritanism had passed—except in sentiment or melodrama. Fielding himself took to the novel, and there seems to have been a distinct relationship, in the century 1750-1850, between the growth of the novel and the decline of the drama.

Part of the trouble was the deterioration in poetic language, which may have been the inevitable result of the gradual disappearance of the old rural order and the development of science. Immense gains were offset by considerable losses, and the gain in rational language was counter-balanced by a loss of dramatic expression . . .

We must now briefly consider certain parts of this long but empty dramatic period ; we can take it under two heads, poetic drama and prose drama. We can start the former with the Romantic Revival, the latter with the death of Sheridan in 1816, and take both into mid-Victorian times. Then we can discuss in some detail what might be called the Victorian "compensation" for their dramatic mediocrity —the work of Charles Dickens, who is not only connected with past drama, as we shall see, but who has a claim to be considered the most Shakespearean writer of the nineteenth century.

Regency and Victorian Poetic Drama

In a sense, there was no Regency or Victorian poetic drama : that is, no writer in this long period ever wrote a play in verse that both held the stage and was valuable as literature. The nearest exceptions are Coleridge, whose *Remorse* (1813), in the style of Schiller's *Robbers*, had a fair run ; Shelley, whose *Cenci* (1819) has been performed

with some success ; Browning, whose *Strafford* (1837) is more
vital than most literary plays ; and Tennyson, whose *Becket*
(1879) has its impressive moments. It should also be recorded
that one of the best Shakespearean critics of our time is convinced that the verse plays of Lord Byron are great drama.
Perhaps this rash verdict is due to their being so seldom
performed.

Wordsworth wrote one play, *The Borderers*, composed in
1795, published 1842. Coleridge wrote, besides *Remorse*,
Zapoyla, "in humble imitation of the *Winter's Tale*", and,
in collaboration with Southey, *The Fall of Robespierre*.
Byron's works in dramatic form are interesting rather than
successful ; they are often divided for convenience into two
groups, romantic and classical, the latter being deliberate
attempts to break loose from the domination of the Elizabethans and to fashion tragedy on the neo-classic principles—
observance of the Unities, and so forth—of Racine and Dryden. To the former group belong *Manfred* (1817), *Cain*
(1821), *Werner* (1822), *Heaven and Earth* (1823), and *The
Deformed Transformed* (1824); to the latter, *Marino Faliero*
(1820), *The Two Foscari* (1821), and *Sardanapalus* (1821).
The last-named has been considered to be his most successful
play, but admirers of Byron no more deem his dramatic work
superior to his *Don Juan* than admirers of Coleridge his
Remorse to his *Ancient Mariner*.

Keats wrote one play, *Otho the Great*, intended to keep
Kean in England, as later Browning was to keep Macready
from the United States with his *Strafford*. Landor and his
brother Robert Eyres Landor both wrote verse dramas.
Joanna Baillie wrote nine *Plays on the Passions* between
1798 and 1836; her tragedy *De Montfort* (1800) had a success, probably due to the acting of John Kemble and his
sister Mrs Siddons.

The three most celebrated writers of stage tragedy in the
first part of the century were Richard Lalor Sheil, whose
chief plays are *Adelaide* (1814) and *Bellamira* (1818); Charles
Robert Maturin, an Irish clergyman, whose three tragedies—

Bertram, Manuel, Fredolfo (1816-17)—are influenced by German romance ; and Henry Hart Milman, better known as Dean of St Paul's and author of *The History of the Jews*, whose tragedy *Fazio* (1818) had a long stage life. James Sheridan Knowles—one of the amazing Sheridan family—attempted to steer clear of verbiage and German extravagance ; his chief tragedies (he also wrote prose comedies)—*Caius Gracchus* (1815), *Virginius* (1820), *William Tell* (1825)—had genuine success in the theatre, as did *The Death of Marlowe* (1837) by R. H. Horne, and *Ion* (1835) by Sir Thomas Talfourd, the biographer of Lamb. J. W. Marston was the first to attempt a poetic tragedy of contemporary life—*The Patrician's Daughter* (1842).

It is safe to say that the majority of the plays mentioned are to the majority of modern readers merely names in literary history. That is, if once successful on the stage, they have not been revived and have little value as literature for reading ; or, if not primarily intended for the stage, they are considered inferior to the poets' other works. A partial exception is Shelley's *The Cenci*, a drama more actable than any of Byron's, but which is seriously weakened by the author's unconscious plagiary of Shakespeare.

The Elizabethan-Jacobean drama was the work of professional dramatists, the leading figures of which—Marlowe, Shakespeare, Jonson—had also been professional actors, like Molière later, at some period of their lives. Both the Regency and the Victorian poetic drama was mainly the work of amateurs—Gentlemen, as it were, who were certainly not Players. In addition to those named, we must record the fact that such people as Godwin, Mary Russell Mitford, and Disraeli also composed poetic tragedies—none of which has added to the reputation of its author.

Macready, of course, was quite right to urge his young friend Browning to try his hand at writing for the stage. In his early verse Browning had shown certain dramatic qualities which might well have led to distinguished work in the theatre ; as a matter of fact, he found his real but limited genius in dramatic monologues, the best of which are superior to his six more theatrical pieces—*Strafford* (1837), *King Victor and King Charles* (1842), *The Return of the Druses* (1843), *A Blot on the 'Scutcheon* (1843), *Colombe's Birthday* (1844), *Luria* (1846)—all of which were acted, but without great success.

Other amateur poetic dramatists were Sir Henry Taylor, the author of *Philip van Artevelde* (1834) ; Thomas Lovell Beddoes, nephew of Maria Edgeworth, who wrote *Death's Jest Book* (1829); and Charles Jeremiah Wells, whose *Joseph and his Brethren* (1824) was rewritten in 1876 and published with an extravagant eulogy by Swinburne. We can leave Swinburne's own dramatic work, which includes *Bothwell* (1874), with speeches hundreds of lines long, to our general consideration of him as a poet. We can adopt the same procedure in the case of Tennyson, whose stage work is unimportant compared with his lyric poetry.

Prose Drama After 1816

The former section has resembled a catalogue rather than a history, for the simple reason that it has had to deal with many talented authors on about the same level of mediocrity. This section is likely to be similar, for a similar reason, the only difference being that in poetic drama the work, as we have observed, was mainly amateur, while in prose it was mainly professional.

Few prose dramatists of the period belong to literature, though many are important in the history of the stage. They include the novelists Bulwer-Lytton and Charles Reade ; the burlesque-writer James Robinson Planché ; J. M. Morton, the author of the famous farce *Box and Cox* ; and Douglas William Jerrold, later a frequent contributor to *Punch*, who scored a great success with *Black-ey'd Susan* (1829). Dion Boucicault was the most talented writer of melodrama—for instance, *The Colleen Bawn*—and also had success in comedy. Tom Taylor was a capable dramatist, who wrote *The Ticket-of-Leave Man* (1863) among many other melodramas, and one famous comedy, *Our American Cousin* (1858), which has the incidental notoriety of being the play at whose performance in Washington in 1865 John Wilkes Booth assassinated Abraham Lincoln.

A vein of realism, foreshadowing the later work of Pinero and Galsworthy, was explored by T. W. Robertson, whose chief plays are *Society* (1865), *Ours* (1866), and *Caste* (1867). He was followed by Henry James Byron, who wrote the celebrated comedy *Our Boys* (1875), and James Albery, the author of *Two Roses*, in which Henry Irving made his first big success. In *The Silver King* (1882) the young Henry Arthur Jones raised melodrama almost to the level of art; his more realistic work belongs to the 'nineties and can be considered in our final chapter, with the plays of Pinero, Wilde, and Shaw.

The Dramatic Genius of Dickens, 1812-70

We have attempted above to give in a short space the main features of a long but extremely dull period in English drama. Compared with the achievements of Wordsworth and others in non-dramatic poetry, the Regency drama is hardly worth troubling about; and in the Victorian age, even including the 'nineties, the achievement in the theatre was vastly inferior to the achievement in the novel.

The most famous Victorian novelist, and the most popular of all English literary geniuses, is, of course, Charles Dickens. He is not only the central figure of the early Victorian literary age, he is the most dramatic writer, and it was probably only the accident of his birth that led him to achievements in prose fiction (which, it has often been noticed, have poetic qualities) rather than to successes on the stage.

His interest in the theatre, and the influence of the theatre upon himself and upon his writings, have rightly formed a part of every biography, from his friend John Forster's onwards. But if we accept the proposition that the dramatic genius which might have gone into playwriting, had the drama been in a more healthy state, spent itself instead, like Fielding's, on the novel, then we need to know why, on the face of it, Dickens would appear likely to have been so *bad* a dramatist. Not, of course, by the evidence of his amateur dramatic efforts, nor of the stage versions of his novels, but by the evidence of the novels themselves. How unlikely it seems, on the face of it, that the creator of Nancy, Ralph Nickleby, Sir Mulbery Hawk, Tom Pinch, Paul Dombey, Mr Carker—to name a few of his less credible figures—would have been able to produce any drama that was not of the most melodramatic sort.

But might not the creator of Mrs Gamp, Pecksniff, Flora Finching, Jefferson Brick, Chadband, Buzfuz, Micawber . . . have produced comedy nearer in kind to Ben Jonson's than to the usual Victorian farce ? This seems as likely as the contention that he could not, by any evidence, have produced a serious play that would not have been grossly sentimental and melodramatic. We have noted that Walpole drove Fielding from the theatre by the institution of the censorship. The novels he subsequently wrote owed a large debt to *Don Quixote*. But they must also have been influenced by his own dramatic experience ; indeed, the influence of the stage upon his novels has even been urged as a point of criticism against them. (As Ruskin remarked that Dickens ''chose to work in a circle of stage fire.'') So that we have a link, if a slight one, to connect the novels of Fielding with the course of English stage comedy, from his own plays back to those of Jonson and Shakespeare. That the connection extends to Dickens we know, of course, from his early reading of Fielding mentioned in *Copperfield* and in Forster's *Life*, quite apart from the stylistic evidence of the novels.

So that the writer of comedy, actually in fiction but conceivably in drama, is connected, however slightly, with the masters of the art. There is no such connection discoverable on the ''serious side.'' What connects the Elizabethan-Jacobean tragedy with the Victorian melodrama is merely the long and tedious degeneration between the two, represented (at various stations down the line) by Shirley, Otway, Lee, Addison, Lillo, Knowles, etc. The dissociation is almost complete, even though the best melodrama, like *The Silver King*, may bear some slight resemblance to *Macbeth*.

Dickens was a writer very much influenced by his surroundings, by the taste and sentiment of his time ; this would be expected of one whose most obvious distinction, as an American philosopher has remarked, was "a vast sympathetic participation in the daily life of mankind." He could be critical of his time and its manner when the question was one of social reform : he wrote *Oliver Twist* and *Hard Times*. He could oppose the money-grabbing and the pretentiousness that were the darker side of "our commercial greatness": he wrote *Little Dorrit* and *Our Mutual Friend*. He was not patient of the law's delay : he wrote *Bleak House*. But the things that did not arouse either his indignation or his sense of the ridiculous slipped through his guard unobserved. The sentimentality of the age he accepted with open arms ; and his love of the theatre became a liability as well as an asset when it took over *en masse* the conventions of its debased melodrama.

His Melodrama and his Comedy

Perhaps it is as well to get the bad over at once. When Ralph Nickleby dies, crying to the church bell, "Lie on, with your iron tongue ! Ring merrily for births that make expectants writhe, and for marriages that are made in hell, and toll ruefully for the dead whose shoes are worn already ! Call men to prayers who are goodly because not found out, and ring chimes for the coming-in of every year that brings this cursed world nearer to an end. No bell or book for me ! Throw me on a dunghill, and let me rot there, to infect the air !"—when the villain of *Nickleby* dies like this, we are bound to be reminded of the dying speeches of some Elizabethan villains ("Tongue, curse thy fill, and die !"); but any idea that this, like Marlowe's *Jew of Malta*, is what a modern critic has called "savage comedy", is dispelled by a recollection of the rest of the book. If the whole novel were on the savage-comic scale, then undoubtedly this ranting would fit in ; but what of the scene where Nicholas defends Smike from the cane of Squeers, a scene which is certainly meant to be taken seriously ?—"Touch him at your peril !

I will not stand by and see it done. My blood is up, and I
have the strength of ten such men as you. Look to yourself,
for by heaven I will not spare you if you drive me on !'' Or
his triumphant cry at the end : ''You are caught, villains, in
your own toils !''; or Ralph Nickleby's stagey hiss : ''My
curse, my bitter, deadly curse, upon you, boy !'' This, surely,
is about the crudest melodrama we get anywhere in Dickens.
The unmasking of Pecksniff (''Hear me, rascal !'') is comparatively credible, and by the time we get to *Copperfield* it
is significant that the exposure of the villain is performed by
a *comic* character, Micawber : ''You Heep of infamy !''

Nothing was ever done again by Dickens as crude as
Nickleby, but he often placed in the crudest context some of
his very finest work. For excellencies embedded in a melodramatic whole, we need look no further than *Oliver Twist*,
the second novel he wrote. The workhouse section stands
quite apart, in merit, from the rest, but even at the end of the
novel there is at least one bright spot—quoted in the epigraph
to this chapter—when Mr Bumble reappears to answer the
charge of stealing the trinkets. The kind of humour here—
''If that's the eye of the law, the law is a bachelor . . .'', etc.
—is not far from that of Shakespeare or Ben Jonson ; and we
should observe that such bright spots in Dickens nearly always
occur when a comic character is *holding forth*, occupying the
stage, as it were, addressing the reader/audience as much as
the other characters in the book.

It is this extra-literary life of his characters that has earned
Dickens his greatest applause and his heartiest abuse. On the
one hand, we have the popular idea of his characters, that
they are as real as life, as our own friends ; on the other, the
criticisms of G. H. Lewes, Taine, and other contemporaries
complain of the undevelopment of the characters psychologi-
cally. Both the uncritical delight and the hypercritical contempt seem indiscriminate when we relate this tendency to
its probable source, the stage. Lewes sneered at Dickens for
having once remarked that ''every word said by his characters was distinctly *heard* by him.'' Bearing in mind the
novelist's obsession with the theatre, the remark seems not

so much the "hallucination" suggested by Lewes as a quite
accurate description of Dickens's method of composition.

Whether such a method of writing novels is the best, is
beside the point; what matters is that this fundamentally
dramatic way of writing was responsible for nearly all that
is best in his comic creation. It was the gift of the dramatist rather than the novelist which enabled Dickens to express
the ramblings of a Mrs Gamp and a Flora Finching, or the
rhetoric of a Jefferson Brick and a General Choke, with
enough reality to convince us and enough exaggeration to
astound. When Mrs Gamp comes *"sidling and bridling* into
the room", when she remarks that "rich folks may ride on
camels but they won't find it easy to get through a needle's
eye", when she remembers "the wooden leg gone likeways
home to its account" and says after the quarrel with Betsy
Prig that "the words she spoke of Mrs Harris lambs could
not forgive, no, nor worms forget"; when Flora Finching,
describing her married life to Little Dorrit, says "Ere we had
yet fully detected the housemaid in selling the feathers out
of the spare bed *Gout flying upward* soared with Mr F. to
another sphere"; when the Young Columbian defies the
British Lion ("Bring forth that Lion! Alone, I dare him!
I taunt that Lion! I tell that Lion, that Freedom's hand once
twisted in his mane, he rolls a corse before me . . .")—when
we come across such things as these, it is not surprising if we
are reminded as much of Mrs Quickly and Pistol, of Juliet's
Nurse, of the characters of *The Alchemist,* as of Fielding or
Sterne or Smollett. Here the talent for the theatre has succeeded in adorning the medium of the novel; here the tradition of English comic writing is taken up by another master;
and there is now no question of "decadent genius" (a phrase
that could be applied to Dickens's melodrama) because the
line of comedy is unbroken. What is remarkable, of course,
is that Dickens should have been able to carry on this tradition while being also so much in tune with his own age; that
he should, in one and the same novel, such as *Chuzzlewit,*
give us this supreme kind of comedy, with its Shakespearean

"suggestiveness", side by side with the more sentimental forms popular in his day.

His Social Criticism

"Figuratively speaking, I travel for the house of Human Interest brothers, and have rather a large collection in the fancy goods way." This celebrated remark from *The Uncommercial Traveller* indicates the nature of one side of Dickens's "interest in social reform." The inverted commas of the latter phrase suggest, perhaps, the distinction we wish to make between this reporting of social conditions and that criticism of society which bears not merely the contemporary, particular reference, but the universal. Dickens is at his very best as a social critic when he is displaying his greatest genius as a literary artist. *Oliver Twist, Martin Chuzzlewit, Bleak House, Hard Times, Little Dorrit*, take the same precedence over *The Uncommercial Traveller* as Fielding's *Joseph Andrews* over his *Proposal for the Poor*.

Nothing could be less sentimental, for instance, than Dickens's words about the Workhouse Board at the beginning of *Oliver Twist*. The irony is refreshingly cool. But the apparent detachment goes along with something very different. It was the particular genius of Dickens that he could always put his finger on the social evil which hurt the sufferer the most. He was always "seeing people", thinking in terms of flesh and blood rather than abstract ideas or institutions. He saw the Workhouse Board, not as an institution, but as so many individuals anxious to assert their authority at someone else's expense, as so many people given by the accident of fortune power over the lives and conduct of others, firmly convinced that their own good fortune meant virtue and the distress of the others vice. He was aware of the fact that the petty regulation—separating husbands from wives and families, for example, in the "reformed" workhouse—was not only the one that hurt the pauper most keenly, but the one the Board got the most pleasure out of inflicting. The exaggeration here is simply the necessary exaggeration of art, what Edgar Allan Poe called the necessary "fine excess."

What the Dickensian theme is a second reference enforces.
Mr Sowerberry, the undertaker, is admiring the brass buttons
on Mr Bumble's coat: "Dear me, what a very elegant button
this is, Mr Bumble; I never noticed it before." "Yes, I
think it is rather pretty," replies the beadle. "The die is the
same as the parochial seal—the Good Samaritan healing the
sick and bruised man. The Board presented it to me on New
Year's morning, Mr Sowerberry; I put it on, I remember,
for the first time, to attend the inquest on that reduced trades-
man, who died in a doorway at midnight."

The offhandedness of that allusion points the moral impli-
cation. It is the very opposite of sentimentality, achieving in
an economical effectiveness what a whole page of pathos
might have failed to do. It is the carelessness here (and later
on, when Bumble refers to "two Irish labourers and a coal-
heaver", as to so much cattle) that gives the irony its force.
It is not only the character of Bumble that is shown up by
these remarks, but the habit of mind of the institution he
represents—the refusal to take into account the individual.

Dickens is not less of a literary artist because he is often
concerned so directly with social issues; on the contrary, he
gains in stature as a writer by the manner in which he presents
his criticism. If this were not so, such parts of his work
would be as dead now as other nineteenth-century "novels
with a purpose." The gift, the gift of the artist, for perceiving
the fundamental beneath the particular, saves him. Most of
the evils he represented in *Oliver Twist*, for example, have
long since been cleared away, but there remains the universal
significance of the relation between Bumble's sort, personifying Authority, and the "two Irish labourers and a coal-
heaver", personifying Dependence. This is one of the
fundamental themes of literature—"the insolence of office"
—and it has never been better developed than in the novels
of Dickens.

Chronology of his Novels, 1836-65

We have considered in some detail two important aspects
of Dickens's work. There are many other aspects, and

Dickens is such a complicated subject and so great a writer
that he really needs a whole chapter to himself. By giving
him half a chapter, and relating him (as he would have
wished) to the English dramatic tradition, we have managed
to combine significant selection with reasonable space. We
have not bothered much with chronology, partly because
Dickens is one of those writers whose best things are scattered
up and down their work, partly because it was imperative that
we should illustrate by several different examples the two
sides of his genius that we were discussing. Now, in conclusion, we must remedy the defect, by glancing, in order, at
his career as a whole.

This corresponds almost exactly with the first half of the
reign of Victoria, for the Queen ascended the throne as the
final adventures of the Pickwick Club were entertaining her
subjects, and Dickens's last completed novel ran in monthly
numbers from 1864 to 1865. (His unfinished novel, *The
Mystery of Edwin Drood*, was influenced by the stories of his
friend Wilkie Collins.)

The main events of his life are as well known as Shakespeare's, and better authenticated. The son of a poor clerk,
who was the son of a servant, he received little formal education, and spent a short period, like his *alter ego* David
Copperfield, in a blacking factory, while his father, like
Little Dorrit's, was imprisoned for debt in the Marshalsea.
He became a reporter, and in 1827 entered the gallery of the
House of Commons for the *Morning Chronicle*, to which he
contributed the *Sketches by Boz*, published in book form in
1836. In the same year he married his editor's daughter,
Katherine Hogarth, a descendant of the great artist who was
in some ways to the eighteenth century what he was to be
to the nineteenth, and began his first novel, *The Pickwick
Papers*.

Curiously enough, as the beginning of a great career in
English fiction, this was not originally intended to be a novel
at all, but merely an accompaniment to a series of sporting
illustrations. Luckily, the adventures of Pickwick outgrew their

setting,* and with the creation of Sam Weller the sales began to advance rapidly, reaching eventually 40,000 an issue. (This, like most of Dickens's novels, came out originally in monthly parts.) *Pickwick* is a comic masterpiece, but only develops one side mainly, the farcical, of the author's comic genius. A comparison of any scene from *Pickwick* with a typical Gamp-scene from *Chuzzlewit* is a useful indication of the difference between great farce and great humour.

It is usual for talented "best-sellers" to go on repeating a success; it is no less usual for writers of genius immediately to try their hand at something else. Before *Pickwick* was finished, Dickens was editing—in association with the Irish novelist and song-writer Samuel Lover—a new magazine, *Bentley's Miscellany*, and contributing a serial, *Oliver Twist* (1837). For months *Pickwick* and *Oliver* ran side by side, and by their contrast secured for the author a reputation as a master alike of farcical comedy and of grotesque melo-drama. We have noted the compensating virtues of *Oliver*, and all Dickens's novels have their own merits; but much of the criticism we applied to *Nicholas Nickleby* (1838) applies also to *The Old Curiosity Shop*—which he wrote, together with the historical novel *Barnaby Rudge*, as part of an ill-considered periodical venture, *Master Humphrey's Clock* (1840-1).

In 1842 he paid a visit to the United States, and on his return published *American Notes* (1842) and began *Martin Chuzzlewit* (1843-4). Both contained severe criticism of the U.S.A., but a good deal of it was the natural reaction of a liberal mind against what seemed to him mere empty pro-fessions of liberty in a country where slaves still existed. The fact that he was enthusiastically received on his second visit in 1867—after the Civil War—proves, like the war, how much of his criticism was latent in the American mind.

* Dickens, of course, throughout his career, owed much to his illustrators. The chief of these was Hablot Knight Browne, "Phiz", who illustrated the greater part of *Pickwick*, and about a dozen other Dickens books. It is an extremely common error to suppose that George Cruikshank was the chief illustrator of Dickens. Actually he illustrated of Dickens only *Sketches by Boz* and *Oliver Twist*.

Chuzzlewit has claims to be Dickens's best humorous novel, perhaps the greatest comic achievement in the language. Mrs Gamp in herself would be sufficient to make any novel memorable ; but there are also her companions in "this Piljian's Projiss of a mortal wale", and the American interludes—quite apart from the basis of the whole book, the selfishness-hypocrisy theme. This, of course, is "humorous" in the older or Jonsonian sense. "The notion of taking Pecksniff for a type of character," Forster tells us, "was really the origin of the book, the design being to show, more or less by every person introduced, the number and variety of humours and vices that have their root in selfishness."

Whether Pecksniff be a human being or only the personification of a vice, we are confronted with the absolute perfection of this presentation of hypocrisy. It is brilliant at a distance, from one's casual recollection, but the idea of the writer's comic genius becomes a certainty when we look at the detail, the actual language, in which this figure is given to us. One of the strangest paradoxes in the artistry of Dickens is that this most verbose of novelists, who gloried in his long-windedness and never used one word where ten would do, was also a master of the pithy, illuminating phrase. He can give us a couple of lines that say as much about the ruling vice of Mr Pecksniff as the rest of the hypocrite's adventures put together. During his conversation with Mrs Lupin at the Blue Dragon, he pulls off his gloves to warm his hands before the fire—warming them, says Dickens, "*as benevolently as if they were somebody else's, not his*", and his back "as if it were a widow's back, or an orphan's back, or an enemy's back, or a back that any less excellent man would have suffered to be cold."

The year 1843 also saw the publication of *A Christmas Carol*, the first and favourite of the five little annuals known as "the Christmas Books", which include *The Chimes* (1844) and *The Cricket on the Hearth* (1845). In 1846 Dickens became the first editor, for a short period, of the Liberal newspaper *The Daily News*. The rather gloomy novel, *Dombey and Son*, came out in monthly parts from 1846 to 1848, and this was followed by his greatest success, the partly-auto-biographical *David Copperfield* (1849-50). This contains a certain amount of melodrama and sentimentality, as does *Chuzzlewit*, but the best parts are generally regarded as among the author's finest achievements. *Bleak House* (1852-3), with its impressive delineation of London, has also been widely considered one of Dickens's very best.

That brief neglected masterpiece, *Hard Times*, first appeared during 1854 in the pages of *Household Words*, a weekly magazine which Dickens reorganised in 1859 as *All the Year Round*. (Under the new title, it started off with the serial *A Tale of Two Cities* and the articles afterwards collected as *The Uncommercial Traveller*.) His married life had long been unsatisfactory, and in 1856 he and his wife agreed on a separation, his sister-in-law remaining with him to look after the children, while he himself formed an association with the actress Ellen Ternan. In 1858 he began making public readings from his novels, which proved a tremendous success both here and in the States, but which probably cut short, by the excitement, his already over-worked life.

Some of his last novels, while inferior to many of the earlier in comic creation, are the best of all from the psycho-logical point of view. The father in *Little Dorrit* (1855-7) and Pip in *Great Expectations* (1860-1) are his most consider-able attempts at producing a character "in the round." *Our Mutual Friend* (1864-5), the last novel to be completed, is one of the most interesting. The scene in the penultimate chap-ter, where the schoolmaster Bradley Headstone, bullied by Rogue Riderhood, "turned his face to the blackboard and slowly wiped his name out", reminds us, in its simple use of symbolism, of some of the scenes in the late Victorian novelist Thomas Hardy.

It is an immense field of work, this of Dickens's, and, for all the space we have given him, there is much left unsaid. He is as central to the early Victorian age as Shakespeare to the Elizabethan, and the popular verdict of these two writers as being the most "English" of geniuses can be justi-fied in detail by their use of the language. With Shakespeare, it was a language based on the country, on the rural tradition ; with Dickens, it is pre-eminently the language of the city and the street. "The final stress", to quote a recent critic, "may fall on Dickens's command of word, phrase, rhythm and image : in ease and range there is surely no greater master of English except Shakespeare."

CHAPTER VI

EARLY VICTORIAN NOVELISTS
1826-1866

"Whether it is right or advisable to create beings like Heathcliff, I do not know : I scarcely think it is. But this I know ; the writer who possesses the creative gift owns something of which he is not always master —something that, at times, strangely wills and works for itself."

CHARLOTTE BRONTË: Editor's Preface to *Wuthering Heights*.

"I mentioned to G. that I had thought of the plan of writing a series of stories, containing sketches drawn from my own observation of the clergy, and calling them *Scenes from Clerical Life*, opening with *Amos Barton*. He at once accepted the notion as a good one —fresh and striking ; and about a week afterwards, when I read him the first part of *Amos*, he had no longer any doubt about my ability to carry out the plan. The scene at Cross Farm, he said, satisfied him that I had the very element he had been doubtful about —it was clear I could write good dialogue. There still remained the question whether I could command any pathos."

GEORGE ELIOT : *Journal*.

Between Scott and Dickens

We have noticed how the literary career of Dickens corresponds almost exactly with the first half of the reign of Victoria. Some of the other "early Victorian" novelists began writing ten years or so before the Queen ascended the throne ; that is, in literary history, between the last distinguished works of Scott and the publication of *Pickwick* and *Oliver Twist*. These pre-Victorian Victorians—Mary Russell Mitford, Harriet Martineau, Bulwer-Lytton, Disraeli, G. P. R. James, Ainsworth, Marryat, Surtees—are, conveniently for this chapter, of less importance, not only than Dickens, but than the other chief Victorian novelists, so that they can be discussed briefly before we proceed to Thackeray and the Brontës and George Eliot.

Where to end "early Victorian" and start "late Victorian" is, of course, largely a matter for each historian or critic to decide for himself. Some of the Victorian novelists took an example from the throne, and lived and wrote to a ripe old age. But it is inconvenient, and unnecessary in most cases, to split up a writer between two chapters; it only becomes necessary where a writer's later work is distinct from his earlier, and where, in this later work, he exerts a great influence on succeeding writers. The most striking, if not the only, instance of this among the Victorian novelists is George Eliot, whose *Middlemarch* and *Daniel Deronda* are usually considered distinct from her early work (there was a six-year gap between the publication of *Felix Holt* and *Middlemarch*) and whose late novels were a great influence on Henry James. So this chapter can begin with the "pre-Victorian" Victorian novelists, go on to Thackeray, the Brontës, the early George Eliot, among others, and leave to Chapter X the consideration of the later George Eliot, together with Henry James, Hardy, Meredith, and other novelists who did most of their work after 1866.

The pre-Victorian Victorians are, as we have noted, not very important, compared with the chief Victorian novelists. The ambition of Mary Russell Mitford (1787-1855) was to write verse tragedies, such as her *Rienzi* (1828); but these are forgotten, while her sketches of *Our Village* (1824-32) are remembered as genuine achievements in the lesser Jane Austen manner. Harriet Martineau (1802-76) tried to blend economics and fiction in her *Illustrations of Political Economy* (1832-4) and *Illustrations of Taxation* (1834). Her two novels, *Deerbrook* (1839) and *The Hour and the Man* (1841), are not—it has been wittily observed—"economic in any sense." Her tales for children were very popular; she wrote articles for learned reviews; and her friend Marian Evans, later George Eliot, called her "a *trump*—the only Englishwoman that possesses thoroughly the art of writing."

On the historical novel, the influence of Scott was, of course, tremendous. James, Ainsworth, and Marryat, were among his most considerable successors. G. P. R. James (1799-1860) wrote about a hundred historical romances, for example *Richelieu* (1829) and *The Smuggler* (1845). William Harrison Ainsworth (1805-82) had a much longer popularity, and it can be said that *Rookwood* (1834), *Jack Sheppard* (1839), *The Tower of London* (1840), and *Old St Paul's* (1841) are almost equal in merit to the *Waverley Novels*, with certain distinguished exceptions. Frederick Marryat (1792-1848) has a touch of Smollett's influence as well as Scott's ; he wrote many popular adventure stories, including *Peter Simple* (1834), *Mr Midshipman Easy* (1836), *Masterman Ready* (1841), and *The Children of the New Forest* (1847). Some of his stories were expressly written for boys, others not, but most of them, like most of Ainsworth's, were extremely popular with young readers right up to recent generations and are still found well-thumbed in juvenile libraries to-day. Captain Marryat has another claim to our esteem : his novels were one of the reasons why a romantic young Pole named Teodor Jósef Konrad Korzeniowski—who later became one of the greatest English novelists—joined the British merchant service in 1878.

Bulwer-Lytton and Disraeli

Politics and fiction—paradoxical as it may seem to cynics —are not very commonly allied. The Victorian age can boast of two exceptions, both of whom started their popularity with what has been called "the dandiacal-Byronic style" in novel-writing, Disraeli with *Vivian Grey* (1826) and Bulwer-Lytton with *Falkland* (1827) and *Pelham* (1828).

Edward Bulwer-Lytton (1803-73), who was created Lord Lytton, managed to combine the production of fiction, verse, drama, etc., with a distinguished record in politics and a prominent place in society. His novels successfully followed every turn of the public taste, and he achieved success as a playwright with *Richelieu* (1838), *The Lady of Lyons* (1838), and *Money* (1840). His historical romances are his best-known works, particularly *The Last Days of Pompeii* (1834).

The Caxtons (1849) is a good example of his more realistic novels on contemporary society. In 1871 he broke fresh ground with *The Coming Race*, a forerunner in some ways of later romances of the future. It is not known for certain whether it was a mere coincidence that Butler's satirical *Erewhon* came out the year after.

Even more striking than the career of Lytton—or of his son, who became Earl of Lytton, Viceroy of India, and a poet under the name "Owen Meredith"—was the career of Benjamin Disraeli (1804-81), who became Prime Minister and Earl of Beaconsfield. The son of Isaac Disraeli, a distinguished Jewish man of letters, he was baptised a Christian at the age of thirteen. After a period abroad as a Byronic dandy, he turned to literature, producing seven novels between 1826 and 1836. These are not important, and it was only after he had entered Parliament in 1837, and had formed, in opposition to his party leader Peel, the "Young England" group, that he wrote novels reflecting—admittedly with some absurdities still—the interests of an intelligent politician. The "Young England" trilogy—*Coningsby* (1844), *Sybil* (1845), *Tancred* (1847)—represent his most considerable achievement in literature, his later successes in the political field preventing him from adding much more to it. In this trilogy, as in life, he began to ask awkward questions of the Tory party. What did they wish to preserve? he asked. "Our glorious institutions"? But those institutions, he maintained, had been broken: "The Crown has become a cipher; the Church a sect; the Nobility drones; and the People drudges."

The ideal feudalism of which he dreamed never existed, and it was certainly not the England which the Chartists and the Trade Unions were struggling to achieve. There is a conservatory atmosphere about Disraeli's Conservatism: his heroes are hot-house plants, and only his villains come to life. For instance, in *Coningsby*, Lord Monmouth and Rigby—not to mention Tadpole and Taper—are observed with a master's eye. It is not often we get the chance of reading political novels by someone behind the scenes; even Dickens, right as he often was, as it were by instinct, over fundamental

points, never got closer to political details than the gallery
of the House of Commons.

What strikes a modern reader unpleasantly is Disraeli's
anticipation, in *Coningsby*, of the Hitler doctrine. It is super-
ficially the opposite of the Aryan legend, for Disraeli main-
tains, through his *alter ego* Sidonia, that the purity of the
Jewish race entails a constant triumph over "the mixed
persecuting races." But it is fundamentally as barbarous a
creed—and was a curious, exotic growth in the Young
England conservatory.

Surtees and the Sporting Novel

Nothing exotic about the Old England of Surtees. For
plain English humour, he is in the direct line from Fielding
to Dickens. It was, in fact, the success of the grocer-hunts-
man Mr Jorrocks—who first appeared in the *New Sporting
Magazine* in 1831—that led to the idea of *Pickwick*. (The
collected volume of sketches was published in 1838 as
Jorrocks's Jaunts and Jollities.) Though Surtees published
most of his stories in the Victorian period, his humour marks
a transitional stage between the bawdiness of Fielding and the
Dickensian comic. For instance, in *Handley Cross* (1843)
Mr Jorrocks is returning home from an unfortunate hunting
expedition, and has to run the gauntlet of the neighbours. "Old
Fatty's had a fall!" observes the landlady of the Barley-mow.
"He's always on his back, that old fellow," says the barber's
pretty wife. Mr Jorrocks overhears this last remark, and
caps it with an "obserwation" owing more to Squire Western
than to Sam Weller: "Not 'alf so often as you are, old
gal!" he retorts.

Robert Smith Surtees (1803-64) was a Durham squire,
who edited the *New Sporting Magazine* from 1831 to 1856.
Other books of his, mostly illustrated by John Leech or
"Phiz" (H. K. Browne), are *Hawbuck Grange* (1847), *Mr
Sponge's Sporting Tour* (1853), *Ask Mamma* (1858), and *Mr
Facey Romford's Hounds* (1865).

He is the best of the sporting, Old English writers. There
were many others: for instance, Charles James Apperley,

"Nimrod" of the *Sporting Magazine*, who wrote *The Life of a Sportsman* (1842); Francis Smedley, who wrote the celebrated comic novel *Frank Fairlegh* (1850); Major Whyte-Melville, who wrote both sporting and historical fiction; and Pierce Egan, whose *Life in London* was illustrated by the brothers Cruikshank and who is generally considered to be the chief inventor of that florid "Corinthian" style of sporting journalism which still talks about "the visiting custodian literally hurling himself at the leather."

Borrow, 1803-81

"The bruisers of England" are praised in a famous chapter of *Lavengro*, but George Borrow belongs to the European picaresque romantic tradition rather than to English sporting literature. He knew many languages, including Romany, and travelled on foot through England, France, Germany, Russia, and the East. For several years—incongruously enough—he acted as agent for the British and Foreign Bible Society in Catholic Spain. On his return to his native Norfolk, he wrote *The Zincali* (1840), an account of the Spanish gipsies, and *The Bible in Spain* (1843). In 1844 he toured the Balkans, and then wrote the books by which he is best known, *Lavengro* (1851) and its sequel, *The Romany Rye* (1857). These unique works are a blend of autobiography and romance—to which he added topographical information in *Wild Wales* (1862).

He is a pleasant and intelligent writer of the open-air life, who is really like no other writer of the nineteenth century; he himself expressed his indebtedness to Defoe. He has been compared with Cobbett, and also with Stevenson; a combination of Defoe and Byron may be nearer the mark.

Thackeray, 1811-63

Almost the exact contemporary of Dickens, William Makepeace Thackeray was for many years considered a rival to him. The claim to rivalry was rather absurd, for the two novelists had nothing fundamentally in common—save, from a modern point of view, that taste for sentimentality which was shared by nearly every writer of the Victorian age. What is more important is that Dickens's stature and popularity have increased with the years, while Thackeray's have declined. It has been said that, out of the long line of Thackeray's works, only three—*Vanity Fair, Esmond,* and *Pendennis*—"remain in the general repertory of 'the great variety of readers'"; and even this may be an over-estimate by some two-thirds.

Born near Calcutta, the son of a civil servant, Thackeray was educated at Cambridge and in Paris, where he studied art. The loss of his small private fortune through unfortunate investments led him to enter journalism, and he wrote and drew in various papers and magazines, using such pseudonyms as "Michael Angelo Titmarsh" and "George Savage Fitz-Boodle." Another personal misfortune — or rather tragedy—was the insanity of his wife, through childbirth, in 1840, four years after their marriage.

It is best to take his journalism and his novels separately. He was a superb journalist, and the chief follower of Peacock in burlesque. *The Yellowplush Papers*, contributed to *Fraser's Magazine* in 1837, and *The Book of Snobs*, which came out originally in *Punch* in 1846-7, are among his best periodical pieces. *Catherine, by Ikey Solomons junior* (1839-40) was a burlesque of the romantic highwayman stories of Ainsworth and Bulwer-Lytton, and this vein was extended in the series known as *Punch's Prize Novelists* (1847). *A Shabby Genteel Story* (1840) and *The Luck of Barry Lyndon* (1844)—both in *Fraser's*—are interesting precursors of *Philip* and *Vanity Fair* respectively.

The best of the Christmas stories, which began in 1847, is the last—a classic fairy-tale—*The Rose and the Ring* (1855). Of his two series of lectures, delivered in Britain and America, *The English Humorists of the Eighteenth Century* (1851-2) and *The Four Georges* (1855), the former is much the superior, for the simple reason that, as Trollope said, "the lecturer was a man of letters dealing with men of letters . . . a prince among humorists dealing with the humorists of his own country and language. One could not imagine a better subject . . ."

Thackeray's Best Novels

Authors are proverbially bad at self-criticism, but when in 1847 Thackeray put his own name, for the first time, to the first monthly part of a novel called *Vanity Fair*, his abandonment of frivolous *noms-de-plume* was well justified by the text. *Vanity Fair*, completed in 1848, remains his most considerable achievement—a classic, if not a great one—and Becky Sharp and Rawdon Crawley his most subtle characters. It is a realistic portrayal of the cadging, toadying sort of life that goes on—or went on in the eighteenth and nineteenth centuries—on the fringe of smart society. Dickens did a similar thing in a few chapters of *Dombey and Son, Little Dorrit,* and *Our Mutual Friend,* but Thackeray is more convincing than his "rival" here, probably because he was nearer, in social origin, to the class he was satirising.

Vanity Fair was followed by *Pendennis* (1848-50), which has a considerable autobiographical element, and *The History of Henry Esmond* (1852). While neither novel comes up to the first great achievement, partly because Thackeray was reacting against his own realism and went too far in the opposite direction, they are worth study as instances of the novelist's wider range. Hogarth was the artist, Thackeray tells us, whom he tried to follow when first meditating art as a profession, and in *Esmond* he has attempted to recapture the "contemporary" Hogarthian spirit in picturing in prose fiction an age slightly earlier, the age of Addison and Swift. The picture is by no means a complete success, but probably it is Thackeray's best work after *Vanity Fair*.

His later novels are not considered very important, even by those few modern readers who deem him superior to Dickens. (His relationship to Trollope is more convincing.) *The Newcomes* (1853-4) and *The Virginians* (1857-9) are both sequels to more successful books, the former being supposedly edited by Pendennis, the latter being a chronicle of the American descendants of Henry Esmond. In 1857 Thackeray tried unsuccessfully to enter Parliament; in 1860 he became the first editor of the very successful *Cornhill*

Magazine. The opening number contained the first instalment of *Lovel the Widower* and the first of the *Roundabout Papers.* His last completed novel, *The Adventures of Philip* —in which he returned to the characters of *A Shabby Genteel Story*—came out in the *Cornhill* in 1862.

He was one of the most versatile of the Victorians: novelist, essayist, humorist, editor, lecturer, rhymester, draughtsman—it is astonishing how little has survived. For most people to-day, he is the author of *Vanity Fair*, or of that and *Esmond*. The readability of *The Book of Snobs* makes one suspect that a modern selection of his other journalistic work would be worth making. *The Rose and the Ring* is recognised as being the best Victorian fairy-tale apart from the *Alice* books and *The Water-Babies*, but for every modern child who has read it, a hundred must have read Carroll's and fifty Kingsley's. It is difficult to avoid the conclusion that Thackeray has been rather unlucky, nearly as unfortunate in his posthumous reputation as he was in his private life. Perhaps the interest aroused by his recently-collected correspondence will lead to a partial resurrection.*

Trollope, 1815-82

The volume on Thackeray in Macmillan's *English Men of Letters* series was written by his friend and fellow-novelist Anthony Trollope. The two writers have something in common ; they are much nearer to each other than either is to Dickens—whom Trollope was inclined to despise. (He wrote of Dickens in the Thackeray volume : "The good opinion which he had of himself was never shaken by adverse criticism ; and the criticism on the other side, by which it was exalted, came from the enumeration of the copies sold.") Once again, it is Trollope, and not Thackeray, who has been successfully revived in the twentieth century, after the literary world had got over the shock of the posthumous *Autobiography* (1883), in which he spoke of his work as something

* Thackeray's eldest daughter, Anne Isabella, who married her cousin Sir Richmond Thackeray Ritchie, wrote novels and reminiscences, notably *The Story of Elizabeth* (1863)

that could be done regularly by the clock, at the rate of a thousand words an hour.

Probably both his candour and his literary convictions were inherited from his mother. Frances Trollope (1780-1863) was the wife of a poor scholar who wrote prolifically to support her home ; she caused an uproar, similar to Dickens's later, by her frank *Domestic Manners of the Americans* (1832). Her chief novels are *The Vicar of Wrexhill* (1837) and *The Widow Barnaby* (1838).

Anthony Trollope (whose elder brother Adolphus also wrote novels) has two claims to enduring fame : as an official in the Post Office, he invented the pillar-box ; and as a novelist, he invented the county of Barsetshire, in which lies the cathedral city of Barchester. It is safe to say that nearly all his sixty novels are highly readable, but the prime favourites have always been the Barsetshire series : *The Warden* (1855), *Barchester Towers* (1857), *Dr Thorne* (1858), *Framley Parsonage* (1861), *The Small House at Allington* (1864), and *The Last Chronicles of Barset* (1867). Others include *Orley Farm* (1862) and the political novel *Phineas Finn* (1869).

Trollope has little of the genius so manifest in Dickens, and no one of his novels quite comes up to *Vanity Fair*, but collectively they give us the best picture of Victorian upper-middle-class society we possess. It was a tribute to his powers, as well as to the contrasting Victorian peace, that, in the midst of the recent war, his novels became so popular that secondhand-book shops on the edge of bomb-craters had in their windows, not collected editions, but notices imploring the purchase of any Trollope novel in reasonable condition.

Collins and Others

The friend and collaborator of Dickens, Wilkie Collins (1824-89) had his greatest popularity in the decade 1857-66, when his mystery novels, *The Dead Secret, The Woman in White, No Name,* and *Armadale,* especially the second, had an immense vogue. He influenced considerably the later novels of his friend, and Dickens took the part of the hero in his famous melodrama *The Frozen Deep*. Collins may also be said to have invented the typical English detective-story, partly by *The Woman in White* (1860) but more by *The Moonstone* (1868). A combination of Collins and the American mystery-writer Edgar Allan Poe is behind much of the later work of Conan Doyle. A novelist dealing, like Poe, with the super-natural as well as the mysterious was Joseph Sheridan Le Fanu (1814-73)—one of the Sheridan family—who is mainly remembered to-day for *The House by the Churchyard* (1863) and *Uncle Silas* (1864).

It was a great age for the novel, the Victorian, both in quality and quantity. The popular novelists of the time were sometimes of lasting value ; the most obvious example is Dickens, and both Trollope and Collins are not only still very readable to-day, but have distinctly literary merits. Inevitably there are many others, however, whose popularity has not been sustained or who have not much value as litera-ture. Among the widely-read novels of the early Victorian age whose interest now is chiefly historical, we may mention here such varied things as Samuel Lover's *Handy Andy* (1838), Charles Lever's *Charles O'Malley* (1841), Mrs Clive's *Paul Ferrol* (1855), Mrs Craik's *John Halifax, Gentleman* (1857), Major Lawrence's *Guy Livingstone* (1857), Mrs Henry Wood's *East Lynne* (1861), Miss Brad-don's *Lady Audley's Secret* (1862), Mrs Oliphant's *Salem Chapel* (1863), and James Payn's *Lost Sir Massingberd* (1864). The last named, and several others in this list, have attained the dignity of being included in a famous "classic" series—along with Scott, Dickens, etc.—and can still be picked up here and there on secondhand-book stalls.

Reade and Kingsley

We have observed how Dickens was saved, by his genius for the universal, from sharing the fate that normally over-takes those who write "novels with a purpose." Reade and Kingsley are good examples of excellent men who wrote on social problems, but who are chiefly remembered for their other work.

Charles Reade (1814-84) is famous for his historical romance *The Cloister and the Hearth* (1861), but most of his fiction, which in certain of its methods anticipates Zola, deals with contemporary life and was intended to further social reform. Thus, *It is Never too Late to Mend* (1856) embodies criticism of the horrible "model" prisons; *Hard Cash* (1863) exposes the abuses of lunatic asylums; *Foul Play* (1869) attacks "ship-knacking"; and so forth. Reade was also a dramatist, and liked to turn novels into plays and plays into novels; his first novel, *Peg Woffington* (1853), was a version of his play *Masks and Faces*. He had a great success with the melodrama *The Lyons Mail*.

Charles Kingsley (1819-75) is important in literary history in several different ways, and will come briefly into later chapters. As a novelist, he shares the fate of Reade : he is remembered for his classic fairy-tale *The Water-Babies* (1863), a work of genius that admittedly contains some social criticism, and for his *Westward Ho!* (1855), an adventure story in the Scott-Ainsworth-Marryat juvenile tradition, while his campaigning novels of contemporary life, which earned him the title of "the Chartist clergyman", are almost forgotten. *Yeast, a Problem* (1848) deals with the degrading conditions under which the agricultural labourer lived and worked; *Alton Locke, Tailor and Poet* (1850) with the stresses of the town artisan. They are not very good as novels, rather sincere pamphlets in fictional form.

Kingsley's other works include numerous forgotten tracts ; a drama, *The Saint's Tragedy* ; a few poems which are celebrated in anthologies, notably *The Sands of Dee* ; a book of Greek legends for children, *The Heroes* (1856); and two historical novels, *Hypatia* (1853) and *Hereward the Wake* (1866), neither of which has attained the popularity of *Westward Ho!*.

Several other members of the Kingsley family became known as writers. Charles's daughter, Mrs Harrison, published novels under the name of Lucas Malet ; his brother Henry Kingsley, who emigrated to Australia, wrote two popular novels, *Geoffrey Hamlyn* (1859) and *Ravenshoe* (1862);

while their neice Mary Kingsley, who travelled widely in
Africa, wrote *Travels in West Africa* and other books.*

Mrs Gaskell, 1810-65

The social novels of Elizabeth Cleghorn Stevenson, who
married the Rev. William Gaskell, are more important than
either Reade's or Kingsley's. In *Mary Barton* (1848) and
North and South (1855) she makes good use of her knowledge
of the industrial life of Lancashire, and the miseries of the
factory system, to create works that are genuine novels, not
simply fictional tracts. The deserved success of *Mary Barton*
brought her into contact with Dickens, to whose *Household
Words* she contributed the series of amusing sketches afterwards collected as *Cranford* (1853). This intimate record of
a few lives in a Cheshire village became her most popular
book, and is generally regarded as a minor classic. Her later
novels include *Ruth* (1853), *Sylvia's Lovers* (1863-4), *Cousin
Phillis* (1865), and the unfinished *Wives and Daughters*,
posthumously published in 1866. She was a correspondent
of George Eliot, and a friend of Charlotte Brontë, whose
Life she wrote.

The Brontës

The achievement of women novelists in the nineteenth
century is very remarkable. There were women poets—Mrs
Hemans, Mrs Browning, Christina Rossetti, and others—but

* Kingsley's friend and fellow-crusader, Thomas Hughes (1822-
96), is chiefly remembered for his classic boys' book *Tom Brown's
School Days* (1857). The Victorian age was the great age for juvenile literature. Worthy of mention also are such admirable things
as R. M. Ballantyne's *Coral Island*, W. H. G. Kingston's *Peter the
Whaler*, G. A. Henty's *With Clive in India*, Mayne Reid's *Rifle
Rangers*, Anna Sewell's *Black Beauty*, Mrs Gatty's *Parables from
Nature*, Dr Brown's *Rab and his Friends*, and Mrs Ewing's *Jan
of the Windmill*, besides magazines such as *Chatterbox* and the
Boys' Own Paper, American books like *Little Women*, and the works
by Marryat, Thackeray, Kingsley, Lewis Carroll, etc., already
referred to. The post-Hughes type of school story was begun by
Talbot Baines Reed, reacting against, not only *Tom Brown*, but
Dean Farrar's *Eric, or Little by Little* (1858).

no one would compare their work with that of Wordsworth or Keats. The work in fiction, however, is not only comparable to the male achievement, a good case could be made out for deeming it superior. Dickens is unique in comedy, it is true, but *Emma, Wuthering Heights*, and *Middlemarch* set a standard in serious fiction which few novels by male contemporaries attain.

The astonishing story of the Brontë sisters* may be presumed to be known to everyone. We shall content ourselves here with a brief outline. They were the daughters of a Yorkshire parson who was one of the ten children of an illiterate Irish peasant; born Patrick Prunty, Brunty, or O'Prunty, the father, when at Cambridge university (to which his own exertions and friendly help had brought him), took the style of "Brontë", which he liked to think was the classical form of the Irish original. After their mother's death, the girls with their brother were brought up by an aunt; they roamed the moors around Haworth, and amused themselves with writing. They got their early education from their father; later they were sent to a cheap boarding school, probably the model for Lowood in *Jane Eyre*.

For some years the sisters earned their living as governesses, and then in 1842 Charlotte and Emily entered Professor Heger's school at Brussels. Emily returned to Haworth on their aunt's death, but Charlotte, who was in love with the married Heger, did not finally leave Brussels until 1844. Meanwhile their brother Branwell, a rather Byronic figure who dabbled in painting and poetry, had become a drunkard and an opium-addict.

Charlotte now discovered by accident some poems by Emily which impressed her greatly, and in 1846 the sisters published a joint collection under the pseudonyms of Currer, Ellis, and Acton Bell. Charlotte was convinced, and rightly, that Emily's poems were strikingly original, but only two copies of the book appear to have been sold. It is astonishing that the reviewers should have failed to admire one at least

* Charlotte Brontë (1816-55), Emily Brontë (1818-48), Anne Brontë (1820-49).

of Emily's poems, that called *Remembrance,* which contains the lines :

> Cold in the earth—and fifteen wild Decembers,
> From these brown hills, have melted into spring . . .

but the only adequate review seems to have been that in the *Dublin University Magazine,* a comparatively obscure journal which is chiefly honoured now by this association.

The sisters, probably under the stimulus of Charlotte, now each decided to attempt a novel. Charlotte's first, *The Professor,* failed to find a publisher, but Emily's *Wuthering Heights* and Anne's *Agnes Grey* were accepted. Charlotte's second novel, *Jane Eyre,* was quickly accepted, and it was published, with great success, a few weeks before *Wuthering Heights* and *Agnes Grey* came out together. (The Victorian fashion was for novels in three volumes : Anne's story made up the third, to the two volumes of *Wuthering Heights.*)

During 1848-9 Branwell, Emily, and Anne all died, the sisters of consumption, the brother of bronchitis—possibly consumption—aggravated by his dissipated life. Anne had written a second novel, *The Tenant of Wildfell Hall,* which was published in 1848. Her writing has its own modest charm, but is mainly interesting to-day through her association with her greater sisters.

Charlotte was now left alone as companion and housekeeper to her father—who, though blind and ill, survived all his children. Her later novels were *Shirley* (1849), whose chief character was based on Emily, and her finest achievement, *Villette* (1853), mainly about the Brussels experience. In 1854 she married her father's curate Arthur Nicholls, but died a year later. She left two chapters of a novel called *Emma*—a rather astonishing title for one who, on the urging of G. H. Lewes, read Jane Austen but remained, as we have seen, decidedly unimpressed.

Emily and Charlotte

The genius of the family, it is now generally agreed, was Emily. Several poems of hers are memorable, but her achievement rests upon that astonishing work *Wuthering*

Emily Greater than Charlotte — proved in Wuthering Heights.

*Heights.** It is not very surprising that many of her Victorian contemporaries found this novel appalling; reviewers spoke of its "coarseness." Some later critics have rightly considered it one of the finest novels in any language, and for generations now it has been a favourite with the general reader.

For some time it was described, in both academic and professional circles, as "full of constructional faults"—whatever that phrase may precisely mean. Modern criticism has mainly agreed with D. H. Lawrence, some of whose novels met a similar objection from Arnold Bennett: "Tell Arnold Bennett," wrote Lawrence, "that all rules of construction hold good only for novels which are copies of other novels. A book which is not a copy of other books has its own construction."

It is interesting to see that Charlotte Brontë's words about *Wuthering Heights*—quoted in the epigraph to this chapter—are confirmed by a modern novelist and critic, Virginia Woolf, when she contrasted the two sisters on the occasion in 1916 of the centenary of Charlotte's birth:

> *Wuthering Heights* is a more difficult book to understand than *Jane Eyre*, because Emily was a greater poet than Charlotte. When Charlotte wrote she said with eloquence and splendour and passion "I love", "I hate", "I suffer." Her experience, though more intense, is on a level with our own. But there is no "I" in *Wuthering Heights* . . . Emily was urged by some more general conception . . . She looked out upon a world cleft into gigantic disorder and felt within her the power to unite it in a book. That gigantic ambition is to be felt throughout the novel—a struggle, half thwarted but of superb conviction, to say something through the mouths of her characters which is not merely "I love" or "I hate", but "we, the whole human race" and "you, the eternal powers . . ." the sentence remains unfinished.

In other words, Emily has that impersonal quality in her art which informs great dramatic poetry like *King Lear* or

* "Wuthering" is a Yorkshire dialect word meaning "storming" and is correctly pronounced with a deep resonant "u", as in the word "full".

Antony and Cleopatra, a quality which Charlotte lacked, or comparatively lacked, but which she nevertheless immediately recognised in her sister when she wrote those words about the creative gift sometimes overmastering the creator.

George Eliot, 1819-80

The two quotations which form the epigraph to this chapter were deliberately chosen as a contrast. For not all novelists—indeed, very few—work in the manner of Emily Brontë. It is possible to attain great achievement in fiction, though probably not in poetry, by a process of deliberate effort and revision. This is not a matter of "rules of construction" contrasted with "untaught genius"; it is rather the creator in full possession of the creative gift as opposed to those few "poetic" novelists—they include such varied geniuses as Bunyan, Dickens, Emily Brontë, D. H. Lawrence, T. F. Powys—who "own something that, at times, strangely wills and works for itself."

Mary Ann Evans, usually called "Marian", who took the name of George Eliot, is the supreme example among the Victorians of a novelist who deliberately and by great effort worked her way from the apprenticeship of *Scenes from Clerical Life* ("There still remained the question whether I could command any pathos . . ."), through the contemporary "best-sellers" *Adam Bede* and *The Mill on the Floss,* to the superb *Middlemarch*—a work that has been frequently described, by critics of varying schools of thought, as "the finest novel of the Victorian age." *

It is her early fiction that concerns this chapter, if "early" is the word for a writer whose first story was published at the age of thirty-eight. She was the daughter of a carpenter who became an estate-agent, the original of Adam Bede and (more exactly) Caleb Garth in *Middlemarch.* Brought up in the strictest tenets of the Puritan faith, her

---

* Rather curiously, this verdict was first given by John Buchan, Lord Tweedsmuir, a biographer and in some ways a follower of Scott—the author of the *Waverley Novels* being a novelist at the other extreme from the mature George Eliot, who nevertheless admired him greatly throughout her life.

sincerity of mind led her through varied spiritual experiences, including a period of devotion to ascetic ideals. This was inspired by the example of an aunt, a Methodist preacher, whose religious enthusiasm was to suggest the character of Dinah Morris in *Adam Bede* and an anecdote by whom was the germ of that novel.

On moving to Coventry in 1841, she was led gradually to an agnostic view of religion, through her friends, the Hennell sisters, and their brother and brother-in-law. (Charles Hennell was the author of *An Enquiry concerning the Origin of Christianity*; Charles Bray, the brother-in-law, wrote *The Philosophy of Necessity*.) She took over from Sara Hennell a translation of Strauss's *Leben Jesu*, then the last word in unorthodoxy. This was published in 1846 by John Chapman, who had acquired the *Westminster Review* from Mill; and after her father's death, Marian Evans became assistant editor—virtually editor—lodging in the Strand with the curious Chapman *ménage*, which consisted of the publisher, the publisher's wife, the publisher's mistress, and the publisher's mistress's lady friend. Through Chapman she met the philosopher Herbert Spencer, and through Spencer the journalist George Henry Lewes. Lewes was married, but separated from his wife (divorce was then illegal), and in 1854 Marian Evans entered upon a union with him which she regarded as a true marriage and which continued until his death.*

This union may be said to have created George Eliot. It was in 1856 that the conversation quoted in the epigraph took place, "G" standing for Lewes. *The Sad Fortunes of the Rev. Amos Barton* appeared in *Blackwood's Magazine* during 1857, and it was followed by *Mr Gilfil's Love Story* and *Janet's Repentance*. The collected work, *Scenes of Clerical Life*, was published in 1858. The name "George Eliot" was

---

* G. H. Lewes (1817-78) was a versatile writer, well known in his day as essayist, novelist, biographer, and expounder of popular science. He had been an actor in early life and wrote much on the theatre. His chief works are *The Biographical History of Philosophy* (1845-6), *The Life and Works of Goethe* (1855), and *Problems of Life and Mind* (1874).

chosen almost at random ; George was Lewes's Christian name and "Eliot was a good mouth-filling, easily-pronounced word."

The *Scenes* were successful, and in the following year, 1859, George Eliot won immediate popularity with *Adam Bede*, which, like its successors *The Mill on the Floss* (1860) and *Silas Marner* (1861), was set in her native Midlands and owed much to personal experience. *Romola*, serialised in the *Cornhill* in 1863, was much less successful as a novel ; it is a story of Florence at the time of Savonarola, and as a literary creation it suffers under a weight of laborious research. "I began *Romola* a young woman," the author recorded ; "I finished it an old woman."

Felix Holt, the Radical (1866) is a very interesting novel, but rather uneven ; and then we get the long gap referred to above, before the publication of her masterpiece, *Middlemarch*, in 1872. *Daniel Deronda* followed in 1876. The blank-verse drama *The Spanish Gypsy* (1868), and her other minor works and translations, are only important for students of her writing. Much more interesting is *George Eliot's Life as related in her Letters and Journals*, a posthumous semi-autobiography, edited by J. W. Cross, an old friend of Lewes and herself whom she married in 1880, eight months before she died.

Her Early Novels, 1857-66

The pre-*Middlemarch* George Eliot was a novelist of great powers rather than complete achievement ; she was one of those writers who develop gradually as they go along, like Jane Austen and unlike Dickens, Thackeray, and Trollope. Dickens's great things are scattered throughout his work ; Thackeray's best novel was his first under his own name ; while Trollope, once he had found his feet early on, produced novel after novel on a remarkably sustained level of accomplishment.

The *Scenes of Clerical Life* were admittedly experiments, and need not detain us here. That they were a success is their chief importance, for they encouraged George Eliot to write a long novel, *Adam Bede*, which is her first important work. It has often been noticed that this great story was a rather curious thing to come from "the advanced intellectual" of the *Westminster Review*—a young lady who, on meeting Dickens in 1852, was very disappointed in his phrenological development: "the anterior lobe not by any means remarkable." But there were two forces in George Eliot, the intellectual and the emotional; the intellectual found expression in the essays for the *Westminster*, in the translations of Strauss and Feuerbach, and in the research for *Romola*, the emotional is most obvious in *Adam* and in *The Mill on the Floss*. Sometimes the emotional habit was a weakness, it degenerated into sentimentality. It was not until *Middlemarch* that the two forces combined in great achievement—*Silas Marner* being, indeed, a classic, but a minor one.

"She is no satirist," observed Virginia Woolf, and a more recent critic adds rightly: "She sees too much and has too strong a sense of the real (as well as too much self-knowledge and too adequate and constant a sense of her own humanity) to be a satirist." Her superiority, not only to Samuel Butler and George Meredith, but to Jane Austen herself, lies in that reverence for human life, that Shakespearean breadth, which is only equalled in her period, in his very different way, by the novelist with the unremarkable anterior lobe. A purely "intellectual" George Eliot could not have written either *Adam Bede* or *Silas Marner*, a purely "emotional" could not have written the best parts of *Felix Holt* or her masterpiece *Middlemarch*. Pondering her own life, with its early stresses and humiliations—she wrote at the end of 1857: "Few women, I fear, have had such reason as I have to think the long sad years of youth were worth living for the sake of middle age"—she could have said, with Dickens, "all these things have worked together to make me what I am."

Her gradual development being recognised—and most critics have agreed upon this—to discuss the merits of her various novels in any brief space seems almost redundant. It was not, it is true, an entirely logical development: *Romola* is a failure, but probably a failure by which George Eliot profited. *Scenes of Clerical Life, Adam Bede, The Mill on the Floss, Silas Marner,* represent a steady improvement in what is virtually the same field : the tender observation, the "recollection in tranquillity", of the past. She refers in *The Mill* to "the loves and sanctities of our life" having "deep immovable roots in memory." She has been compared with Wordsworth in these books, and the judgment is sound ; so much so that, being wise after the event, we are astonished that Lewes should have doubted whether she "could command any pathos." The Wordsworthian pathetic strength that is the bright side of the Victorian sentimental medal is the chief virtue of her early achievement ; in the Transome scenes of *Felix Holt* she went on to something more difficult, a vein of interest that was exploited more fully in *Middlemarch* and *Daniel Deronda.*

CHAPTER VII

EARLY VICTORIAN POETRY [1]

1830-1869

"Let knowledge grow from more to more,
But more of reverence in us dwell;
That mind and soul, according well,
May make one music as as before."

TENNYSON : In Memoriam.

Between Byron and Tennyson

Most modern readers, if asked to name a few typical "early Victorian" poems, would mention *Recollections of the Arabian Nights*, or the Song beginning "A spirit haunts the year's last hours", or *The Lady of Shalott*, or *Oenone*, or *The Palace of Art*, or *The Lotos-Eaters*, or *A Dream of Fair Women*, or the ballad with the memorable refrain, "For I'm to be Queen o' the May, mother, I'm to be Queen o' the May."

Of these eight poems by Tennyson, the first two were originally published in 1830, the year that George IV died and William IV succeeded; and the rest came out in 1832. The Victorian age did not begin till 1837.

Yet the modern reader would not be so far out. We have observed, in the first chapter, the great importance of the early deaths of Keats in 1821, Shelley in 1822, Byron in 1824. Such a triple loss could not possibly have been made up by their immediate successors. What poetry, we must ask, was produced between the years 1825 and 1830—the period when, by rights, Byron, Shelley, and Keats would have been in their prime ? The catalogue is extremely meagre : some minor work by the veteran Wordsworth; *The Christian Year* by Keble ; *Poems* by Thomas Hood ; *The Shepherd's Calendar* by Clare ; *The Omnipresence of the Deity* by Robert Montgomery ; *The Village Patriarch* by Ebenezer Elliott ; *The Course of Time* by Robert Pollok ; *The Improvisatore* by "L.E.L." (Letitia Elizabeth Landon); "From Greenland's

icy mountains" by the Bishop of Calcutta ; *Poems by Two
Brothers* by the three Tennysons ; some poetic dramas mentioned in Chapter V ; and the last part of Samuel Rogers's
long blank-verse poem *Italy*. The preceding five years had
produced *Don Juan*, *The Vision of Judgment*, Wordsworth's
River Duddon sonnets, and the final, most mature work of
Keats and Shelley. The end of the decade is evidently far
inferior to the beginning, and, in fact, the period 1825-30
marks a real resting-place between the Age of Wordsworth
and Byron and the Age of Tennyson and Browning. What
we normally call "the Romantic Movement" virtually ended
with the death of Byron and the degeneration of Wordsworth ;
there was a gap of five years, partly filled by minor poetry,
of which perhaps the best is Clare's ; and then "the early
Victorian age" began seven years before its time.

So it is not surprising that it was, in some respects, rather
a stunted growth. In the 1830 and 1832 collections Tennyson
was influenced greatly by Keats. But not, unfortunately,
by Keats's best work ; rather by those charming minor poems,
Isabella, *The Eve of St Agnes*, etc., which Keats himself
criticised as weak and inexperienced and which he was reluctant to publish. Early Victorian poetry, like the minor work
of Keats, has its genuine charm and its occasional strength ;
but it cannot be compared with the finest achievements of the
great period 1786-1824, it can only be considered an advance
on the minor poetry of the transitional period and on the
sentimental verse admired by the Regency reviews.

Tennyson, 1809-92

All three Tennysons contributed to the juvenile volume
called—rather curiously—*Poems by Two Brothers*, published
in 1827. But it is no great disparagement to Frederick and
Charles to claim, for general purposes of literary history,
the name Tennyson for the younger, more sensitive, more
intelligent brother Alfred alone ; for he was not only the most
popular of Victorian poets, fittingly raised to the peerage in
1884, he was the most representative. Though he is typical
above all of the early Victorian age, his work spanned almost

the entire period—beginning, as we have noted, some years before the period opened. There is nothing of value in the 1827 volume ; his real work began in 1830. Of his brothers' subsequent poetry, we can mention Frederick's *Days and Hours* (1854) and the sonnets of Charles, who took the name of Turner on succeeding to some property.

Like George Eliot, his great admirer, Tennyson was a very careful worker, whose self-criticism was rigorous. Of *Poems, Chiefly Lyrical* (1830) and *Poems* (1832) he rejected thirty-two out of the original eighty-six, and revised some others, when he published in 1842 the two volumes of *Poems* which first made him widely known to the general public. To revised versions of the poems mentioned in the first paragraph of this chapter, he now added such immediately popular things as *Ulysses, Sir Galahad, Morte d'Arthur, Locksley Hall, The Gardener's Daughter, The Day-Dream, The Beggar Maid,* "Break, break, break," and "Of old sat Freedom on the heights."

The Princess, first published in 1847, was less successful. It is the first of three long poems where the poet, as in part of *Locksley Hall*, attempts to set forth in verse his views on the problems of the time. He considered most of the poetry of the day lacking in intellectual interest, and in *The Princess, In Memoriam,* and *Maud* he hoped to supply what was needed. *The Princess*, dealing with the position of women in social life, is the least valuable of the three, mainly known to-day by the charming lyrics—for instance, "The splendour falls on castle walls" and "Now sleeps the crimson petal, now the white"— added to the third edition.

In Memoriam A.H.H. is a more important poem. It was the product of much thought and of many years, having been begun in 1833, on the death of Arthur Henry Hallam, the intimate friend of Gladstone at Eton, of Tennyson at Cambridge, and the fiancé of the poet's sister. It was published in 1850, the year of Tennyson's marriage and his succession to Wordsworth as Poet Laureate.

At this time, as we have noticed briefly when speaking of George Eliot, the scholarship of Germany and the discoveries of scientists were leading thoughtful men and women to question, and in some cases to abandon, the old religious faiths. The death of his closest friend brought Tennyson face to face with those eternal problems about which natural science—by definition—has nothing to say. George Eliot became an Agnostic—to use the word later coined by Thomas Huxley—who nevertheless saw in Christianity "the highest expression of the religious sentiment that has yet found its place in the history of mankind." Tennyson, though in painful doubt, was more orthodox, speaking, as he did so often, for the mass of his contemporaries when he wrote in this poem of the strife between God and Nature and the "lame hands of faith":

> Are God and Nature then at strife
>   That Nature lends such evil dreams ?
>   So careful of the type she seems,
> So careless of the single life ;
>
> That I, considering everywhere
>   Her secret meaning in her deeds,
>   And, finding that of fifty seeds
> She often brings but one to bear,
>
> I falter where I firmly trod,
>   And, falling with my weight of cares
>   Upon the great world's altar-stairs,
> That slope through darkness up to God,
>
> I stretch lame hands of faith, and grope
>   And gather dust and chaff, and call
>   To what I feel is Lord of all,
> And faintly trust the larger hope.

It was passages like this that made *In Memoriam*, despite the personal nature of the original impulse, a true cry from the Victorian heart. The poem was annotated by clergymen, and quoted from pulpits and lecture platforms. It was the start of that combination of Christianity and Evolution which is seen at its most striking in a famous picture in an Edwardian encyclopaedia for children, where the story of life is given in pictorial perspective, the ape-man on the horizon and the Cross in the middle distance.

Maud (1855) was the third of these longer poems. Like *The Princess*, it is mainly known to-day by its interspersed lyrics, rather than by its intellectual theme, the denunciation of materialism and social evil. The celebrated "Come into the garden, Maud" was a favourite song for generations :

> She is coming, my own, my sweet ;
> Were it ever so airy a tread,
> My heart would hear her and beat,
> Were it earth in an earthy bed ;
> My dust would hear her and beat,
> Had I lain for a century dead ;
> Would start and tremble under her feet,
> And blossom in purple and red.

Tennyson had been early attracted by the romances of Malory, and had published his first poetic version of them, *Morte d'Arthur*, in the second 1842 volume. Now he undertook a whole series of Round Table legends, the twelve *Idylls of the King*, published between 1859 and 1885. It is generally recognised that the eleven new poems, charming as they are in many respects, are not of so high a standard as the reprinted *Morte d'Arthur*. The characterisation, in general, is not subtle enough for such an ambitious undertaking ; most of the heroes and heroines are too faultless to carry conviction, though it has been rightly observed that the characters fail, not because they are Victorian (Malory's are late medieval, yet the date usually given to the legendary Arthur is the sixth century), but because they are not alive. The virile *Morte d'Arthur* of 1842 exposes the mawkish nature of the later work.

Tennyson's Best Period, 1842-64

Though Tennyson wrote much of interest throughout his long life—he was eighty when he wrote *Crossing the Bar*— his best poetry, on the whole, is to be found in the period 1842-64 : in the new material of the 1842 volume, in *In Memoriam*, in the lyrics of *Maud* and *The Princess*, and in the *Enoch Arden* volume. *Enoch Arden* itself is a tragedy of village life, recalling some of Crabbe's and Wordsworth's narrative pieces ; it is more dramatic than most of the *Idylls*, and this dramatic interest is shared by the dialect poems, *The Grandmother* and *The Northern Farmer—Old Style*, in the same 1864 volume.

In many of the poems in this period Tennyson has occasional lines of dramatic rhetoric—for instance, "Now lies the Earth all Danae to the stars"—which remind the reader of the early Marlowe. But of his dramas proper—*Queen Mary* (1875), *Harold* (1876), *Becket* (1879)—it is sufficient to observe that they have no proper dramatic quality. *Becket* is the least wordy, and has been performed several times with fair success; more recently, *Queen Mary* has been given on the B.B.C.'s Third Programme.

Some of Tennyson's most popular work was in the patriotic vein. He was sometimes as arrogant an Englishman as Thackeray; both men can be contrasted with Dickens in this respect. But the final stress should be laid, not on the insular arrogance of such a piece as *The Third of February, 1852* (lines on the *coup d'état* of Napoleon III), nor on the "Crimean" opening of *Maud*, nor even on the rightly celebrated *The Revenge: A Ballad of the Fleet* (1878), but on the wiser and better poet of *Locksley Hall*.

This poem is perhaps the finest in Tennyson's most important volume of shorter pieces, the second of 1842. Like Wordsworth's *Leech-Gatherer*, it contains a certain amount of unconscious humour, and unfortunately the metre lends itself as readily to bathos as to parody. But the famous prophecies in the sixtieth verse onwards represent a considerable achievement, both as poetry and as prediction. The "ghastly dew" is an astonishing prevision of the Battle of Britain and the Atomic Bomb, and we can only hope that "the Parliament of man, the Federation of the world" will be as accurate a forecast:

> For I dipt into the future, far as human eye could see,
> Saw the Vision of the world, and all the wonder that would be;
>
> Saw the heavens fill with commerce, argosies of magic sails,
> Pilots of the purple twilight, dropping down with costly bales;

> Heard the heavens fill with shouting, and there rain'd
>   a ghastly dew
> From the nations' airy navies grappling in the central
>   blue ;
>
> Far along the world-wide whisper of the south-wind
>   rushing warm,
> With the standards of the peoples plunging thro' the
>   thunder-storm ;
>
> Till the war-drums throbb'd no longer, and the battle-
>   flags were furl'd
> In the Parliament of man, the Federation of the world.

FitzGerald, 1809-83

The contemporary and friend of Tennyson, Edward Fitz-
Gerald is remarkable as a poet who wrote scarcely any original
work but who became famous for his free translation of the
Rubaiyat of Omar Khayyam (1859). The adjective "free"
qualifies somewhat, of course, the previous statement ; good
translations of poetry, as distinct from those of prose, are
always "original" to a large extent, and we need not suppose
that FitzGerald's version owes much in poetry, though probably something in philosophy, to the work of the Persian
astronomer-poet who lived in the eleventh century. The publication of 1859 was, in fact, an English poem of seventy-
five quatrains based upon selections and combinations of the
original Persian stanzas. In later editions—the poem became
popular with the younger generation—FitzGerald revised the
expression and extended the length.

We can see, at this date, why the *Rubaiyat* appealed so
strongly to many of the generation that followed Darwin—
whose *Origin of Species* came out the same year. The scepti-
cism of the early Victorians was reluctant and sorrowful—
George Eliot translated the unorthodox Strauss with a cast
of Thorwaldsen's risen Christ constantly before her—but Fitz-
Gerald in his version of Omar comforted many of the younger
generation by his very frankness and courage. *In Memoriam*
was the favourite poem of a generation of believers who,
though perplexed, consoled themselves with the thought :

> There is more faith in honest doubt,
> Believe me, than in half the creeds.

The *Rubaiyat* became the favourite poem of a generation who were weary of the struggle between faith and doubt, and who even got a certain satisfaction out of their own perplexity and a certain amusement out of the vain strife of their elders :

> Myself when young did eagerly frequent
> Doctor and Saint, and heard great Argument
>   About it and about : but evermore
> Came out by the same Door as in I went.

> With them the Seed of Wisdom did I sow,
> And with my own hand labour'd it to grow :
>   And this was all the Harvest that I reap'd—
> "I came like Water, and like wind I go."

After FitzGerald's death, the poem became even more popular, with a wide variety of readers. It is still one of the few poems of any merit—though some of it is crude enough—from which quotations are recognised by people who don't as a rule read poetry at all. In the 1914-18 War it shared with the Service edition of Kipling's *Barrack-Room Ballads*, a place in the kitbags of soldiers at the front, and parodies of the poem are still found in regimental magazines. Its appeal to soldiers can perhaps be explained by the opening verses :

> Awake ! for Morning in the Bowl of Night
> Has flung the Stone that puts the Stars to Flight :
>   And Lo ! the Hunter of the East has caught
> The Sultan's Turret in a noose of Light.

> Dreaming when Dawn's left Hand was in the Sky
> I heard a Voice within the Tavern cry,
>   "Awake, my little ones, and fill the Cup
> Before Life's Liquor in its Cup be dry."

> And, as the Cock crew, those who stood before
> The Tavern shouted —"Open then the Door !
>   You know how little while we have to stay,
> And, once departed, may return no more."

Elizabeth Barrett Browning, 1806-61

Elizabeth Barrett Moulton Barrett, who married Robert Browning in 1846, was before their marriage, and for some time after, the more celebrated poet. When Wordsworth died in 1850, it was Mrs Browning, not her husband, who was suggested by the *Athenaeum* as the new Poet Laureate, partly on her own merits, partly as a subtle compliment to the Queen. The eldest child of a prosperous business man whose means were derived from slave plantations in the West Indies—and who, as is well known, treated his numerous family as if he were himself an overseer to slaves—she had an accident in girlhood which led to her being treated as an incurable invalid. Her juvenile poem in heroic couplets, *The Battle of Marathon* (1820), was succeeded in 1826 by *An Essay on Mind and other Poems*. Then in 1833 came a translation from Aeschylus, *Prometheus Bound*, and in 1838 *The Seraphim and other Poems*. Probably more valuable than this early work in verse was her critical writing for the *Athenaeum* and her collaboration with R. H. Horne in *A New Spirit of the Age*, a series of criticisms, after the style of Hazlitt, of the principal writers of the day.

The two volumes of *Poems* which she brought out in 1844 finally established her reputation as a poet, the sentimental poem *Lady Geraldine's Courtship*, of which she herself was none too proud, becoming a particular favourite. It was in the passage of this poem describing the poetry which Lady Geraldine read with her lover that the mention of Browning occurs :

> Or at times a modern volume—Wordsworth's
>   solemn-thoughted idyll,
> Howitt's ballad-verse, or Tennyson's exhausted
>   reverie—
> Or from Browning, some "Pomegranate"
>   which, if cut deep down the middle,
> Shows a heart within blood-tinctured, of a
>   veined humanity.*

This reference led to Browning's first letter to his future wife, to their voluminous correspondence, and two years later

* The Browning pun alludes to his plays and dramatic lyrics which he published in a series of pamphlets called—after *Exodus* XXVIII—*Bells and Pomegranates*. William Howitt, who, with his wife Mary, wrote many children's books, was an author greatly esteemed in his time—so much so that there was for generations a favourite joke among schoolboys, about a man watching a blazing building who uttered the names of three "great" writers in a single exclamation : "Dickens ! how it burns !"

to their marriage "without benefit of father." Elizabeth Barrett replied regularly to Browning's often obscure letters, but the love-poems she wrote at the same time—and which were often private answers to the letters—were not published till 1850, and only then under the camouflage title of *Sonnets from the Portuguese*. Browning declared characteristically that these sonnets were "the finest in any language since Shakespeare's"—an opinion which bears rather hardly on Milton and Wordsworth and Keats, to mention no others. What is certain is that these forty-four poems represent—together with such pieces as *The Cry of the Children* and the Napoleon sonnet—the finest talent of Elizabeth Barrett, her more ambitious work as Mrs Browning (*Casa Guidi Windows*, 1851; *Aurora Leigh*, 1857) hardly matching the relatively economic sentiment of this series. It is inferior to the best work of Emily Brontë and Christina Rossetti—a better comparison is with Mrs Hemans—but such a sonnet as this, for example, has its own sentimental charm:

> If thou must love me, let it be for nought
> Except for love's sake only. Do not say
> "I love her for her smile . . . her look . . . her way
> Of speaking gently . . . for a trick of thought
> That falls in well with mine, and certes brought
> A sense of pleasant ease on such a day."
> For these things in themselves, Beloved, may
> Be changed, or change for thee,—and love so wrought
> May be unwrought so. Neither love me for
> Thine own dear pity's wiping my cheeks dry,
> Since one might well forget to weep who bore
> Thy comfort long, and lose thy love thereby.
> But love me for love's sake, that evermore
> Thou may'st love on through love's eternity.

Browning, 1812-89

The son of a clerk in the Bank of England, Robert Browning was educated privately, his family's position as Dissenters preventing him—at this date—from attending the public school and university normal to his class. His first poem to be published was the anonymous *Pauline* (1833), written under the influence of Shelley. This "crude pre-liminary sketch", as he afterwards called it, is interesting because, like his later best work, it was—as he put it—"dramatic in principle", though narrative in form. During the same year, he visited Russia and applied unsuccessfully for a diplomatic post in Persia. The next year he contributed poems to the *Monthly Repository*, and then in 1835 published *Paracelsus*, an ambitious poem for a young man of twenty-three. It was damned with faint praise by the *Athenaeum*—"Not without talent, but spoiled by obscurity, and only an imitation of Shelley"—but it gained Browning the apprecia-tive notice of such readers as Wordsworth, Dickens, Landor, and Carlyle.

After an interval in which he was writing those plays for the theatre which we have briefly mentioned in Chapter V, Browning followed *Paracelsus* with another long poem with a philosophic interest, *Sordello* (1840). This is not so success-ful : *Paracelsus* is obscure in places, *Sordello* is almost totally obscure. "Its radical defect," says a sympathetic critic, "is, simply, that the reader cannot follow the author, and the fault is the author's."

Browning's publisher thought he might stand a better chance with the general public if his new works were issued cheaply in parts. So there appeared between 1841 and 1846 that series of poetic pamphlets, *Bells and Pomegranates*, which we have mentioned in connection with *Lady Geraldine's Courtship*. There were eight of these pamphlets, six being published versions of the stage plays referred to in Chapter V. The two others were *Dramatic Lyrics* (1842) and *Dramatic Romances and Lyrics* (1845). In the 1863 edition of his poems—dedicated to John Forster, the future biog-rapher of Dickens—Browning collected and redistributed the pieces in these two books, together with those in *Men and Women* (1855), and it is safe to say that this collection con-tains the majority of his most popular work—poems such as *The Lost Leader*, "*How they brought the good news from Ghent to Aix*", *The Laboratory*, *Evelyn Hope*, *Love Among the Ruins*, "*De Gustibus—*", *Home-Thoughts from Abroad*,

Home-Thoughts from the Sea, Any Wife to Any Husband, Memorabilia ("Ah, did you once see Shelley plain"), *Incident of the French Camp, The Patriot, My Last Duchess, The Last Ride Together, The Pied Piper of Hamelin* (written for the small son of the actor Macready, it remains a favourite with schoolchildren), *A Grammarian's Funeral, Porphyria's Lover, "Childe Roland to the Dark Tower came", How it Strikes a Contemporary, Fra Lippo Lippi, The Bishop orders his Tomb at Saint Praxed's Church, Bishop Blougram's Apology,* and *One Word More,* a poem written in tribute to his wife and originally appended to *Men and Women,* as the opening lines suggest :

> There they are, my fifty men and women
> Naming me the fifty poems finished !
> Take them, Love, the book and me together :
> Where the heart lies, let the brain lie also.

These poems, published between 1842 and 1855, have always been more widely read than his more ambitious work ; many of them are comparatively short and easy to understand, and a case could be made out for deeming them his best poetry. (One of the shortest, *Home-Thoughts from Abroad,* has those lines about "the wise thrush" which Keats himself might have been proud of.) *Bishop Blougram's Apology* is a fairly long poem, but the majority of readers know of it only a few celebrated passages, such as this :

> Just when we are safest, there's a sunset-touch,
> A fancy from a flower-bell, some one's death,
> A chorus-ending from Euripides,—
> And that's enough for fifty hopes and fears
> As old and new at once as Nature's self,
> To rap and knock and enter in our soul,
> Take hands and dance there, a fantastic ring,
> Round the ancient idol, on his base again,—
> The grand Perhaps !

Browning, it has been said, was his own Bishop Blougram, and he uttered on behalf of a good many of his contemporaries a cruder, more robust version of the Tennysonian religious compromise.

In 1864 he published *Dramatis Personae*, a volume containing the rest of his famous shorter poems—such as *Dis Aliter Visum, Abt Vogler, Rabbi Ben Ezra, Prospice*—and during 1868-9 an enormous poem, *The Ring and the Book*, based on an Italian murder story. Originally issued in four volumes, containing over twenty thousand verses, this poem was surprisingly well received, but Browning—to quote a judicious admirer—"having won what seemed like a reward of popularity, proceeded to squander it." During the next fifteen years he produced volume after volume, each proving more unpopular than the last. These books—for instance, *Prince Hohenstiel-Schwangau* (1871), *Red Cotton Night-Cap Country* (1873), *La Saisiaz and the Two Poets of Croisic* (1878)—are hardly read at all now, even by his warmest admirers. His work virtually ended in 1869, though his last volume, *Asolando*, was published twenty years later, on the day he died at Venice.

The Brownings and Hopkins

Browning is much to be respected for his efforts to get the current idiom into his verse, and some modern poets have studied him with profit in this respect—and also his American contemporary, Walt Whitman, with whom he has much in common. But it is not possible to praise his celebrated "colloquial style" without severe qualification. In many of his poems, indeed, "colloquial style" seems a misnomer, in view of his studied "Renaissance" language, his melodramatic attitudes, his "in't"s and "ha"s, his feminine fondness for dots, dashes, and exclamation marks. No Victorian could ever have used in non-alcoholic social intercourse the style peculiar to Browning and the melodramatic stage, as no Victorian lady could ever have used in real life the Elizabethan word "certes" in the sonnet by Elizabeth Barrett we have quoted.

But where the Brownings failed—or comparatively failed —no other Victorian poet entirely succeeded. It was pre-eminently an age of short lyric verse and of anthologists—like Tennyson's friend Francis Turner Palgrave who published his famous *Golden Treasury* in 1861—who sincerely thought that lyric verse was, not merely one of the main strands in English poetry, but the major, if not the sole, achievement. But English is a language essentially dramatic, its characteristic idiom muscular and energetic; and it is no accident that the greatest English poet was a professional dramatist and that some of the best lyric poems in the *Golden Treasury* itself are nearer to the speaking voice than to song. There is no doubt that the Brownings were among the few Victorian poets who felt the need of regaining the sort of dramatic strength that is found in poets so otherwise dissimilar as Shakespeare and Dryden, as Pope and Keats, as Herbert and Byron; but the only contemporary poet who may be said to have succeeded in this attempt, and then only in a few poems, was a poet completely unknown to the general public—Gerard Manley Hopkins, who ended his brief life in the same year as Browning but who remained virtually unpublished till the twentieth century.*

He wrote most of his poetry in the 'seventies and 'eighties, so will come into a later chapter. But it is worth while just to mention here his relation to the Brownings, because all three poets were trying, in their different ways and with varying degrees of consistency, a more contemporary, colloquial style than the usual Victorian romantic. The relation, it is true, is antithetic, so far as general achievement is concerned; Hopkins's poetry would probably have bewildered the Brownings, and he expressed to his friend Bridges his own reaction to Browning's poetry: "I greatly admire the touches and the details, but the general effect, the whole, offends me, I think it repulsive."

Mrs Browning's ten-thousand-line "novel in blank verse", *Aurora Leigh*, is interesting in this connection. It was admired by George Eliot, and a recent critic has over-praised it in a

* Some short extracts from a few of his poems were printed in A. H. Miles's anthology *Poets of the Nineteenth Century* (1893). The first literary historian to give him notice was George Saintsbury, who referred, in the revised third edition of his *History of Nineteenth Century Literature* (1901), to "the remarkable talents of Mr Gerard Manley Hopkins, which could never be mistaken by any one who knew him, and of which some memorials remain in verse.'

manner reminiscent of Browning's glorification of the *Sonnets from the Portuguese*: "*Aurora Leigh* may well be the finest achievement by any woman in any art: it may also be the most successful long poem (in English) since *Paradise Lost*." The first judgment seems needlessly hard, not so much on the legendary Sappho, as on *Emma*, *Wuthering Heights*, and *Middlemarch*; while as for the second, the critic had doubtless compared, unfavourably, extracts from *The Dunciad*, *Don Juan*, and *The Prelude* with this typical passage (selected by him for recommendation) from Mrs Browning's novel:

> Ay, but every age
> Appears to souls who live in't (ask Carlyle)
> Most unheroic. Ours, for instance, ours:
> The thinkers scout it, and the poets abound
> Who scorn to touch it with a finger-tip:
> A pewter-age—mixed metal, silver-washed;
> An age of scum, spooned off the richer past,
> An age of patches for old gaberdines,
> An age of mere transition, meaning nought
> Except that what succeeds must shame it quite
> If God please. That's wrong thinking, to my mind,
> And wrong thoughts make poor poems.

It is the heroine-narrator, the author's *alter ego*, speaking; and the passage is typical in that breathless energy which informs the whole, a mainly factitious energy which, after the first two or three thousand lines, becomes as insupportable as Browning's parentheses, exclamation marks, his rhyming of "rims on" with "crimson", and his emotional dots and dashes—a private Morse Code to signalise that words failed even him. A distinguished American philosopher has called this sort of writing "the poetry of barbarism", and the judgment seems more accurate than that quoted above, if we realise in it, not simply disparagement, but the sincere appeal of such poetry to people of eminent action (both the Brownings are quoted in a recent article by a famous Antarctic explorer), and if we also couple the judgment with a tribute to the understanding of the poetic problem which these poets generally had and of their vigorous efforts towards a solution. Possibly one reason for Hopkins's superiority in this field was the comparative modesty of his undertaking; his entire work is less in volume than the ambitious *Aurora Leigh*, to say nothing of *The Ring and the Book*.

Arnold, 1822-88

It is best to consider Matthew Arnold, as we have considered Coleridge, in two parts; and fortunately this is very easy to do, for he wrote most of his poetry in early life and most of his criticism afterwards.

He was the eldest son of Thomas Arnold, headmaster of Rugby, whose influence on public-school education was profound, and who was also one of the leaders of the Liberal party in the Anglican Church. He was educated under his father and at Oxford, and became one of His Majesty's Inspectors of Schools. From 1857 to 1867 he was professor of poetry at Oxford.

Nearly all his best poetry was written during the busiest years of his school inspectorate. His first volumes, *The Strayed Reveller and other Poems* (1849) and *Empedocles on Etna and other Poems* (1852), were published anonymously and were unsuccessful. In 1853 he published under his own name a new volume, with a preface on the function of poetry. This included many of the poems already printed, with such notable additions as *Sohrab and Rustum*, his best narrative piece, and the famous *Scholar-Gipsy*. A second volume, containing only two new poems, came out in 1855. Then in 1858 appeared *Merope*, an attempt at an English-Greek drama, and in 1867 *New Poems*, the last of his separate volumes of verse. This collection includes the typically impressive poem *Dover Beach*, which ends:

> The sea of faith
> Was once, too, at the full, and round earth's shore
> Lay like the folds of a bright girdle furl'd.
> But now I only hear
> Its melancholy, long, withdrawing roar,
> Retreating to the breath
> Of the night-wind down the vast edges drear
> And naked shingles of the world.

> Ah, love, let us be true
> To one another ! for the world, which seems
> To lie before us like a land of dreams,
> So various, so beautiful, so new,
> Hath really neither joy, nor love, nor light,
> Nor certitude, nor peace, nor help for pain :
> And we are here as on a darkling plain
> Swept with confused alarms of struggle and flight,
> Where ignorant armies clash by night.

After 1867 Arnold wrote nothing but occasional pieces, and it is characteristic of him that when he felt he had said all he had to say in poetry, he gave up writing it regularly and turned to prose.

There have been several critic-poets in English literature : Ben Jonson, Dryden, Dr Johnson, Coleridge, and, in our own time, T. S. Eliot. In all these writers a distinct relationship is apparent between their poetry and their criticism. What Arnold tried to do, in a romantic age, was to regain, both in verse and prose, some of the classical virtues. He was much more successful in this attempt in his criticism than in his poetry—which was, as we have noted, the work of a younger man. A good deal of his poetry seems to a modern eye to be typically early Victorian in some respects ; for instance, in its romantic nostalgia for the past, its sense of isolation in

> this iron time
> Of doubts, disputes, distractions, fears.

Where he is distinguished in his melancholy is in the clarity of his vision of some aspects of Victorian society, as in the famous phrase,

> this strange disease of modern life,
> With its sick hurry and divided aims,
> Its heads o'ertaxed, its palsied hearts.

It is the poetry of a young man, reminiscent, somewhat ironically, of some of the verse of Shelley—a poet whom the later, critical Arnold ranked far below Wordsworth and Byron and whom he described as a "beautiful and ineffectual angel, beating in the void his luminous wings in vain." *The Scholar-Gipsy* (owing more to Keats) is his most popular poem, and one of the best ; it is the story of the seventeenth-century scholar who left Oxford to find the secret of life among the gipsies, and became immortal through his faith in the search :

> Still nursing the unconquerable hope,
> Still clutching the inviolable shade . . .

He is contrasted with the people of the modern world :

> But fly our paths, our feverish contact fly ;
> For strong the infection of our mental strife,
> Which, though it gives no bliss, yet spoils for rest ;
> And we should win thee from thy own fair life,
> Like us distracted, and like us unblest.
> Soon, soon thy cheer would die,
> Thy hopes grow timorous, and unfixed thy powers,
> And thy clear aims be cross and shifting made :
> And then thy glad perennial youth would fade,
> Fade, and grow old at last, and die like ours.

Clough, 1819-61

The Scholar-Gipsy is in part a reminiscence of Oxford, of the university which Arnold later described in one of his prefaces as "the home of lost causes, and forsaken beliefs, and unpopular names, and impossible loyalties." Arnold's Oxford, of course, as we can judge from this description, was not quite that of Newman, the leader of the Anglo-Catholic "Oxford Movement"; it was rather the more sceptical Oxford of his elegy *Thyrsis*, written in memory of his friend Arthur Hugh Clough.

Clough, three years the senior of Arnold, preceded him at Rugby and the university. Unlike Arnold, he remained in Oxford as a tutor till 1848, when he resigned his fellowship on grounds of conscience, his early leanings towards religious orthodoxy having changed to doubt. He became the head of an educational institution in London, later received a post in the Education Office, and died at Florence in his forty-second year.

His poetry is of a minor order, but is very interesting, partly as a record of spiritual and mental struggle,* partly, in some

---

* The American critic, Lowell, the friend of many Victorian men of letters, considered that later generations would find in Clough's poetry "the truest expression in verse of the moral and intellectual tendencies, the doubt and struggle towards settled convictions, of the period in which he lived."

cases, for its satirical, Byronic qualities. His first published work was the serio-comic poem *The Bothie of Toper-na-Fuosich* (1848), afterwards called *The Bothie of Tober-na-Vuolich*; which version is more easily remembered or spelt is as difficult to say. He had already written some shorter poems, including the well-known *Say not, the struggle nought availeth*, and these appeared in *Ambarvalia* (1849). His later works include *Amours de Voyage*, *Dipsychus*, and *Songs in Absence*; and there was a posthumous collection entitled *Poems and Prose Remains* (1869) which contains the Byronic piece *The Latest Decalogue*:

> Thou shalt have one God only; who
> Would be at the expense of two?
> No graven images may be
> Worshipped, except the currency:
> Swear not at all; for, for thy curse
> Thine enemy is none the worse:
> At church on Sunday to attend
> Will serve to keep the world thy friend:
> Honour thy parents; that is, all
> From whom advancement may befall;
> Thou shalt not kill; but need'st not strive
> Officiously to keep alive:
> Do not adultery commit;
> Advantage rarely comes of it:
> Thou shalt not steal; an empty feat,
> When it's so lucrative to cheat:
> Bear not false witness; let the lie
> Have time on its own wings to fly:
> Thou shalt not covet, but tradition
> Approves all forms of competition.

Of his non-satirical short poems *Say not, the struggle nought availeth* remains the most popular; it received a new lease of life during the recent war, when Mr Winston Churchill, with his usual superb histrionic sense, ended one of his broadcasts—with obvious reference to Russian victories and American aid—with the last lines:

> And not by eastern windows only,
>   When daylight comes, comes in the light,
> In front, the sun climbs slow, how slowly,
>   But westward, look, the land is bright.

Minor Poets and Light Verse

The most distinguished poets of the generation after Tennyson—the Rossettis, Morris, Swinburne—will come in our next chapter, where we shall be considering those twin movements, the Oxford and the Pre-Raphaelite.* We can close this chapter with a brief word on some of the minor poets and light-verse writers of the early Victorian age.

George Darley (1795-1846) was the author of a charming lyric *It is not beauty I demand* which Palgrave, by mistake, included in the first edition of the *Golden Treasury* as an anonymous song of the Caroline period. His poems, of which the chief was the unfinished *Nepenthe* (1839), became popular during the 'nineties, as did also the work of his contemporary Thomas Lovell Beddoes (1803-49), whom we have mentioned in Chapter V.

William Barnes (1801-86) was a clergyman whose literary labours are perhaps more interesting to the student of philology than of poetry. He published grammars of the Dorsetshire dialect, and three collections of verse—*Poems of Rural Life in the Dorset Dialect* (1844), *Hwomely Rhymes* (1859), *Poems of Rural Life in Common English* (1868)—in which he tried to replace every word of Latin origin by a purer English word, no matter how uncouth or ridiculous the result.† Another West-country parson, the vicar of Morwenstow, Robert Stephen Hawker (1803-75), is celebrated for his revival of the harvest festival and for his authorship of *The Song of the Western Men*, in *Cornish Ballads* (1869).

Ballads of various kinds were an important feature in the minor poetry of the period. In Scotland we have a notable

* The first biographer of Rossetti remarked : "Primarily, the Pre-Raphaelite movement had its impulse in the Oxford religious revival ; and however strange it may seem to say that such men as Holman Hunt and Rossetti . . . followed directly in the footsteps of Newman and Pusey and Keble, it is indubitably so."

† Some of his revivals or coinings were *folk-wain* for *omnibus, markword of suchness* for *adjective, starlet* for *asterisk, outshapen* for *perfect, deemstery* for *criticism, gleecraft* for *music, wortlore* for *botany, two-horned redeship* for *dilemma, fireghost* for *electricity,* and *foredraught* for *programme.* Like all foredraughts to make English pure and simple, Barnes's vocabulary—if we may venture a deemstery—tends to make it more artificial than before.

group of women—including Lady Anne Lindsay, Joanna Baillie, Lady Nairne, Lady John Scott—who either wrote original ballads or modern versions of the old. With them can be mentioned William Motherwell, who collected ballads in *Minstrelsy Ancient and Modern* (1827) and wrote *Poems Narrative and Lyrical* (1832); William Aytoun, a regular contributor to *Blackwood's Magazine*, who wrote *Lays of the Scottish Cavaliers* (1848); and Allan Cunningham, who compiled four volumes of the songs of Scotland but who is best known for his original ballad *A wet sheet and a flowing sea*, often to be met with in anthologies.

In England the productions of "Barry Cornwall", B. W. Procter, were popular, particularly *English Songs* (1832); but they have not survived. What have survived in almost their Victorian popularity are the fine ballads of the historian Lord Macaulay, especially *The Armada, The Battle of Naseby*, and *The Lays of Ancient Rome* (1842). These are simple pieces, which we all remember from our early schooldays, but unsurpassed of their kind. Worthy of mention also, in much the same field, are Sydney Dobell's ballad *Keith of Ravelston* and Sir Francis Doyle's military pieces, *The Private of the Buffs, The Loss of the Birkenhead*, and *The Red Thread of Honour*.

Two prominent Chartists, of the same name but widely different backgrounds, produced verse, including ballads: the Byronic orator Ernest Jones wrote *Songs of Democracy* (1856); Ebenezer Jones, a London clerk, wrote *Studies of Sensation and Event* (1843). Gerald Massey, a self-educated man whose career is said to have given George Eliot some hints for *Felix Holt, the Radical*, wrote a considerable quantity of verse, none of which can be said to have endured. His eclipse is shared by Alexander Smith, the author of *City Songs* (1857), and by Martin Tupper, whose *Proverbial Philosophy*, first published in 1838, went through forty editions and is said to have brought in twenty thousand pounds.

The Irish poet James Clarence Mangan, who wrote many songs and translations—and sometimes poems of his own "translated" from non-existent authors—is mainly remembered for his *Dark Rosaleen*. Two other poets known for a solitary achievement are Jean Ingelow, for her *High Tide on the Coast of Lincolnshire*, and William Johnson Cory, for his *Heraclitus*. The chief Australian poet, Adam Lindsay Gordon (1833-70), was educated in England and has always been a favourite with English anthologists; his best work is to be found in *Sea Spray and Smoke Drift* (1867) and *Bush Ballads and Galloping Rhymes* (1870).

Light verse, including serio-comic verse, was popular throughout the nineteenth century, from the *Rejected Addresses* (1812) of James and Horace Smith, through the children's masterpieces of Edward Lear and Lewis Carroll—*A Book of Nonsense* (1846), *Alice in Wonderland* (1869), *Through the Looking-Glass* (1871), *The Hunting of the Snark* (1876)— to the comic operas of W. S. Gilbert. The most distinguished writer of light verse before Carroll was Thomas Hood (1799-1845), who became sub-editor of the *London Magazine* about 1820. He wrote both serious and comic work, but found that, while the latter was welcomed, the former was neglected. So he made up his mind, in the words of his own pun, to be "a lively Hood for a livelihood." His *Comic Annual* came out from 1830 to 1839, in 1843 he started *Hood's Magazine*, and the same year began to contribute to *Punch* (founded in 1841 by Henry Mayhew and Mark Lemon). His best-known poems, *The Song of the Shirt* and *The Bridge of Sighs*, date from these last years; they are rightly remembered with respect, as are the earlier *Dream of Eugene Aram* and the *Ode on a Distant Prospect of Clapham Academy*, and his chief social satire, *Miss Kilmansegg and her Precious Leg*.

Other popular writers of light or serio-comic verse were W. M. Praed, who founded the *Etonian* and was later elected to some of the best London clubs, including the House of Commons; C. S. Calverley, best known for his parodies; and "Thomas Ingoldsby", the pen-name of a clergyman R. H. Barham, whose *Ingoldsby Legends*, first collected from magazines in 1840, retained their popularity throughout the nineteenth century.

CHAPTER VIII

THE OXFORD MOVEMENT AND THE PRE-RAPHAELITES

1833-1883

"The flood is round thee, but thy towers as yet
Are safe, and clear as by a summer's sea
Pierce the calm morning mist, serene and free,
To point in silence Heavenward."

KEBLE : on Oxford ; 1833.

"When I remember the contrast between the Oxford
of to-day and the Oxford which I first saw thirty years
ago, I wonder I can face the misery (there is no other
word for it) of visiting it, even to have the honour of
addressing you to-night."

MORRIS : speaking on *Art under Plutocracy*
at University College, 1883 ; Ruskin being in the chair.

Relation to Early Victorian Poetry

The poetry of the early Victorian age can be criticised sympathetically for its nostalgic sense of the past, its withdrawal from "this iron time" to a dream-world owing more to romantic imagination than to the reality of previous centuries. Tennyson, for all his keen contemporary sense of the struggle between science and religion, wrote a good deal about the Middle Ages—not the period of history, but that of romance. Browning wrote the majority of his poetry about the Renaissance, and even when he tackled a contemporary theme he was apt to indulge in archaic language and melodramatic attitudes. While Arnold the poet—the young Arnold —wrote some of his best verse either about classical times or about the Oxford of the past.

With Oxford are partly associated the twin movements in mid-century life and literature which made a deliberate return, in place of the earlier largely unconscious return, to the

146

philosophy of previous eras, in particular of the Middle Ages. The Oxford Movement, which is also known as the Tractarian Movement and (in general terms) the Catholic Revival, is, of course, pre-eminently important in the history of nineteenth-century religion; but it has its literary importance, too. The Pre-Raphaelite Movement, as its name implies, is mainly relevant to the history of art, but it had a distinct influence on the poetry and prose of the mid-Victorian age.

Brief Sketch of the Oxford Movement

Religion and theology in themselves are outside the scope of this book, but to understand the literary career of such men as Keble and Newman, and such women as Christina Rossetti and Charlotte Mary Yonge, it is necessary to prefix our discussion of individuals by a sketch of the complicated Movement as a whole.

Newman dated it from Keble's sermon at Oxford in 1833. An historian adds that it was provoked by a false alarm. The Reform Bill of 1832 had created a new electorate containing a large body of Dissenters and Evangelicals, and the following year a Bill was introduced in Parliament for the suppression of some of the sees of the Irish Protestant Church, then regarded by orthodox churchmen as an integral part of the Church of England. The cry was raised that the Church was in danger, and from the pulpit of St Mary's, Oxford, John Keble—already widely known as the author of *The Christian Year*—denounced the Irish Church Bill as "a direct disavowal of the sovereignty of God" and an act of "national apostasy." It was the duty of every Christian, he urged, to dissociate himself from this national crime. The revolt of the State against the divine authority did not, indeed, justify the Christian in disobeying the authority of the State. He must submit to it as to any other tyranny, but under protest: "This seems the least that can be done," Keble concluded; "unless we would have our children's children say: 'There was once here a glorious Church, but it was betrayed into the hands of libertines for the real or affected love of a little temporary peace and good order.'"

The next year, 1834, Keble and Newman—in association with Hurrell Froude, Isaac Williams, Pusey, the brothers Mozley, and others—began to publish a series of pamphlets called *Tracts for the Times*. In the first of these Newman warned the clergy that disestablishment, disendowment, and perhaps actual persecution, might lie ahead of them.

But the Church was not in real danger—or not in that kind of danger. Its enemies in England were a smaller minority than the Protestants in Ireland, and the strong Evangelical party, who certainly wanted reform, would have strenuously opposed any religious revolution. The Oxford Movement survived its original negative purpose—or the negative purpose of its first public protest—by laying stress on conceptions which had been long neglected in Protestant England. It took as its main text a clause of the creed that had been almost forgotten: "I believe in the Holy Catholic Church." As Newman himself put it in *Apologia pro Vita Sua* (1864): "I have ever kept before me that there was something greater than the Established Church, and that was the Church Catholic and Apostolic, set up from the beginning, of which she was but the local presence and organ."

During the eighteenth century the Church had sunk into stagnation, becoming almost a branch of the Civil Service, with the sort of hunting, tippling, and wenching parson— reminiscent of Chaucer's monk and friar—described in the novels of the period. The Wesleys at Oxford and in London found themselves regarded at first as eccentric fanatics, and the defection of the Methodists at the end of the century left the Church more and more a mere department of the State— a department, in the first quarter of the nineteenth century, with similar corruption and nepotism to that existing in other spheres.

The Romantic Movement may be said to have paved the way for the success of the Oxford Movement's reaction, by making pre-Reformation worship and philosophy mysteriously attractive. Coleridge's interest in the old English divines gave new life to Anglican theology, and in 1829 an Act was passed by Parliament—opposed, ironically enough, by some of the future leaders of the Oxford Movement, including Newman—emancipating the English Roman Catholics from the various social disabilities they had formerly suffered.

The Oxford leaders were not at first admirers of the Church of Rome ; indeed, most of them never became so. But, on the other hand, they could hardly be described as Protestants. Some of the more headstrong, such as Hurrell Froude, made insulting remarks about the Protestant martyrs, and many Englishmen who recalled the Gordon Riots and the cry of "No Popery", and who may have regretted the welcome to the French priests after the Revolution and the recent emancipation of the Catholics, failed to understand how an anti-Protestant could be anything but a Papist in sheep's clothing. The young theologians of Oxford—still a "medieval" city in many ways—attained a scandalous notoriety, which some of the more superficial of them, attracted to the latest spiritual fashion, may have welcomed and sought to extend. We must remember that theological discussion was popular in the nineteenth century ; sermons and tracts reached a wide public. When Newman published in 1841 the ninetieth and last of the *Tracts for the Times*—arguing that the Thirty-nine Articles, though "the offspring of an uncatholic age, are, through God's providence, to say the least, not uncatholic, and may be subscribed by those who aim at being Catholic in heart and doctrine"—the sensation was great. And when, four years later, he fulfilled the prophecy of the Evangelicals by going over to Rome, the event created almost as much stir as Peel's conversion to Corn-Law Repeal a few months afterwards.

With that secession of Newman in 1845, much of the attraction of the Movement seems to have gone out of it. But Pusey remained steadfast, and, with the assistance of Keble, Samuel Wilberforce, and others, maintained the High-Church cause and lived to see it become the greatest and almost the dominant party in the Church of England. At this distance of time it is possible to see a good deal of benefit in both the Evangelical and the Oxford movements. The Evangelicals, as we have briefly noticed in Chapter IV, were prominent in reform but were inclined to be narrow and insular—which qualities and defects were shared by the Nonconformists (who produced, in Victorian times, such admirable figures as Livingstone, Bright, Dr Barnardo, and General Booth). The Oxford High-Church movement was responsible for a good deal of spurious medievalism, but it did recover some connection both with the Continent and with the English past, and it brought to many of the younger generation the revelation of a grander and more romantic conception of Christianity. And it helped, in alliance with the Pre-Raphaelites, to introduce some colour—if also some colourful nonsense—into the rather drab religious art and literature of the Victorians.

Keble, 1792-1866

We must now consider, individually, those leaders of the Oxford Movement who have an importance in literature as well as in religion. We can proceed roughly in chronological order, and begin with Keble.

A brilliant scholar and regarded by many as one of the holiest men in modern times, John Keble was ordained in 1815. In 1827 he published the popular volume of poems called *The Christian Year*, and from 1831 to 1841 he was professor of poetry at Oxford. His sermon of 1833 is taken, as we have seen, as the beginning of the Oxford Movement, and he wrote four of the *Tracts for the Times*. From 1835 he was vicar of Hursley, in Hampshire, and resided there entirely from 1841 to his death.

There had not been much important religious poetry in England since the great period of the seventeenth century, the time of Herbert, Donne, Vaughan, Crashaw, Milton, Traherne. Keble's verse—*The Christian Year, Lyra Innocentium*, and *Miscellaneous Poems*—cannot be compared with the achievements of these poets; but it has a gentle, modestly inspiring charm of its own and probably influenced a more distinguished poet in Christina Rossetti. Keble's prose works, apart from his sermons, are a collection of criticisms in Latin, *Praelectiones Academicae*, and some reviews in English of contemporary poetry.

Pusey, 1800-82

The members of the High-Church Movement in its middle years were often called by their enemies "Puseyites." Newman had gone over to Rome, Hurrell Froude was dead, Keble was of a very retiring disposition, so it fell largely to Pusey to bring the High-Church party out of the wilderness of contempt into a land flowing with incense and celebrity.

Of noble connections, Edward Bouverie Pusey was educated at Eton and Christ Church, studied theology in Germany, and was made Professor of Hebrew at Oxford at the early age of twenty-seven. As Keble had aided the Movement by his personal virtues and the continuing popularity of *The Christian Year*, so Pusey brought to its service, not only a scholarly share in the *Tracts for the Times* and many sermons urging a return to a more primitive and Catholic theology, but the great enterprise in translation called the *Oxford Library of the Fathers* (1836-85), of which he executed parts and edited others.

His example of resolution against both contempt from the Church and something like persecution from the University —in 1843 he was suspended, for a sermon on the Eucharist, from preaching for three years—makes him important in religious history. In literature his importance is theological only, and not so great, even in this field, as that of Newman, who is also important in poetry and polemic.

Newman, 1801-90

For the majority of modern readers, the Oxford Movement means, paradoxically, John Henry Newman, who, after twelve years' spiritual struggle, left it and went over to Rome. He is probably the most important religious writer of the nineteenth century, and we have to return—as he himself did—to the religious writers of the sixteenth and seventeenth centuries, to such men as More, Hooker, and Lancelot Andrewes, to get any English parallel.

He was ordained in 1824, and in 1827 became vicar of St Mary's, Oxford. His sermons there—deeply influenced themselves by his conversations with Hurrell Froude—were the foundation and mainstay of his influence, and, in printed form, constitute the largest item in his work. Nominally intended as parish sermons, they were really addressed to the undergraduates, who soon flocked to hear him—as, about the same time, those of Cambridge did to the sermons of the Evangelical leader Charles Simeon. Compared with Pusey and Keble, Newman had no great learning, but he had a singular charm of manner and was a master of both the spoken and the written word.'

In 1834, as we have seen, he published the first of the *Tracts for the Times*, which culminated in 1841 in the famous or notorious ."Tract 90", arousing a great storm of indignation and making his position in the Church of England untenable. He resigned the vicarage of St Mary's in 1843, and two years later published the *Essay on the Development of Christian Doctrine* and was received into the Roman Catholic Church. The Oxford Movement as such—according to some historians —ended with his secession, but the High-Church Movement continued, as we have seen, under the leadership of some of his former colleagues.

A short period as Rector of the ill-fated Catholic University in Dublin produced one of his best works, *The Idea of a University* (1852); but it was not until the 'sixties that he wrote his masterpiece and, incidentally, came once more into the public eye. This masterpiece, *Apologia pro Vita Sua* (1864-5), would probably not have been written but for the accident of a rather foolish provocation. In 1863 Charles Kingsley, reviewing in *Macmillan's Magazine* J. A. Froude's *History of England*, accused Newman of having said that the pursuit of truth for its own sake was not necessarily a virtue. Newman denied the allegation ; and after an exchange of letters Kingsley apologised. Newman then published the correspondence, with a witty summary of its drift. Part of this summary may be quoted, as showing Newman's mastery of the ironic style (a mastery that has been compared, rather ironically, with Matthew Arnold's style in discussing the translation of Homer by Newman's brother Francis) :

Mr Kingsley begins then by exclaiming, "Oh, the chicanery, the wholesale fraud, the vile hypocrisy, the conscience-killing tyranny of Rome ! We have not far to seek for an evidence of it ! There's Fr Newman to wit : one living specimen is worth a hundred dead ones. He a priest, writing of priests, tells us that lying is never any harm." I interpose, "You are taking a most extraordinary liberty with my name. If I have said this, tell me when and where." Mr Kingsley replies, "You said it, Reverend Sir, in a sermon which you preached when a Protestant vicar of St Mary's, and published in 1844, and I could read you a very salutary lecture on the effects which that sermon had at the time on my own opinion of you." I make answer, "Oh . . . *Not* it seems as a priest speaking of priests ; but let us have the passage." Mr Kingsley relaxes :— "Do you know, I like your *tone*. From your *tone* I rejoice, greatly rejoice to be able to believe that you did not mean what you said." I rejoin, "*Mean* it ! I maintain I never *said* it, whether as a Protestant or as a Catholic." Mr Kingsley replies, "I waive that point." I object :—"Is it possible ? What ? Waive the main question ? I either said it or I didn't . . ." "Well," says Mr Kingsley, "if you are quite sure you did not say it, I'll take your word for it, I really will." My *word* ! I am dumb. Somehow I thought it was my *word* that happened to be on trial. The *word* of a professor of lying that he does not lie !

With the theological details we are not here concerned ; Kingsley published a pamphlet *What then did Dr Newman mean ?*, and, after the publication of the *Apologia,* a supporter of Kingsley produced a pamphlet entitled *But was not Kingsley right after all ?*. It is the *Apologia* itself that concerns us : it came out originally in seven parts in 1864, and was then issued as a volume the next year, Newman ommitting the most controversial parts of the Preface and making the work virtually "A History of his Religious Opinions", in accordance with the sub-title. It is a masterly exposition, a spiritual autobiography undistorted by polemic ; it was immediately successful and restored its author to his rightful place as one of the leaders of Christian thought. It also helped

Englishmen of various beliefs to form a more kindly opinion of the Church of Rome.

Newman's chief poem, *The Dream of Gerontius*, was published in 1866. It relates the passing of a man's soul from his body to the divine presence, and its musical setting by Elgar has made it the most widely appreciated of his poetry —with the exception of the famous hymns *Lead, kindly Light* and *Praise to the Holiest in the height*, found to-day in most English hymn-books, High-Church, Low-Church, and Nonconformist. The collection entitled *Verses on Various Occasions* (1868) contains most of his poems.

The Grammar of Assent, an analysis of the nature of belief, came out in 1870. Nine years later he was created a Cardinal. In his last years he lived in retirement at Edgbaston, and died in 1890.

Of his forty volumes, most are theology. Some of his sermons are regarded as among the best in English, while Leslie Stephen adduces him with Mill as "probably the two greatest masters of philosophical English in recent times." *

The Newmans and the Froudes

The Newman family is very interesting to the student of Victorian philosophic literature, because the three literary brothers went such widely different ways. Francis Newman (1805-97) came under the influence of James Martineau (brother of Harriet) and adopted Unitarian views. He was professor of Latin at University College, London, and wrote the autobiographical *Phases of Faith* (1850). Charles Robert Newman contributed essays to Holyoake's agnostic journal *The Reasoner*.

* For a fair criticism of Newman from the agnostic point of view, see Stephen's essay, "Newman's Theory of Belief", in the collection *An Agnostic's Apology* (1893). In *Some Early Impressions*, Stephen explains what it was about the future Cardinal, the hero of Oxford, that so disgusted the Cambridge intelligentsia of the 'fifties. "I have never known a Cambridge man who could appreciate Newman," he was once told "by a reverent disciple of the prophet." "Our version of the remark was slightly different," Stephen continues. "We held that our common sense enabled us to appreciate him only too thoroughly by the dry light of reason and to resist the illusions of romantic sentiment."

We find a similar thing with the two brothers Froude, friends of the Newman family. Richard Hurrell Froude (1803-36) had a great influence on the future Cardinal and, through Newman, on others. His bringing together of Newman and his tutor Keble may be said to have started the Oxford Movement in its spiritual sense, as in the public sense it was begun by the Irish Church Bill. Froude died too soon to leave much work, but his travels in the Mediterranean in search of health, during 1832-3, seem to have marked the turning-point in the career of Newman, his companion—as we learn from the joint volume of poems called *Lyra Apostolica*, published as a volume in 1836. After his death appeared the two volumes of his *Remains* (1838-9), which, attacking the Reformation and all its works, caused a great sensation. "Froude's *Remains* acted as a purge," says an historian. "The timid were driven from the Movement, the vigorous were strengthened to proceed."

The younger Froude, James Anthony, who belongs to the next chapter, was at first strongly influenced by his brother and Newman, but he subsequently turned sceptical and was affected by the teaching of Carlyle, whose *Life* he wrote. He travelled so far from the Oxford Movement that in his *History of England* he made heroes of Henry VIII and John Knox.

Minor Tractarians and Charlotte Yonge

There were many distinguished men in the Oxford Movement, or connected with its later High-Church development, who have here to be mentioned very briefly. They are none of great importance in literature, though important in the history of the Anglican or the Roman Church. Of those who followed Newman to Rome, we may mention the future Cardinal Manning, the hymn-writer Frederick William Faber, and W. G. Ward, commonly known as "Ideal" Ward from his important book *The Ideal of a Christian Church* (1844).

The rector of Hadleigh, Hugh James Rose, was a Cambridge scholar to whom the first Oxonians looked for light; the "Hadleigh conferences" have led some historians

to say that the Oxford Movement really began at Cambridge !
But these conferences were a failure, and Rose's importance
is rather that he founded in 1832, as the official organ of the
High-Church party, the *British Magazine,* in which some of
the best theological work of Newman and Hurrell Froude
originally appeared.   The *British Critic,* which was founded
a few years later, was more the organ of the extremist group ;
it was edited first by Newman, and afterwards by Thomas
Mozley.

Isaac Williams was a disciple of Keble who, like his
master, wrote poetry, notably *The Cathedral* (1838); he was
the author of Tracts 80 and 87, *On Reserve in Communicating
Religious Knowledge,* which created almost as much indignation as Newman's Tract 90.

In the later development, we can mention Bishop Wilberforce, son of the great Evangelical reformer ; Bishop Stubbs,
a disciple of Pusey, who wrote the *Constitutional History of
England* ; Dean Church, one of the founders of the *Guardian*
(1846), who wrote a brief history of the Oxford Movement ;
Henry Parry Liddon, who gave the Bampton Lectures *On
the Divinity of Our Lord* (1867); and J. M. Neale, who wrote
the *History of the Holy Eastern Church* and adapted from old
sources many well-known hymns, including *Jerusalem the
Golden* and *Good King Wencelas.**

The religious public of those days was, as we have
observed, very great ; the public for romantic and didactic
novels was also extensive, and yearly becoming more so.   It is
not surprising, therefore, that one of the most popular influences connected with the High-Church Movement was the fiction
of Charlotte Mary Yonge (1823-1901), who lived in Keble's
parish in Hampshire most of her life.   She was extraordi-
narily prolific, producing between 1844 and 1900 a hundred
and fifty-six fictional works, also twenty-one essays, biographies, etc. ;   she edited three magazines, including the

* Though not to be compared with the great period of hymn-
writing in the seventeenth and eighteenth centuries, the nineteenth
was a distinguished century in this field.   Among noted hymn-
writers can be mentioned Henry Francis Lyte, author of *Abide with
me,* and Christopher Wordsworth, nephew of the poet.

Monthly Packet, and found time to superintend the religious education of the local children. The high claims made for her novels in recent years by Anglo-Catholic critics are not justified ; she seems very naïve by the side of her "heretical" contemporary George Eliot, to say nothing of Jane Austen, with whom she has been compared. On the other hand, she is probably the only novelist of any value at all in the long line of practitioners of "the High-Church novel" who were particularly active between the years 1835-60, and some of her work for children—*The Lances of Lynwood, The Little Duke*, etc.—is among the very best in this extensive field. Of her more adult novels, *The Heir of Redclyffe* (1853) and *The Daisy Chain* (1856) attained immense popularity, lasting many years. Among the contemporary admirers of *The Heir* were William Morris, the Pre-Raphaelite, and Canon Dixon, who wrote that it was "unquestionably one of the finest books in the world."

Patmore, Dixon, and Christina Rossetti

With Coventry Patmore, Canon Dixon, and Christina Rossetti, we reach distinguished, if minor, poets who are connected on the one hand with the Oxford Movement and on the other with the Pre-Raphaelites. It is best perhaps to consider them here, before going on to discuss the Pre-Raphaelite Movement in general and the poets D. G. Rossetti, Morris, and Swinburne in particular. The Jesuit poet, Gerard Manley Hopkins, among whose friends were both Patmore and Dixon, is also connected with the Oxford Movement, in so far as he followed Newman from the Anglican Church to the Roman in 1866. But, as we have noted when speaking of Browning, Hopkins was a poet almost completely apart, having virtually no influence, so it is probably better to consider him in the chapter on late Victorian poetry rather than with the Oxford and Pre-Raphaelite poets.

Coventry Patmore (1823-96) was a librarian at the British Museum for twenty years, and wrote two very different works, *The Angel in the House* (1854-6) and *The Unknown Eros* (1877), besides other poetry and some criticism. A poem in

praise of domestic happiness, telling a simple story in deliberately simple verse, *The Angel in the House* was bound to
gratify some tastes and to infuriate or tickle others. *Blackwood's* described the poetry as "the spawn of frogs" and
referred, as inaccurately as tastelessly, to "the life into which
the slime of the Keatses and Shelleys of former days has
fecundated"; while the *Athenaeum* called the work "goody-
goody muddle." It is certainly not a poem which can be
read with much enjoyment to-day, though parts of it have
appeared in some modern anthologies. More interesting is
the work he produced after his conversion to Rome, the book
of odes entitled *The Unknown Eros*. Instead of the smooth,
trim metre of *The Angel*, we have here abrupt, unconventional versification and diction that has been described as
"rugged." Hopkins, though offering in his letters some
detailed criticisms, liked this later manner so much as to
say to the author: "Your poems are a good deed done for
the Catholic Church, for England, for the British Empire."

Richard Watson Dixon (1833-1900) was Canon of Carlisle
for many years, and wrote, besides ecclesiastical history, some
religious verse partly in the manner of Blake, partly in that
of the Pre-Raphaelites. The first part of *Dream*, in the collection *Christ's Company* (1861), is a good example of his
poetry and of the relation between the High-Church and the
Pre-Raphaelite movements:

> With camel's hair I clothed my skin,
>   I fed my mouth with honey wild ;
> And set me scarlet wool to spin,
>   And all my breast with hyssop filled ;
> Upon my brow and cheeks and chin
>   A bird's blood spilled.
>
> I took a broken reed to hold,
>   I took a sponge of gall to press ;
> I took weak water-weeds to fold
>   About my sacrificial dress.
>
> I took the grasses of the field,
>   The flax was bolled upon my crine ;
> And ivy thorn and wild grapes healed
>   To make good wine.

I took my scrip of manna sweet,
    My cruse of water did I bless ;
I took the white dove by the feet
    And flew into the wilderness.

The sister of the artist and poet who founded the Pre-Raphaelite Movement, Christina Georgina Rossetti (1830-94) lived a retired life and was a devout Anglican. She has been described in a modern encyclopaedia as "probably the greatest of English women poets", and a literary historian writes that "It is difficult to find any who can contest her claim to be the finest of English poetesses." She is a minor poet compared with Blake and Wordsworth and Hopkins, but what makes her so superior to Mrs Hemans and Mrs Browning is the economy of her emotion and her unforced use of the speaking voice. (Emily Brontë has some of the same quality.) Her first volume of verse was *Goblin Market and other Poems* (1861), which, like its successor *The Prince's Progress* (1866), was illustrated by her brother. *Sing-Song* (1872) was a collection of simple rhymes for children ; then followed *A Pageant and other Poems* (1881) and the posthumous volume of *New Poems* (1896). One of her most popular pieces has always been the Song beginning "When I am dead, my dearest." It is brief enough to be quoted in full :

When I am dead, my dearest,
    Sing no sad songs for me ;
Plant thou no roses at my head,
    Nor shady cypress tree :
Be the green grass above me
    With showers and dewdrops wet ;
And if thou wilt, remember,
    And if thou wilt, forget.

I shall not see the shadows,
    I shall not feel the rain ;
I shall not hear the nightingale
    Sing on, as if in pain ;
And dreaming through the twilight
    That doth not rise nor set,
Haply I may remember,
    And haply may forget.

The Pre-Raphaelite Brotherhood, 1848-53

It was in 1848, the year of Continental revolutions and the *Communist Manifesto*, that a few young artists and men of letters in London united to oppose the conventional or academic approach to art, calling themselves, as an act of homage to the early Italian painters, "the Pre-Raphaelite Brotherhood." The name, in fact, was not new, for in 1810 two German religious painters had founded a society in Rome called the German Pre-Raphaelite Brethren; but the genesis of the English movement seems to have been in a letter written in 1848 by Dante Gabriel Rossetti to his brother William. He says that he has been reading Lord Houghton's *Life and Letters of Keats*, then just published:—"Keats seems to have been a glorious fellow, and says in one place (to my great delight) that, having just looked over a folio of the first and second schools of Italian painting, he has come to the conclusion that the early men surpassed even Raphael himself!"

It was particularly appropriate that the name of the movement should have come originally from Keats, for, so far as poetry is concerned, the Pre-Raphaelites owed an enormous debt—as they acknowledged—to those charming minor poems of the great poet that we have mentioned in speaking of Tennyson, and also to some of the early work of Tennyson himself. Keats's unfinished *Eve of St Mark*, which has been called "a Pre-Raphaelite poem by anticipation", was unknown to the public till the Houghton volume of 1848; and Houghton also reprinted from the original number of the *Indicator* the ballad *La Belle Dame sans Merci* which deeply influenced the Rossettis, Dixon, and Morris.

The general aim of the Movement found a champion in Ruskin, the first volume of whose *Modern Painters* had partly influenced it. In 1850 the Brotherhood published a short-lived magazine entitled *The Germ: Thoughts towards Nature in Poetry, Literature and Art*. On the literary side, the main interest of the magazine was the verse of the Rossettis and Patmore—including the celebrated poem, *The Blessed Damozel*, by D. G. Rossetti—and a prose romance, *Hand and Soul*, by the same author.

The original members of the Brotherhood were D. G. Rossetti, Millais, and Holman Hunt. Later were added the sculptor Woolner, the critic Stephens, the painter Collinson —who afterwards became a Roman Catholic—and W. M. Rossetti, who was to uphold the principles of the Brotherhood in literature and was appointed secretary. In the early 'fifties, other artists came under their influence, notably Madox Brown, Arthur Hughes, and Burne-Jones. It is sometimes reckoned that the Brotherhood, as such, broke up in 1853, when Millais became an A.R.A. and abandoned the Pre-Raphaelite technique. But in literature, and in the general development of ideas on life and art, the Pre-Raphaelite Movement may be said to have dominated a good deal of the poetry and prose of the later nineteenth century.

It dominated, immediately, a group of undergraduates at Oxford in the early 'fifties, including Morris, Burne-Jones, and Dixon. These young men all had High-Church leanings — Morris and Burne-Jones, as well as the future Canon, intended taking holy orders—and their favourite reading was Chaucer, Malory, Keats, Tennyson, Ruskin, the *Tracts for the Times*, and Charlotte Yonge. In 1856 Morris edited and largely financed what was called the *Oxford and Cambridge Magazine*, though it was entirely an Óxonian product; its main literary interest was some poetry by D. G. Rossetti and a good deal of work, in both verse and prose, by the editor.

In the account of individuals which follows, we shall be concerned, of course, mostly with literature, and we shall be taking "the Pre-Raphaelite Movement" in its widest meaning. We can begin with one who was not a Pre-Raphaelite at all, but whose influence upon both the original Brotherhood and the later Movement, especially on Morris, was profound.

The Influence of Ruskin, 1819-1900

The first paintings of the Pre-Raphaelite Brotherhood were quite well received, but in 1850 one of Rossetti's pictures was severely criticised by the *Athenaeum* and in 1851 *The Times* attacked the work of the Brotherhood in general, speaking of "affected simplicity, senile imitations of a cramped style, false perspective, crude colours, morbid infatuation, and the sacrifice of beauty, truth, and genuine feeling, to mere eccentricity." It was then that John Ruskin, appealed to by Patmore, wrote his famous letters to *The Times* in which he defended the Brotherhood and said that "both as studies of drapery and of every minor detail, there has been nothing in art so earnest or so complete as these pictures since the days of Albert Dürer." This intervention by a respected art critic turned the current of public feeling, and, besides the personal patronage of Rossetti and others by Ruskin himself, paved the way for their later success.

But the influence of Ruskin upon the general Pre-Raphaelite Movement was more profound than a mere generous impulse of defence and patronage. He was not only the most famous art critic in England, he had definite views on the relation of art to society—views which were in accordance with some of the vaguer notions of the Pre-Raphaelite Brotherhood and which were later developed by William Morris. In *Modern Painters* (1843-60) he examined the principles of painting with a thoroughness and insight never before attempted; in *The Stones of Venice* (1851-3) he performed the same service for architecture. His influence for good on the public taste was only surpassed by that of his disciple Morris, and we have an interesting line of thought here from Carlyle to Ruskin and from Ruskin to Morris.

Like Carlyle, though in very different social circumstances, Ruskin was intended by his parents for holy orders; and, like Carlyle, he refused to make preaching his profession, though he made it his practice throughout life. His art criticism led him to social and economic criticism; he preached the fundamental doctrine that art was not a thing apart from the public and private life of a nation, it was dependent on that life and essential to it. Great art could only be produced in a healthy nation; and a nation that did not produce things of beauty was not healthy. In the final volume of *Modern Painters* he wrote:

> In these books of mine their distinctive character
> as essays in art is their bringing everything to a root
> in human passion or human hope. Every principle of
> painting which I have stated is traced to some vital or
> spiritual fact; and in my works on architecture, the
> preference accorded finally to one school over another is
> founded on a comparison of their influence on the life of
> the workman—a question by other writers on the subject
> of architecture wholly forgotten or despised.

His first quarrel with his age was that it neglected beauty;
and this objection soon developed into the further objection
that beauty was impossible in such an age. He quarrelled with
the utilitarian ideals which influenced statesmen, and in the
essays collected under the title *Unto this Last* (1859), and in
later volumes like *Sesame and Lilies* (1865) and *The Crown
of Wild Olives* (1866), he attacked the comfortable notion that
mere self-interest, enlightened or unenlightened, would work
out unaided the solution of every social problem. "Government and Co-operation," he wrote, "are in all things the laws
of life; Anarchy and Competition the laws of death."

His social writing, like Carlyle's, can be fairly criticised
on several points, but his protest was valuable and had valuable results in different fields. His rhetorical style is often
irritating to read, but we must remember that many of his
later books were first delivered as lectures; his extravagant
prose, like Carlyle's, seems to have been suited to his material.
His enthusiasm in art makes him sometimes an unsafe guide,
and his dispute with Whistler in 1877 shows that he could
be unreceptive of new ideas.

From 1867 to 1870 he was professor of art at Oxford, and
he made a number of experiments for the establishment of
industry on socialist lines. He is fittingly commemorated
by Ruskin College, Oxford, founded in 1899 by an American admirer to provide education in the social sciences for
working-men.

D. G. Rossetti, 1828-82

Dante Gabriel Rossetti was one of the four children of an
Italian poet and critic (son of a blacksmith) who had become
involved in revolutionary activities and had had to flee to

England. All four children made contributions to English literature: we have seen that the majority of critics place Christina Rossetti in the foremost position among English women poets; it was her brother William, secretary of the Brotherhood and himself a minor poet, who edited her posthumous poems and wrote some interesting reminiscences and criticism; the elder daughter Maria wrote an introduction to Dante.

To *The Germ*, we noted, Rossetti contributed the first version of the poem *The Blessed Damozel*; he revised this for the *Oxford and Cambridge Magazine* in 1856, together with a longer poem, *The Burden of Nineveh*. In 1861 he published his first volume, *The Early Italian Poets*, rearranged in 1874 as *Dante and his Circle*. Most of the poems he wrote in the late 'fifties and early 'sixties he copied into a manuscript book, which, when his wife died tragically in 1862, was buried with her. Rossetti himself became a victim of insomnia, ending his life with an overdose of narcotic. Most of the *Poems* published in 1870 had lain undisturbed in his wife's grave until he had yielded to entreaty and consented to their exhumation. His last volume, *Ballads and Sonnets*, appeared in 1881.

He and Swinburne were attacked by Robert Buchanan (under the guise of "Thomas Maitland") in an article in the *Contemporary Review*, afterwards expanded into a pamphlet, entitled *The Fleshly School of Poetry*. Though Rossetti replied suitably in an article in the *Athenaeum* entitled *The Stealthy School of Criticism*, it is thought by his biographers that the incident preyed on his mind and contributed to the delusion of organised conspiracy against him that was one of the afflictions of his last years. The attack seems to have little relevance now; even the poem *Nuptial Sleep*, which was subsequently omitted after being printed in the 1870 collection, appears mild enough to a modern eye:

> At length their long kiss severed, with sweet smart:
> And as the last slow sudden drops are shed
> From sparkling eaves where all the storm has fled,
> So singly flagged the pulses of each heart.

Their bosoms sundered, with the opening start
Of married flowers to either side outspread
From the knit stem ; yet still their mouths, burnt red,
Fawned on each other where they lay apart.

Sleep sank them lower than the tide of dreams,
And their dreams watched them sink, and slid away.
Slowly their souls swam up again, through gleams
Of watered light and dull drowned waifs of day ;
Till from some wonder of new woods and streams
He woke, and wondered more : for there she lay.

Typical of Rossetti in the more mystic vein—religiose
rather than religious—is the well-known sonnet *Soul's Beauty*
from the sequence *The House of Life* :

Under the arch of Life, where love and death,
Terror and mystery, guard her shrine, I saw
Beauty enthroned ; and though her gaze struck awe,
I drew it in as simply as my breath.
Hers are the eyes which, over and beneath,
The sky and sea bend on thee,—which can draw,
By sea or sky or woman, to one law,
The allotted bondman of her palm and wreath.

This is that Lady Beauty, in whose praise
Thy voice and hand shake still,—long known to thee
By flying hair and fluttering hem,—the beat
Following her daily of thy heart and feet,
How passionately and irretrievably,
In what fond flight, how many ways and days !

Morris, 1834-96

The parents of William Morris were wealthy, so he was
able to dispose of his time as he pleased when he left Oxford.
His early enthusiasm for the Middle Ages had appeared likely
to lead him into the Church, but the reading of Ruskin's
famous chapter, "The Nature of Gothic", in *The Stones of
Venice*, decided him to study architecture. Under the influence of Rossetti, he turned for a time to painting, and then
in 1859 found his true vocation, after his marriage to Jane
Burden, the subject of many of Rossetti's pictures. He wanted
to furnish himself a house, but found that beautiful wood-
work, glass, and fabrics were not obtainable in England ; so

he founded the firm of decorative artists, Morris and Company, which he controlled from 1861 to his death, and which gradually revolutionised public taste in fabrics and furniture.

The range of the domestic arts he practised was astonishingly wide : wall-hangings, wallpaper, chintz, carpets, tapestry, tiles . . . all these things were manufactured by or for him, and in every case he prepared himself for the work of designing by mastering thoroughly the technique of the craft. The Anglo-Catholic revival, too, called for church decoration in something different from the "ecclesiastical outfitter" style ; so stained glass, painted decoration, tapestries, church embroidery came within the work of Morris and Co. The final achievement of his crowded career was the founding of the Kelmscott Press in 1891.

His revolt against the products of commercialism led him to revolt against commerce itself, and in later life he became a Socialist, devoting himself with characteristic energy to the work of propaganda. His fine romances, *A Dream of John Ball* (1888) and *News from Nowhere* (1891), are the chief literary products of this phase of his activity. Paradoxically, though, in one who believed so strongly—with Ruskin—in the organic relation between life and art, his literary career as a whole is singularly free from traces, not merely of his own practical interests, but of any contemporary interest at all. The other extraordinary fact about Morris as a writer is that most of his works were written after a hard day in office or workshop. Some of them were even composed while he was engaged upon something else ! "If a chap can't compose an epic poem while he's weaving tapestry," he remarked, "he'd better shut up, he'll never do any good at all."

Four of the five poems he had written for the *Oxford and Cambridge Magazine* appeared in his first volume of poetry *The Defence of Guenevere and other Poems* (1858). This contains some of his best-known pieces, including *The Haystack in the Floods*, the sonnet *Summer Dawn* ("Pray but one prayer for me 'twixt thy closed lips . . ."), and the ballad with the refrain "Two red roses across the moon." After a long interval, devoted to his house and business, came *The Life* *and Death of Jason* (1867), the first of a series of romantic narrative poems which form the bulk of his contribution to literature.* From the fourth book of *Jason* comes the well-known lyric *A Garden by the Sea*.

In 1868-70 appeared the greatest collection of his verse stories, *The Earthly Paradise*. A stanza from the *Apology* prefixed to these volumes is often quoted as an "Apologia pro Vita Sua", as Morris's consciousness of the futility of his efforts—rather paradoxical in view of the vigour and success of many of his activities :

> Dreamer of dreams, born out of my true time,
> Why should I strive to set the crooked straight ?
> Let it suffice me that my murmuring rhyme
> Beats with light wing against the ivory gate,
> Telling a tale not too importunate
> To those who in the sleepy region stay,
> Lulled by the singer of an empty day.

That was undoubtedly one side of Morris : the man who felt that he was born out of his true time and who "had the courage", as a modern admirer puts it, "to make no compromise with the social system he condemned." But some of us will prefer to see the true Morris, and a greater courage, in the magnificent series of lectures he gave in the 'seventies and 'eighties. A good example is his address to the Birmingham Society of Arts and School of Design, delivered in 1879. We have room here for only a short extract, and must take up Morris in full stride. He is speaking about the Dark Ages :

> . . . That is pretty much the sum of what so-called history has left us of the tale of those days—the stupid langour and the evil deeds of kings and scoundrels. Must we turn away then, and say that all was evil ? How then did men live from day to day ? How then did Europe grow into intelligence and freedom ? It seems there were

---

* Most of the later narrative poems were on Scandinavian epic themes, notably *Sigurd the Volsung* (1876). Towards the end of his life, he wrote prose romances, with occasional verse, in an artificial, archaic dialect, about primitive Scandinavian society. *The House of the Wolfings* (1889) was the first of the seven ; *The Sundering Flood* (published posthumously, 1897) the last.

others than those of whom history (so called) has left us the names and the deeds. These, the raw material for the treasury and the slave-market, we now call "the people", and we know that they were working all that while. Yes, and that their work was not merely slaves' work, the meal-trough before them and the whip behind them; for though history (so called) has forgotten them, yet their work has not been forgotten, but has made another history —the history of Art. There is not an ancient city in the East or the West that does not bear some token of their grief, and joy, and hope. From Ispahan to Northumberland, there is no building built between the seventh and the seventeenth centuries that does not show the influence of the labour of that oppressed and neglected herd of men. No one of them, indeed, rose high above his fellows. There was no Plato, or Shakespeare, or Michael Angelo amongst them. Yet scattered as it was among many men, how strong their thought was, how long it abided, how far it travelled ! . . . History (so called) has remembered the kings and warriors, because they destroyed; Art has remembered the people, because they created.

Swinburne, 1837-1909

With Algernon Charles Swinburne, a younger member of the Rossetti circle, we get the true link between the Pre-Raphaelites and the "decadent" poets of the 'nineties. He announced his allegiance to Rossetti in the dedication of his first book, *The Queen Mother and Rosamond* (1860), two poetical dramas written in elaborate blank verse. A considerable portion of his work is dramatic, in form if not in spirit, but his dramas were never welcomed like his lyric poems, and his most famous work, *Atalanta in Calydon* (1864-5), a drama on the Greek model, is chiefly known by its lyrical choruses, particularly the one beginning :

> Before the beginning of years
>   There came to the making of man
> Time, with a gift of tears ;
>   Grief, with a glass that ran ;
> Pleasure, with pain for leaven ;
>   Summer, with flowers that fell ;
> Remembrance fallen from heaven,
>   And madness risen from hell ;

> Strength without hands to smite ;
> Love that endures for a breath ;
> Night, the shadow of light,
> And life, the shadow of death.

Of aristocratic descent, Swinburne, like Shelley before him,
sympathised deeply with the republican ideals of Europe, the
Italian struggle for liberty inspiring some of his most characteristic verse, notably *A Song of Italy* (1867) and *Songs before
Sunrise* (1871). That he later, during the Boer War, rivalled
the jingoism of Kipling—exulting, when he heard about the
mortality in the Kitchener concentration camps, that "the
whelps and dams of murderous foes" were no more—can
probably be dismissed as the aberration of old age.

Between *Atalanta* and the *Song of Italy* appeared the work
that made him both celebrated and notorious, the first series
of *Poems and Ballads* (1866). It was violently attacked by
several reviewers on account of the alleged sensuality of some
of the poems. John Morley in the *Saturday Review* spoke
of Swinburne as "an unclean fiery imp from the pit" and
accused him of exhibiting "the feverish carnality of a schoolboy." But "the curious fact is," says a literary historian,
"that as Rossetti's religious poems had everything except
religious conviction, so Swinburne's sensual poems had everything except sensual conviction." They became popular with
the younger generation, particularly such things as

> Could you hurt me, sweet lips, though I hurt you ?
> Men touch them, and change in a trice
> The lilies and langours of virtue,
> For the raptures and roses of vice.

Perhaps the favourite poem of this collection was the famous
Garden of Proserpine, the penultimate stanza of which is
typical of one aspect of the Pre-Raphaelite Movement :

> From too much love of living,
> From hope and fear set free,
> We thank with brief thanksgiving
> Whatever gods may be
> That no life lives for ever ;
> That dead men rise up never ;
> That even the weariest river
> Winds somewhere safe to sea.

It is generally agreed that most of Swinburne's best work belongs to the period 1865-78, that is from *Atalanta* to the second series of *Poems and Ballads*. Later verse included *Songs of the Springtide* (1880), *Tristram of Lyonesse* (1882), a third series of *Poems and Ballads* (1887), and a number of dramas. The *Tristram* volume contains, besides the Morris-like narrative title-piece, a series of sonnets on the Elizabethan dramatists; and we must mention, in this connection, that Swinburne, in later life—when he was living in retirement under the roof of his friend, the minor poet and critic Theodore Watts-Dunton—wrote several volumes of literary criticism and many essays and introductions, notably on the lesser Elizabethans. The introduction to the *Mermaid* selection of Middleton is a good example of his work in this field, which continues, in some respects, the work of Lamb. It is both remarkable and admirable that Swinburne, one of the most lyrical and least dramatic of our distinguished poets, should have opened this essay with the following sentence: "If it be true, as we are told on high authority, that the greatest glory of England is her literature, and the greatest glory of English literature is its poetry, it is not less true that the greatest glory of English poetry lies rather in its dramatic than its epic or its lyric triumphs."

Dating of the Pre-Raphaelites

It is difficult to fix any definite period to the Pre-Raphaelite Movement, in the general sense here used. Our closing date to this chapter, 1883, may be taken as including, from 1848, all the work of Rossetti and most of the best work of Morris and Swinburne. A modern critic has extended the following of the Pre-Raphaelites to include the Greek translations of Professor Murray, written during the Edwardian age; but as a general rule we can take the movement as belonging to the mid-Victorian age. The poets who wrote partly in that period, but who are not usually regarded as having much connection with the Pre-Raphaelites, are to be considered in our chapter on Late Victorian Poetry, 1869-98.

There were some minor poets in or around the Movement.
The Irish poet, William Allingham, wrote *The Music Master*
(1855), a volume of lyrical poems illustrated by woodcuts
from designs by Rossetti, Millais, and Arthur Hughes ; and
another friend of Rossetti, Arthur O'Shaughnessy, wrote a
good deal of Swinburnian verse, for example *An Epic of
Women* (1870). The opening lines of O'Shaughnessy's
famous *Ode*—

> We are the music makers,
>   And we are the dreamers of dreams,
> Wandering by lone sea-breakers,
>   And sitting by desolate streams ;
> World-losers and world-forsakers,
>   On whom the pale moon gleams . . .

—can perhaps be cited not unfairly in conclusion, as typical
in its charming remoteness of the kind of thing that has
"dated" the Pre-Raphaelites.

CHAPTER IX

SCIENCE AND CULTURE

1859-1890

"We live in a wonderful age ; the enlargement of the circle of secular knowledge just now is simply a bewilderment, and the more so, because it has the promise of continuing, and that with greater rapidity, and more signal results. Now these discoveries, certain or probable, have in matter of fact an indirect bearing upon religious opinions, and the question arises how are the respective claims of revelation and of natural science to be adjusted."

NEWMAN : *Apologia pro Vita Sua.*

"The whole scope of the essay is to recommend culture as the great help out of our present difficulties ; culture being a pursuit of our total perfection by means of getting to know, on all the matters which most concern us, the best which has been thought and said in the world ; and through this knowledge, turning a stream of fresh and free thought upon our stock notions and habits, which we now follow staunchly but mechanically, vainly imagining that there is a virtue in following them staunchly which makes up for the mischief of following them mechanically. This, and this alone, is the scope of the following essay. And the culture we recommend is, above all, an inward operation."

ARNOLD : Preface to *Culture and Anarchy.*

Importance of the Year 1859

The Victorian Age was an age of great intellectual activity. We observed something of this at the end of Chapter IV, when we were stressing the reaction of several early Victorian writers against the general "machine" philosophy that had followed the Industrial Revolution. We saw it again in subsequent chapters, in dealing with the work of such writers as Dickens, George Eliot, Tennyson, Newman, Ruskin. These writers are,

indeed, very different in their individual outlook, but they
share a distrust of certain aspects of the material progress of
their time. The later Victorian period is so bulky in what may
be briefly described as "general prose literature" that we must
take it here under several comprehensive headings, only considering individual writers separately in the few instances
where their strictly literary importance warrants it.

We can begin with the scientists and with the year 1859, when
Charles Darwin published *The Origin of Species by means of
Natural Selection*. This date is a good starting point in other
ways : it was in the final years of the 'fifties that Ruskin
turned his main attention from art to economics and succeeded
Carlyle as the bitter opponent of Victorian commerce ; it was
in the late 'fifties and early 'sixties that Matthew Arnold began
to bombard the "Philistines" with verbal weapons as shrewdly
aimed as they were witty ; and it was in January 1860, as
we have noted when speaking of its editor Thackeray, that
the first number was published of the *Cornhill Magazine*, in
which some of the most important work of both Ruskin and
Arnold originally appeared.

Science and Philosophy

It is no part of literary history to trace in detail the controversies concerning the doctrine of organic evolution, still
less even to summarise the complicated development of
natural science and scientific philosophy in the later Victorian
age. It is sufficient to observe here that the fact that Tennyson's *In Memoriam* preceded the *Origin of Species* is one proof
of the falsity of the popular notion that Charles Darwin
(1809-82) "invented Evolution." There were several British
evolutionists before Darwin, including his grandfather Eras-
mus Darwin, who died in 1802, and the publisher Robert
Chambers, whose *Vestiges of Creation* (1844) put strongly
the view that new species of animals were being evolved from
simpler types. As early as the year of Darwin's birth, the
French naturalist Lamarck had advanced a general evolutionary theory ; and Sir Charles Lyell, in his *Principles of*

Geology (1831-3), had demonstrated that past changes, however great, must be interpreted, not in terms of catastrophic convulsions, but in terms of the accumulation of the small changes to be seen operating in the present. It was then that Darwin, influenced both by Lyell and by the Malthusian doctrine of population, conceived—along with Alfred Russel Wallace, who independently arrived at almost the same conclusions—the idea of the struggle for existence and natural selection, and the wealth of evidence brought forward by the *Origin of Species* won over the majority of scientists. The subsequent biological developments are largely concerned with the detailed controversies, not yet ended, between the Darwinians and the followers of Lamarck (who included Samuel Butler); a very interesting and amusing account of this dispute—which centres round the question of how the giraffe got his long neck—is given by Bernard Shaw in the Preface to *Back to Methuselah*.

Darwin himself took little part in the more theological disputes which raged from 1859 for many years.* Only his *Descent of Man* (1871) can be said to have a place in the polemical battle between the more orthodox Christians and the agnostic Evolutionists. It was the scientist and humanist Thomas Henry Huxley (1825-95) who not only coined the word "agnostic" but who became the most prominent champion of Evolution against religious orthodoxy. He it was who, at an Oxford meeting of the British Association in 1860, defended Evolution against the bland attacks of Bishop Wilberforce (coached by the anti-Darwinian biologist Richard Owen), who asked him whether he claimed descent from a monkey on his grandfather's or his grandmother's side. And thirty years later it was Huxley who debated with Gladstone, in the pages of the monthly review, the *Nineteenth Century*,

---

* The Evangelical paper *The Witness* described the Darwinian theory in 1862 as "the vilest and beastliest paradox ever invented in ancient or modern times." This is interesting, because a previous editor of *The Witness*, the geologist Hugh Miller, had remarked that "The clergy, as a class, suffer themselves to linger far in the rear of an intelligent and accomplished laity—a full age behind the requirements of the time."

over the acceptance of the Gospel story of the Gadarene swine. His books include *Man's Place in Nature* (1863), *Lay Sermons* (1870), and *Science and Culture* (1881).

The economist and philosopher Herbert Spencer (1820-1903) applied the evolutionary principle to the whole field of human knowledge. He had been a convinced Evolutionist before Darwin, but it was not till 1860 that he issued his "Programme of a System of Synthetic Philosophy", to the elaboration of which he devoted the rest of his life. In regular succession came *First Principles* (1862), *Principles of Biology* (1864-7), *Principles of Psychology* (1870-2), *Principles of Sociology* (1876-96), and *Principles of Ethics* (1879-92). He also produced such smaller works as *Education* (1861), *The Man versus the State* (1884), and *Factors of Organic Evolution* (1887). In many ways the mouthpiece of his age, his reputation has tended to decline with the years. His philosophy stems to a certain extent from Bentham, Mill, and the Utilitarians ; it has been widely discussed, from various points of view, by such writers as T. H. Green and J. M. Robertson, and by his friend in later life, Beatrice Webb.

History and Natural History

It was not Science itself, but Science interpreted as History, which so upset the traditional ideas. "A rose-red city, half as old as time !" wrote Dean Burgon of the city of Petra in 1845. It was possible to believe then, and most people did believe, that time had begun less than six thousand years ago, that Moses had written his account only a few generations from the creation of the world. Now geology seemed to disprove entirely the literal *Genesis* story, and Darwin cast doubt on whether life had ever been created at all. He made the later Victorians ask such questions as : At what moment in history had evolving man been given a soul accountable to God ? The old proof of the Creator's design which Archdeacon Paley had taught in the *Evidences of Christianity* (1794) seemed to be disproved, too : God had not given the duck webbed feet in order to swim, the duck had evolved its feet or it would have perished.

It is impossible to summarise in a short space the various questions that were asked, the various arguments used by different sections of opinion, the various foreign influences on Victorian thought, for instance the German influence on Biblical criticism and the influence of the French philosopher Comte, whose "religion of humanity" affected J. S. Mill, Frederic Harrison, and George Eliot. Some Victorians rejected the new ideas altogether; some, like the naturalist Philip Gosse, attempted to reconcile the *Genesis* story with geology; a good many followed the middle way of F. D. Maurice and Kingsley, of Tennyson in *In Memoriam*, of Pattison, Jowett, etc., in *Essays and Reviews* (1860); while there arose in the 'seventies a group of Agnostics, including Huxley, Leslie Stephen, John Morley, and W. K. Clifford, who asserted that a man or nation could be moral and yet not acknowledge Christian dogma. Life lays on us a duty, argued Clifford, to doubt and to ask questions; that is how knowledge advances. To stifle doubts is morally wrong.*

Science, history, theology, ethics, economics: they all seemed, as never before, bound up with one another—literally so, of course, in the essays in the various magazines and learned reviews that were a feature of the age. Controversy on all these and related topics was genuinely popular, and the period of rigid specialisation, like the period of "highbrow" and "lowbrow", was in the future. Henry Buckle, in his uncompleted *History of Civilisation in England* (1857-61),

---

* Clifford was a brilliant mathematician, whose sceptical *Essays and Lectures* (1879) had a wide sale and influence. Stephen, like Clough, resigned his fellowship (at Cambridge) on grounds of conscience; until 1871 no one could be admitted to a fellowship at Oxford or Cambridge unless he signed the Thirty-Nine Articles of the Church of England. The resignation of the respected philosopher Henry Sidgwick in 1869 did much to speed up the reforming legislation. To the year 1869 also belongs the founding of the Metaphysical Society, a group of tolerant inquiring men of every variety of opinion—Huxley and Cardinal Manning, Clifford and Gladstone, Stephen and Tennyson, Ruskin and Dr Martineau, Morley and W. G. Ward, the scientist Tyndall and the Archbishop of York. They once debated in correct parliamentary style the question of the existence of God. A member who had not been present inquired anxiously of one who had: "Well, is there a God?" "Yes," came the answer; "we had a very good majority."

applied to history the methods which Darwin was applying to nature and followed Comte in his search for natural laws of growth; his fragment attained extraordinary success. Anthropology — the natural history of Man — developed strongly in all its branches after 1859; Sir Edward Tylor, in *Primitive Culture* (1871), first made its researches familiar to the general reader. Even more popular was that astonishing study of universal history *The Martyrdom of Man* by Winwood Reade, a nephew of the novelist; it was one of the books attacked by Gladstone in his earnest address of protest to the Collegiate Institution of Liverpool during the year of its publication, 1872. Later it was warmly defended by scientists, politicians, and men of letters, and in the 'nineties we find it recommended to Dr Watson by Sherlock Holmes. Less important as literature, but more important as science, was the study of mythology and comparative religion *The Golden Bough*, by J. G. Frazer, the first volume of which appeared in 1890.

History, Political and Religious

Besides anthropology, universal history and historical philosophy, there was a good deal of valuable work done by the later Victorians in the more modest fields of political and religious history. The popular "Whig" historians, Henry Hallam and Lord Macaulay, had both died in 1859; their most widely read successor was James Anthony Froude (1818-94), who has been mentioned in connection with his brother and the Oxford Movement. His virtues and defects as an historian are similar to Macaulay's; that is, he was an ardent advocate rather than an unprejudiced chronicler, and it has been said that there is probably no historian of anything like his calibre who is so dangerous to trust on mere matters of fact. His *History of England from the Fall of Wolsey to the Defeat of the English Armada* (1856-70) showed his genius for dramatic realisation of historic events—a genius that recalls, not only Macaulay, but Carlyle. The volumes of collected essays called *Short Studies in Great Subjects* (1867-82) contain some of his best work; *The English in Ireland in the Eighteenth Century* (1872-4) and the *Life of Carlyle* (1882-4) caused almost as much controversy as the *History of England*.

The assaults upon the *History* were led by Edward Augustus Freeman (1823-92), the author of many careful historical works, notably the *History of the Norman Conquest* (1867-76), an active journalist, especially known for his contributions to the *Saturday Review*, and Professor of Modern History at Oxford from 1884. He and Bishop Stubbs were the principal writers in what came to be known as the Oxford School of Historians,* which later included J. R. Green and also Mandell Creighton, who afterwards maintained the same principles of history while at Cambridge. These writers differed from Macaulay, Carlyle, and Froude, by making scientific and accurate research the end and aim of history. Freeman's chief pupil, John Richard Green (1837-83), may be said to have combined this accuracy with Macaulay's flair for narrative and interest in social and literary development in his most popular work, *A Short History of the English People* (1874).

The Victorian age throughout was a great period of historical writing, in every field; we have mentioned, and are able to mention, only a few of the more eminent or popular historians. Contemporary with Hallam or Macaulay had been several writers who specialised in ancient or early medieval history: Sharon Turner, Sir Francis Palgrave (father of the anthologist), George Grote, Connop Thirlwall, Charles Merivale, George Finlay, Henry Hart Milman, and others. A little later came the laborious research into the ancient East of George Rawlinson; and the lectures on the history of the early Churches by Dean Stanley, better known for his biography of Thomas Arnold.

Contemporary with Froude and Freeman were Thorold Rogers, the economic historian; S. R. Gardiner, the author

---

* Their admiration for each other was long a theme of academic jest; Thorold Rogers wrote:

> See where, ladling from alternate tubs,
> Stubbs butters Freeman, Freeman butters Stubbs.

of histories of England during the seventeenth century ; and Goldwin Smith, whose book *The Empire* (1863) advocated the establishment of the colonies as independent states. The contrary doctrine of Imperialism owed most to Disraeli and to Sir John Seeley's book *The Expansion of England* (1883). Of the many military historians, we can mention Sir William Napier, who wrote the history of the Peninsula War ; the historian of the Crimean War, A. W. Kinglake, more widely celebrated for his book of Eastern travel *Eothen* (1844); and Sir Edward Creasy, whose *Fifteen Decisive Battles of the World* (1851) attained enormous popularity.

Contemporary with J. R. Green were Frederick Seebohm, the author of *The Oxford Reformers* (1867) and *The English Village Community* (1882); W. E. H. Lecky, best known for his anti-dogmatic *History of the Spirit of Rationalism in Europe* (1865); and, last but not least in this brief survey, the strange figure of the admirable Lord Acton, the most learned historian of his age, who planned but never wrote a large-scale history of liberty, who was the first editor of the *Cambridge Modern History*, and who, as leader of the Liberal party among the Roman Catholics in England, opposed the doctrine of Papal Infallibility in 1870 and made no secret of his dislike for Cardinal Newman : "Newman is an avowed admirer of Saint Pius and Saint Charles, and of the Pontiffs who canonised them. This, and the like of this, is the reason of my deep aversion for him."

Liberal Theology

We have seen that the Evangelicals, unlike the Oxford Movement, did not run a great deal to literature, except of the most ephemeral kind. The "Broad Churchmen", the liberal theologians, who were disliked by both Evangelicals and the High-Church party, were more able in this respect—if not more fortunate, for their writings sometimes led to persecution. The "Oriel theologians" at Oxford—Edward Copleston, Richard Whately, Thomas Arnold—had little patience with either Evangelicals or Tractarians (whom Whately described as the Pharisees and the Sadducees) ; and their attitude towards the enthusiasts, and their acceptance of modern methods of Biblical research, were shared by Dean Stanley, Julius Hare, and the historians Thirlwall and Seeley. (Seeley's book *Ecce Homo*, published anonymously in 1865, was described by Lord Shaftesbury as "the most pestilential volume ever vomited forth from the jaws of Hell.")

One of the broadest of the Broad Churchmen was F. D. Maurice (1805-72), whose outspoken *Theological Essays* (1853), repudiating the orthodox views on eternal punishment and the Atonement, lost him his professorship at King's College, London. With Kingsley and Hughes he had founded the Christian Socialist Movement in 1848. It is chiefly to Maurice that we owe the Working Men's College and the Queen's College for Women.

We have mentioned briefly the volume called *Essays and Reviews* (1860), which created as great a sensation, for different reasons, as Newman's Tract 90, and whose authors were described by their opponents as "the Seven Against Christ." Actually, they included Frederick Temple, a future Archbishop of Canterbury, Benjamin Jowett, a future Master of Balliol, and Mark Pattison, a future Rector of Lincoln. The aim of the book was to provoke free discussion among those who were united in a common Christianity, but the bishops issued an official circular to the clergy condemning it and hinting that some of the essays were inconsistent with belief in the Thirty-nine Articles.

Two years later Bishop Colenso of Natal published a book called *The Pentateuch and the Book of Joshua critically examined*, a piece of Biblical criticism which drew upon him a storm of abuse and controversy. In 1863 he was deposed by the Bishop of Cape Town, but was reinstated on appeal to the Privy Council. A similar persecution deprived William Robertson Smith of his professor's chair at Aberdeen in 1881, owing to his Biblical contributions to the *Encyclopaedia Britannica*. It is hardly necessary to add that the criticism of these and other Victorian theologians is accepted now by the majority in the Church of England, though the subsequent "modernist" developments in the Catholic Church

—associated with the Irish theologian George Tyrrell, the French scholar Loisy, and the Anglo-Austrian writer von Hügel—were condemned by the Pope in 1907.

Editors and Critics

A history of the various journals and reviews in the Victorian Age would require a chapter, if not a book, to itself. Mention has been made of several of the most important, and here we can add the names of some of the most prominent editors and critics, before going on to consider in more detail the social, religious, and literary criticism of Matthew Arnold and the Aesthetes.*

Walter Bagehot (1826-77) and R. H. Hutton (1826-97) were contemporaries and friends. Bagehot edited the *Economist* from 1860 ; his *English Constitution* (1867) and *Lombard Street* (1873) are regarded as classics in their fields. In *Physics and Politics* (1869) he attempted to apply the theory of natural selection to the development of human communities. He is best known to-day by his witty *Literary Studies*, published after his death. Hutton, a literary critic of strong theological convictions, was for over thirty years one of the editors of the *Spectator*.

Sir Leslie Stephen (1832-1904) has been mentioned, in connection with his criticism of Newman, for his collection

* Of the Victorian journals which have survived, we can mention, among the newspapers, the *News of the World* (1843), the *Daily News* (1846), and the *Daily Chronicle* (1877), now combined in the *News Chronicle*, *Reynold's News* (1850), the *Daily Telegraph* (1855), the *Liverpool Post* (1855), the *Birmingham Post* (1857), the *Yorkshire Post* (1866), the *People* (1881), and the *Star* (1888). The later Victorian developments, associated with the Harmsworth brothers, will concern our final chapter ; such papers as *The Times*, the *Morning Post*, the *Manchester Guardian*, the *Observer*, *The Scotsman*, are older than the Victorian Age. Of the reviews that survive, we can mention the *Economist* (1843), the *Cornhill Magazine* (1860), the *Fortnightly* (1865), the *Contemporary Review* (1866), the *Nineteenth Century* (1877), the *National Review* (1883), and the *British Weekly* (1886). Such journals as the *Spectator*, the *Dublin Review*, and *Chambers's Journal* are pre-Victorian. The *Saturday Review*, the *Academy*, *Household Words*, *Macmillan's Magazine*, *Temple Bar*, *St Paul's*, the *Pall Mall Gazette*, are among the journals which have not survived ; the *Athenaeum* was absorbed by the *Nation*, which in turn was combined with the *New Statesman*.

of essays *An Agnostic's Apology*. He edited the *Cornhill Magazine*, 1871-82, and was first editor of the *Dictionary of National Biography*, being succeeded by Sir Sidney Lee, the biographer of Shakespeare. Stephen contributed several monographs to the *English Men of Letters* series, and was the author of some of the best literary history and criticism of his time, notably *English Thought in the Eighteenth Century* and *Hours in a Library*. Like his fellow-Agnostic, Richard Garnett, author of *The Twilight of the Gods*, he has a personal link with twentieth-century writing, being the father of Virginia Woolf, as Garnett was the father of Edward Garnett, literary critic and friend of Joseph Conrad and D. H. Lawrence.

Later a prominent Liberal statesman, John, afterwards Viscount, Morley (1838-1923) spent many years in "the higher journalism", as editor of the *Fortnightly Review* and the *Pall Mall Gazette*. He published Lives of Voltaire, Rousseau, Burke, and Gladstone, wrote the celebrated essay *On Compromise*, and edited the first series of *English Men of Letters*. The *Pall Mall Gazette* had been founded in 1865 by Frederick Greenwood. The subsequent history of this and other journals will be our concern when we consider the implications of the "Northcliffe revolution" that took place in the 'nineties.

Worthy of mention with Stephen and John Morley are such admirable journalists as William Minto, editor of the *Examiner* in its last years; C. P. Scott, editor of the *Manchester Guardian*, 1872-1929; and J. A. Spender, of the *Westminster Gazette*. Of less importance in literature, but celebrated in the history of late Victorian journalism, are such figures as G. A. Sala, of the *Telegraph*; W. T. Stead, of the *Pall Mall*; Clement Scott, dramatic critic; and Henry Labouchere, who founded the journal *Truth* in 1877.

The Criticism of Matthew Arnold

We have observed that most of the early work of Arnold had been in poetry, as most of the early work of Ruskin had been in art criticism. It was only from about 1860 onwards that these writers, in their different ways, turned their major attention to general problems of society and culture.

Arnold's criticism was all directed against national insularity and complacency, provincialism of mind. His work as a literary critic and as a social critic was essentially one. The main body of his literary criticism is to be found in the lectures *On Translating Homer* (1861) and *The Study of Celtic Literature* (1867), and in the two volumes of collected articles entitled *Essays in Criticism* (1865, '89). Here we encounter for the first time the phrases used to such effect in his chief work of social criticism, *Culture and Anarchy* (1869). We hear of "the best that is known and thought in the world", "the free play of the mind", and in the borrowing from German literature of the term "Philistines", to denote the middle classes, we have the germ of the later celebrated division of Victorian society into three classes : "The Barbarians", meaning the gentry ; "The Philistines", meaning the middle classes and more especially the Dissenting middle classes ; and "The Populace", meaning the lower classes. Arnold was careful to point out, though, that there existed in all three classes many "aliens", as he called them, whose chief characteristic was their humanity, not their reliance on abstract machinery. The root error of public opinion, he thought, was its faith in mere machinery. Coal and iron were machinery ; a democratic suffrage was machinery : these things were means to an end. To be active about means and disregardful of ends was the essence of "anarchy" and the denial of "culture."

He described his labours as an attempt "to pull out a few more stops in that powerful but narrow-toned organ, the modern Englishman." He sought to arouse interest in some of the great writers and thinkers of modern Europe—in Goethe and Heine, in the French essayists and critics, in Tolstoy. Two of his best *Essays in Criticism* are *The Function of Criticism at the Present Time* and *The Literary Influence of Academies* ; these, together with such later things as the introduction to Wordsworth, the essay on Keats, a few items in *Mixed Essays* (1879), and the best parts of *Culture and*

Anarchy, represent his most enduring work. *Friendship's Garland* (1871) is a series of satirical letters, introducing, like Carlyle in *Sartor Resartus*, an imaginary German; he visits England and derides all the things that most got Arnold's goat: the optimism of our newspapers, the indolent sportsmanship of our public schools, the inadequacy of our elementary education, and so forth. It is an amusing book, but it has not lasted so well as *Culture and Anarchy* or the best of the critical essays, partly because of the excessive adulation of Prussia (similar to that of the Webbs in the 'nineties), with which can be contrasted the more sober and realistic view given by William Lovett in his Autobiography, published five years later.

Arnold's theological criticism—*St Paul and Protestantism* (1870), *Literature and Dogma* (1873), *God and the Bible* (1875)—cannot be said to have lasted well, either, though the depreciation of recent Anglo-Catholic critics should perhaps be resisted by those holding different religious opinions. Arnold was a free-thinker who nevertheless desired to maintain both Church and Bible as cardinal elements in the spiritual life of the nation. Only "culture" could understand the Bible, and a Bible misunderstood or treated as verbally inspired would sooner or later, he prophesied, be a Bible rejected. He saw "Hebraism", the Jewish-Christian spirit, and "Hellenism", the Greek-scientific spirit, as both necessary to the well-balanced life; but he maintained that in the England of his time the stress was laid too much on the former, to the virtual exclusion of the latter.*

The Aesthetic Movement

The "Aesthetic School of Critics" is often thought to be a product of the 'nineties. Certainly it had its most celebrated

---

* In the previous chapter, an essay by Leslie Stephen was recommended, as giving, in its best form, the agnostic view of Newman. For a Christian view of Arnold's agnosticism, the writings of the distinguished philosopher Francis Herbert Bradley (1846-1924) can be recommended: *Ethical Studies* (1876) is a brilliant criticism, among much else, of Arnold's *Literature and Dogma*. Bradley's two other major works are *Principles of Logic* (1883) and *Appearance and Reality* (1893).

period then, with the publicity given to Oscar Wilde and others, with the publication of the *Yellow Book*, above all with the influence on a number of interesting writers of the view of art and life expressed in Walter Pater's *Studies in the History of the Renaissance*. But that famous book was first published in 1873 ; Pater was himself influenced by some of the views of Arnold and some of the philosophy of Ruskin and the Pre-Raphaelites ; and Oscar Wilde, whose *Poems* were published in 1881, began his artistic career as one of the undergraduates who crowded Ruskin's lectures at Oxford and attempted road-making under his direction.

The term "aesthetic", too, is apt to be a cause of confusion. The dictionary definition of an aesthete, "a professed appreciator of the beautiful", does not get us very far ; and it has been said, with a certain degree of truth, that Pater, usually considered an aesthete as opposed to a moralist, was himself a moralist. It is best, perhaps, in the short space at our disposal, first of all to stress the influence of Ruskin and Arnold on what came to be known as "the aesthetic movement", and then to emphasise that, as time went on, the disciples of Ruskin—Arnold's influence was vaguer—tended to give less and less attention to ethics, to accent the emotional element at the expense of the intellectual, and to rest finally in an achievement bearing more relation to the religiose work of Rossetti than to *Unto this Last* or *Literature and Dogma*. Ruskin's fundamental doctrine, that good morality is the foundation of good art, was superseded by the ideal of the new school—"art for art's sake."

Walter Pater (1839-94) became a fellow of Brasenose College, Oxford, and led a retired life which has been described as that of an artistic Benedictine, with literary labour as a kind of rite. His prose was composed with scrupulous care ; it is exquisite, elaborate, languid, and—by comparison with Arnold's—feminine. The conclusion of his *Renaissance* is that, to beings like men, the love of art, for art's sake, is the highest form of wisdom :

> Not the fruit of experience but experience itself, is
> the end. A counted number of pulses only is given to

us of variegated, dramatic life. How may we see in them all that is to be seen in them by the finest senses ? How shall we pass most swiftly from point to point, and be present always at the focus where the greatest number of vital forces unite in their purest energy ?

To burn always with this hard, gemlike flame, to maintain this ecstasy, is success in life . . . While all melts under our feet, we may well grasp at any exquisite passion, or any contribution to knowledge that seems by a lifted horizon to set the spirit free for a moment, or any stirring of the senses, strange dyes, strange colours, and curious odours, or work of the artist's hands, or the face of one's friend. . .

Of this wisdom, the poetic passion, the desire of beauty, the love of art for art's sake has most ; for art comes to you professing frankly to give nothing but the highest quality to your moments as they pass, and simply for those moments' sake.

Pater's work was not confined to criticism of literature and art. The most influential part of it took the form of fiction. *Marius the Epicurean* (1885) was an imaginative reconstruction of the intellectual and spiritual life of the second century, a period which Pater saw as having a relation, in its artistic and religious conflicts, to his own age. The weakness of the case presented, as A. C. Benson pointed out, is that Marius is converted or half-converted to Christianity, not by its truth or its philosophy or its power of sympathy, but by its sensuous appeal, its liturgical solemnities. And this has a connection, not only with the religiosity of some of the Pre-Raphaelites, but with the conversions to Rome of a good many of the aesthetes of the 'nineties.

Pater's later works include *Imaginary Portraits* (1887), *Plato and Platonism* (1893), and the unfinished *Gaston de Latour*, an imaginative picture of the Renaissance in France. A writer with a similar elaborate style, and with similar interests, was John Addington Symonds (1840-93) whose principal work was *The Renaissance in Italy* (1875-86). The early writings of "Vernon Lee" (Violet Paget) are also Paterian : for instance, *Studies of the Eighteenth Century in Italy* (1880) and *Belcaro*, *being Essays on Sundry Aesthetical Questions* (1881). In his Peacockian satire, *The New Republic* (1877), W. H. Mallock presented, under thin disguises, such figures as Pater, Arnold, Ruskin, and Jowett, and set them discussing the problems of art and life.

Travellers, Essayists, etc.

The general prose literature of the middle and late Victorian age is so voluminous, as we have observed, that any adequate account of it would fill many pages. Some of it, including the non-fiction work of the novelists Butler, Jefferies, and Stevenson, will come into subsequent chapters; here we can note, in conclusion, a few examples of the prose written during the period in various fields of thought and action.

Books of travel were very popular. African exploration produced such celebrated accounts as Livingstone's *Missionary Travels in South Africa* (1857), Burton's *Lake Region of Central Africa* (1860), Speke's *Discovery of the Source of the Nile* (1863), and Henry Stanley's *How I found Livingstone* (1872). Burton also wrote books on his Eastern travels and translated the *Arabian Nights* (1885-8). C. M. Doughty concealed his Arabian experiences in the antique prose of *Travels in Arabia Deserta* (1888). South American exploration produced Henry Bates's *Naturalist on the River Amazons* (1863), and *Travels on the Amazon and Rio Negro* (1869) by Darwin's fellow scientist A. R. Wallace. Darwin himself had published before 1859 his *Journal* of his voyage in the "Beagle." Classics of Alpine mountaineering were written by such noted climbers as Leslie Stephen and Edward Whymper.

Scientific and philosophical works, other than those which have a direct bearing on the general problems of the Victorian age, hardly fall within our scope. It is sufficient to observe in passing how many of the great nineteenth-century scientists—including such men as Whewell, Dalton, Davy, Faraday, Miller, George Green, Tyndall—came from humble or comparatively humble stock; how interest in science was fostered by Brougham, Charles Knight, the brothers Chambers, and their successors ; and how popular were the lectures on physics given at the Royal Institution by Davy, Faraday, and Tyndall, and at Working Men's Institutes by the naturalist Frank Buckland, the archaeologist Pengelly, and other experts in various fields. With Glasgow University is associated the name of the eminent physicist Lord Kelvin, and with Cambridge in its great liberal days the names of the scientist Clerk-Maxwell, the economists Fawcett and Marshall, the philosophers Henry Sidgwick and F. W. H. Myers, and the historian Maitland. Both Sidgwick and Myers were friends of George Eliot, and both became interested in psychical research.

The most ambitious biography of the mid-Victorian age was David Masson's *Life of Milton, narrated in connection with the Political, Ecclesiastical, and Literary History of his Time* (1859-80). The later Victorian age was more the period of brief monographs, combining criticism with biography, such as the books on Hogarth, Goldsmith, etc., by Austin Dobson, and the admirable *English Men of Letters* series.* Probably more enduring than the general critical and biographical writing of the age—which included distinguished work on various levels by Edward Dowden, Stopford Brooke, Charles Whibley, Henry Morley, J. W. Mackail—was the work done in literary scholarship, particularly on Chaucer by W. W. Skeat, on the Elizabethan dramatists by A. H. Bullen, on medieval literature by W. P. Ker, and on the

---

* The original series included contributions by the editor Morley on Burke, Trollope on Thackeray, Dean Church on Bacon, J. A. Froude on Bunyan, Huxley on Hume, Leslie Stephen on Johnson, Hutton on Scott, Myers on Wordsworth, Mrs Oliphant on Sheridan, Pattison on Milton, A. W. Ward on Chaucer, Henry James on Hawthorne, W. J. Courthope on Addison, Saintsbury on Dryden, Goldwin Smith on Cowper, Sir Richard Jebb on Bentley, H. D. Traill on Coleridge, J. C. Morison on Gibbon, Sidney Colvin on Keats, Edmund Gosse on Gray, Canon Ainger on Lamb, and J. A. Symonds on Shelley. George Eliot was invited to contribute the volume on Shakespeare, but, unfortunately, declined. Shakespeare was eventually entrusted to Professor Raleigh for the second series, which also included contributions by Augustine Birrell, Frederic Harrison, G. K. Chesterton, A. C. Benson, Emily Lawless, Canon Beeching, and Clement Shorter.

language and dialects by two self-taught scholars, Joseph Wright and Henry Bradley.

Of the many essayists of the period can be mentioned Augustine Birrell, a Liberal politician who found relaxation in writing such things as *Obiter Dicta* (1884); Havelock Ellis, a literary critic and essayist who is more widely known for his work on psychology; and Andrew Lang, the most varied miscellaneous writer of his time, who published essays, criticism, anthropology, verse, history, children's books, and translations from the Greek. His *Myth, Ritual and Religion* (1887) involved him in controversy with his fellow Scot and anthropologist J. G. Frazer.

CHAPTER X

LATE VICTORIAN NOVELISTS

1866-1897

"No themes are so human as those that reflect for
us, out of the confusion of life, the close connection of
bliss and bale, of the things that help with the things
that hurt, so dangling before us for ever that bright
hard metal, of so strange an alloy, one face of which is
somebody's right and ease and the other somebody's
pain and wrong."

HENRY JAMES : Preface to *What Maisie Knew*.

George Eliot's Later Novels

We have observed, at the close of Chapter VI, the long
gap between the publication of *Felix Holt* (1866) and the
novel which is commonly regarded as George Eliot's masterpiece : *Middlemarch, A Study of Provincial Life*, which came
out during 1871-2. We have noticed also the unanimity of
opinion, among critics and fellow-novelists of widely varying
general beliefs, that this work is probably "the finest novel
of the Victorian age." It is true that, between its first overwhelming success (the author noted in her Journal: "No
former book of mine has been received with more enthusiasm
—not even *Adam Bede*") and its high praise by twentieth-
century judgment, there was a period of about thirty years
when the novel was relegated, along with *Romola* and *Felix
Holt* and *Daniel Deronda*, to the second category, the promi-
nence being given to the early work. But now its superiority
is so widely recognised as to be almost a "fact" in literary
history, not simply an opinion in literary criticism.

Middlemarch is first of all remarkable for its range : every
side of "provincial life" is indeed "studied." But the study
would be barren were it not for that Dickensian sympathy and
understanding which are so miraculously combined here with a
psychological penetration that recalls the French and Russian
masters. Whether we consider the contrast between the

two Miss Brookes (owing perhaps something to Jane Austen),
the subtler contrast between the egoism of Dorothea Brooke
and that of Rosamund Vincy, the apparently different yet
related pathos of the scholarly cleric Mr Casaubon and the
Evangelical banker Mr Bulstrode—and we have counted only
a few main heads among the people and the subjects that fill
this novel—we are struck by the association of impersonal
artistic power and radical humour with the kind of inner sympathy that prevents any response of easy superiority to the
characters on the part of the reader.

Casaubon, for instance, is, from one point of view, a comic
figure ; in the hands of Fielding (to whom George Eliot pays
a tribute at the beginning of Chapter XV) he would have been
almost entirely a person for our tolerant amusement ; but,
though George Eliot extracts the utmost humour from his
scholarly predicament ("Mr Casaubon was nervously conscious that he was expected to manifest a powerful mind")
and though from the very start we are made conscious of his
comparative inhumanity ("Everything I see in him," says
Dorothea with approval, "corresponds to his pamphlet on
Biblical Cosmology"), the irony of the contrast between his
pretensions and his performance is no simple matter, treated
from the outside. For George Eliot knows that, however
comic any of us may seem to the world, inside it is apt to look
different ; the reader is not permitted to feel even the mixture
of pity and contempt for Casaubon that is felt by the kindly
but rather conceited young doctor Lydgate, for George Eliot
implies that this kindly patronage is itself partly the product
of inexperience : "Lydgate was at present too ill acquainted
with disaster to enter into the pathos of a lot where everything is below the level of tragedy except the passionate egoism
of the sufferer."

Casaubon is, on the surface, a comic figure : the banker
Bulstrode is, on the surface, an unpleasant figure. It is one
of the most astonishing achievements of *Middlemarch*—again
reminding us of some of the work of the contemporary Russian
novelists, particularly Shchedrin's *Golovlyov Family*—that
George Eliot can so get inside even Bulstrode that we feel

at the close a kind of respect for him. This power of inner penetration we have compared with that of Dickens; but it goes deeper in *Middlemarch* than the usual Dickensian; it is what can only be called, in English, "Shakespearean" insight. It is the kind of power that George Eliot herself was referring to, when she wrote in one of her letters: "Artistic power seems to me to resemble dramatic power—to be an intimate perception of the varied states of which the human mind is susceptible, with ability to give them out anew in intensified expression."

Middlemarch was followed by her last novel, *Daniel Deronda* (1876). There is no tale of first success, then neglect, to be recorded of this, for the simple reason that it has never been really popular. It sold well on first publication, and there was much speculation and interest in the Jewish theme; but there was "some hostile as well as adverse reviewing", the author noted, and parts of it were thought to be so obscure that Samuel Butler, for instance, spoke of buying the latest dictionary "in order to read *Daniel Deronda* in the original." Henry Sidgwick thought it "a bold thing" to write another book after *Middlemarch*, and in general the public seems to have thought so highly of the former novel as hardly to be fair to this.

Henry James, 1843-1916

It is permissible to consider briefly here—because of his connection with George Eliot in interests—the Anglo-American novelist Henry James, before going on to the other Victorian novelists, some of them a good deal older than James, whose work followed George Eliot's in time.

He was born in New York, travelled widely in Europe as a young man, settling finally in England. Part of his work belongs to the Edwardian age, but not the part of it of which it could be truthfully said: "New readers begin here." It is not the extension into the Edwardian age that compels a brief survey: it is the extent of the work itself, the difficulty of much of it, and the sheer impossibility of covering it at all adequately in less than a chapter. James is one of the most

prolific authors in the history of great literature ; his devotion
to his calling was almost superhuman ; he wrote some slight
things, and some others which can only be called heavy, but
of his full-length novels, his scores of short stories, his dozens
of *nouvelles**—to say nothing of his critical works, his various
volumes of reminiscences, he even attempted drama but without success—there is very little indeed that can be described in
lower terms than deeply interesting. His very first volume, *A
Passionate Pilgrim* (1875), contains some good stories ; while
his first novel, *Roderick Hudson* (1876), is one of the best.

He is not, however, a "classic" in quite the same meaning
as when we say Shakespeare, Coleridge, Dickens, are "classics." As we observed with regard to Coleridge, the classic
virtue of the *Ancient Mariner*, like that of *Hamlet* or the
Pilgrim's Progress or *Gulliver's Travels*, is that it can and does
appeal to all levels of intelligence and all ages, from youth
up. The same virtue is obviously true of the novels of
Dickens, or most of them. It is not true of Henry James,
except perhaps with an occasional *nouvelle*, such as the
famous mystery story *The Turn of the Screw* (1898); the
majority of James's work is very difficult reading, though in
most cases well worth the effort of comprehension. Some of
his very latest work—*The Wings of the Dove* (1902), *The
Ambassadors* (1903), *The Golden Bowl* (1904)—almost justi-
fies the phrase of H. G. Wells, when he spoke of James's
style as like a hippopotamus trying to pick up a pea.

Roderick Hudson (1876), *The American* (1877), *The
Europeans* (1878), and *The Portrait of a Lady* (1881), are

---

* The French term *nouvelle* is used in preference to the English
"novelette", to denote a short novel or a long short-story, because
a common meaning of the English word is the kind of cheap fiction
whose "Gothic" origins we mentioned at the beginning of Chapter II.
In the collected New York Edition of 1909, James sometimes printed
nouvelles and short stories. together in one volume, according to
theme ; for instance, in *The Lesson of the Master*, where the stories
all concern the problems of the literary artist in an increasingly commercial environment. Three of these stories originally appeared in
the *Yellow Book*, the organ of the Aesthetic Movement in the 'nineties. But James was hardly a typical aesthete ; indeed, he wrote
to his brother, the distinguished philosopher William James, that
he hated "the horrid aspect and company of the whole publication."

concerned chiefly with the clash between American culture and European; *Washington Square* (1880) and *The Bostonians* (1886) are concerned with America exclusively, the former about New York, the latter about the contrasting cultures of the old New England and the up-and-coming American vulgarity. Possibly the best of the "middle period" is that remarkable story of innocence amid corruption, *What Maisie Knew* (1897). It is a theme that would have attracted George Eliot, as can be seen from the sentence in James's preface that we have quoted as epigraph to this chapter.

Meredith, 1828-1909

George Meredith's best work lies a little after George Eliot's, though it is curious to observe the fact that she reviewed his first fantasy *The Shaving of Shagpat* on the last day of 1855, before attempting her own first fiction during September 1856. His poetry, which will be discussed in the next chapter, had begun as early as 1851, with the publication of *Poems*, a collection that received little notice.

Like George Eliot, Meredith was partly Welsh by descent; he was educated in Germany, and after a short period in the law entered journalism. In 1849 he married the widowed daughter of Thomas Love Peacock. His first realistic psychological novel, *The Ordeal of Richard Feverel* (1859), was followed, among others, by *Evan Harrington* (1860), *Rhoda Fleming* (1865), *The Adventures of Harry Richmond* (1871), *The Egoist* (1879), and *Diana of the Crossways* (1885). Later fiction includes *Lord Ormont and his Aminta* (1894) and *The Amazing Marriage* (1895). Like Hardy, whose last novel also came out in the 'nineties, he devoted his remaining years to verse.

His novels, in general, have not worn so well as either Hardy's or George Eliot's. He lacks the popular appeal of these writers, and, on the other hand, only a few of his works can compare with those of James in more consciously intellectual interest. Probably he was too consciously intellectual, in one sense; his brilliance now appears a little laboured,

like that of Browning, with whom he has often been compared.* "He is in every sense an eccentric," writes a judicious admirer. "The society he depicts is almost feudal in its
caste feeling ; the attitude to the wonderfully attractive women
depicted is almost mediaeval. Only occasionally, when historical events are involved, is it possible to infer a date or
period in the action of his novels. The process of intellectuali-
zation in art, which at times injured the work of Browning, is
in Meredith so fully developed as to become a mere vanity
of display."

The Egoist : A Comedy in Narrative is generally regarded
as his masterpiece. This is a deeply impressive, as well as a
brilliant, novel. The development of the various reactions
to the egoist Sir Willoughby is worthy of Jane Austen, and
the minor characters, particularly the Peacockian cleric Dr
Middleton, are shrewdly observed, their different manners of
conversation being superbly caught. In its brilliant use of
dialogue, The Egoist can rival George Eliot's Deronda or
Henry James's Awkward Age.

Perhaps one weakness of the book is the rather unsatisfactory notion of Comedy which Meredith presents in the
Prelude, and develops in an occasional page of pretentious
writing throughout :—"Comedy is a game played to throw
reflections upon social life, and it deals with human nature in
the drawing-room of civilized men and women, where we have
no dust of the struggling outer world, no mire, no violent
crashes, to make the correctness of the representation convincing . . . The comic Spirit conceives a definite situation
for a number of characters, and rejects all accessories in the
exclusive pursuit of them and their speech."

This definition covers Restoration comedy, among other
examples, but is not of much use when we are considering the
comedy of Shakespeare or Ben Jonson or Dickens. The best
parts of The Egoist itself seem to be on a deeper level than the
comedy of Congreve. The theory had been developed in
more detail in Meredith's essay On the Idea of Comedy and

* "Meredith is a prose Browning," observed Oscar Wilde
characteristically, "and so is Browning."

the Uses of the Comic Spirit (1877)—and it is to this essay that the reader can be referred, for agreement or disagreement.

Hardy, 1840-1928

The work of Thomas Hardy falls neatly into two parts : the whole of his fiction belongs to the nineteenth century, the majority of his verse—to be briefly considered in the following chapter—was not published till the twentieth.

He was born near Dorchester in rather poor circumstances, and received the beginnings of his education in local schools. Afterwards, in London, he studied in the evenings at King's College, and from 1856 to 1861 was the pupil of an architect. In 1863 he gained the prize of the Royal Institute of British Architects ; he did not abandon his profession for literature till 1867.

His first publication was an article in *Chambers's Journal* (1865) entitled "How I built myself a House." He was writing poetry in the 'sixties, but published no collection till 1898. His first novel, *Desperate Remedies* (1871), was followed by *Under the Greenwood Tree* (1872), before he won success with *Far from the Madding Crowd* (1874). Later came, among others, *The Return of the Native* (1878), *The Trumpet-Major* (1880), *The Mayor of Casterbridge* (1886), and *The Woodlanders* (1887). *Tess of the D'Urbervilles* (1891), with its sub-title, "A Pure Woman", outraged a vocal body of public opinion by its portraying as a heroine a woman who had been seduced ; and when *Jude the Obscure* (1896) was hailed as sordid, immoral, and irreligious, Hardy determined to give up fiction for poetry, publishing only one more novel, *The Well-Beloved* (1897).

Of this considerable output in fiction between 1871 and 1897—we have not mentioned the lesser novels or the several collections of short stories—a remarkable number keeps its hold upon the public. Hardy had his most popular period in the Edwardian age, but even now his popularity among Victorian novelists is only exceeded by Dickens and Trollope. Particularly has his popularity been maintained in his native

"Wessex", partly owing, of course, to local, non-literary interest.

There is a general influence of Shakespeare, Scott and Dickens on Hardy, a more detailed influence of the early novels of George Eliot, and, in the case of *The Return of the Native*, of Emily Brontë. Some of his Victorian sentiment no longer appeals to us, and, like Dickens, he was capable of occasional falsity of manner and occasional turgidity of expression. But when these things have been said, much remains. It is impossible for any imaginative person to remain unimpressed by the tragedy of Henchard, the mayor of Casterbridge, or not to feel the almost Shakespearean strength of the best parts of *The Return of the Native*. These two, with the remarkable *Jude the Obscure*, are probably his greatest works ; but there are some fine things in most of the novels, including the comparatively unpopular *Trumpet-Major*, a story of the Wessex villages during the Napoleonic wars.

The intimate personal knowledge of Wessex village and small-town life was, of course, Hardy's principal asset. It can be compared with the intimate Lowland knowledge of his admired Scott, with the brooding tenderness for the Midlands of George Eliot, with the extraordinary sympathy for every aspect of London life and its environs that is so obvious in Dickens. Hardy's "philosophy", as such, is not so important ; it is more impressive as a generally pervading sense of fate, something vague and mysterious that is felt by the imagination on Egdon Heath at dusk or Stonehenge at dawn, than when Hardy brings it into the foreground. The symbolism, too, varies in its value ; sometimes a mechanical device, as Father Time in *Jude*, sometimes as natural and compelling as the symbolism in that more recent Dorsetshire novelist, T. F. Powys.

That Hardy, like Mr Powys, has not been much recognised on the Continent will only seem important to those people in Bloomsbohemia and elsewhere who hold the curious notion that Englishmen need to be told by foreigners the relative status of their native writers.

Jefferies, 1848-87

The Dorsetshireman Hardy is primarily a novelist who is also distinguished in poetry; his Wiltshire contemporary, Richard Jefferies, is primarily a writer on natural history and the countryside, but he also wrote some very interesting novels, so can be considered in this chapter without misrepresentation. In a large-scale history of nineteenth-century literature, there would, of course, be a separate section on the writers of the English farm and country. It would include Cobbett, who has been mainly considered in this book for his general social and cultural importance; the sporting writers like Surtees whom we have mentioned briefly in Chapter VI; Richard Jefferies, in detail; and such writers as W. H. Hudson (1841-1922) and George Sturt (1863-1927), the majority of whose work belongs to the twentieth century in publication, if largely to the nineteenth century in spirit.*

Born near Swindon, the son of a farmer (the original of Mr Iden in *Amaryllis at the Fair*), Jefferies took to local journalism at seventeen. His early stories and novels were a failure, but the publicity afforded in 1872 by his letters to *The Times* on the condition of the Wiltshire labourer, and the subsequent controversy, brought his name to the favourable attention of other papers. He found that the editors of *Fraser's Magazine, Chambers's Journal*, the *Standard*, the *Pall Mall Gazette*, and *Longman's Magazine*, were glad to take his essays on country life; and in 1878 the publication of some of these sketches under the title of *The Game-Keeper at Home* opened the series of collected volumes—*Wild Life in a Southern County*

* Hudson was born in South America and did not come to England till 1869. *The Purple Land that England Lost* (1885), *The Naturalist in La Plata* (1892), *Idle Days in Patagonia* (1893), and *British Birds* (1895), are some of the books belonging to our period. More widely known are such later works as *Green Mansions*, his masterpiece *A Shepherd's Life*, and his autobiography *Far Away and Long Ago*. A writer also connected with South America was the Scots-Spanish traveller and politician R. B. Cunninghame Graham, whose early work included *A Vanished Arcadia* (1901). Sturt came from a family of Surrey wheelwrights, and wrote mostly under the name of "George Bourne." His principal works include *The Bettesworth Book* (1901), *Change in the Village*, and *The Wheelwright's Shop*.

(1879), *The Amateur Poacher* (1879), *Hodge and his Masters* (1880), *Round About a Great Estate* (1880), *Nature Near London* (1883), etc.—by which he is mainly known.

His novels have been comparatively neglected. The stress tends to fall exclusively on his nature books, his spiritual autobiography *The Story of My Heart* (1883), together with his fable *Wood Magic* (1881) and his boys' story *Bevis* (1882). Yet his novels proper, apart from the first three failures, are as interesting as anything he wrote. *Greene Ferne Farm* (1880), *The Dewy Morn* (1884), and *Amaryllis at the Fair* (1887) have robust qualities, akin to the best of the country essays; while *After London, or Wild England* (1885) is a vision of the future that has more in common with Morris's radical tendencies in life than with the comparative day-dreaming of *News from Nowhere*.

It is at once a novel of extraordinary imaginative power and a work of social criticism. The advent of the Atomic Age makes the first part, "The Relapse into Barbarism", curiously "contemporary", for it deals with the aftermath of the destruction of modern (here called "ancient") civilisa-tion; the second part, "Wild England", is the story of Felix Aquila, a young man who is something like the Jefferies of *The Story of My Heart*, and his spiritual loneliness in the midst of a barbaric, semi-feudal society. Though of noble birth, Felix is forced by circumstances to become for a time a groom to a prosperous retainer, and he listens with amaze-ment to the picture of social life painted by his fellows: "Seen thus from below, the whole society appeared rotten and corrupted, coarse to the last degree, and animated only by the lowest motives." These chapters, dealing with Felix's adven-tures in the King's camp and court, have something in com-mon with similar scenes of courtly corruption in *The Near and the Far*, a novel by the twentieth-century writer, L. H. Myers. Both works are concerned with imaginary societies; both have a certain contemporary relevance, to Jefferies's time and our own.

As will be noticed from the dates of his books, Jefferies—as his publishers complained—wrote and published too much.

He found it difficult, even so, to support himself and his family ; and his health broke down in 1882. After his death, five years later, some further sketches were collected in volumes, notably *Field and Hedgerow* (1889) and *The Toilers of the Field* (1892). More have recently been made available. Of the various biographies, probably the best is *Richard Jefferies: His Life and Work* (1909), by the poet and nature writer Edward Thomas.

Butler, 1835-1902

Jefferies may be said to have had his greatest popularity immediately after his early death in 1887 ; Samuel Butler lived half as long again, but had a similar posthumous celebrity when his novel *The Way of All Flesh*, begun as early as 1872, was published in 1903. His *Note-Books* followed in several collections, the first in 1912. For some years, aided by the enthusiasm of Bernard Shaw, who made no secret of his own indebtedness, the reputation of Butler soared. It has now perhaps suffered too much from the inevitable reaction—as Jefferies's did in the 'twenties—but it is at least agreed by most critics and readers that *The Way of All Flesh* is not the supreme masterpiece of the late Victorian age, as it was once thought in the natural enthusiasm that followed its "debunking" of conventional attitudes, but rather a very useful book for its particular purpose, one of the most amusing of English novels, and a permanent classic of what may be conveniently termed "the second class."

Both the son and the grandson of clergymen—his grandfather was the Bishop of Lichfield—Butler, like his character Ernest Pontifex, was intended originally for the Church. There is not much doubt that the early life of Ernest, as recorded in *The Way of All Flesh*, was substantially the same as Butler's own ; but Butler was not so earnest as his *alter ego*, and the various scrapes of the unfortunate Pontifex Minimus, after leaving the Cambridge of the Evangelical revival, are not paralleled in the novelist's own history. Instead, Butler, after a period as sheep-farmer in New Zealand from 1859 to 1864, settled for the remainder of his life in bachelor chambers in Clifford's Inn, London, and became, in fact, the living spit and image of the burlesque-writer Mr Overton, who narrates the story of the Pontifex family. So we have, virtually, the mature Butler, in the guise of the "friend of the family", casting a satirical eye upon his own father and mother and early life, in the guise of the Pontifexes. This has been called a success "won at the cost of heavy assaults on the fifth commandment"; but it is clear that most novelists combine fact with fiction in their characters, and even Dickens, regarded with much truth as the stoutest champion of the Victorian family, satirised his parents, admittedly far more pleasantly, in the persons of Mr Micawber, John Dorrit, and Mrs Nickleby. More important to observe is the fact, felt by most readers, of the unsatisfactory nature of the last part of Butler's novel, compared with the superb opening and middle chapters. The later Ernest is a shadowy figure, hard to believe in, for the simple reason that the original of the boy Ernest had, in fact, changed into the original of the man Overton.

Butler's other works are fairly numerous. They include the famous *Erewhon* (1872), a satire which is only bettered in its field in English literature by *Gulliver's Travels*; the inferior sequel, *Erewhon Revisited* (1901); *The Fair Haven* (1873), a book which was at first taken at its face value, as a defence of Christianity, by some religious papers*; and several works

---

* Summing up its extremely varied reception in the preface to the second edition, Butler remarks that "My previous work, *Erewhon*, had failed to give satisfaction to certain ultra-orthodox Christians, who imagined that they could detect an analogy between the English Church and the Erewhonian Musical Banks. It is inconceivable how they can have got hold of this idea; but I was given to understand that I should find it far from easy to dispossess them of the notion that something in the way of satire had been intended . . . In spite of all my precautions, the same misfortune which overtook *Erewhon* has also come upon *The Fair Haven*. It has been suspected of a satirical purpose. The author of a pamphlet entitled *Jesus versus Christianity* says: '*The Fair Haven* is an ironical defence of orthodoxy at the expense of the whole mass of Church tenet and dogma, the character of Christ only excepted. Such at least is our reading of it, though critics of the *Rock* and *Record* order have accepted the book as a serious defence of Christianity, and proclaimed it as a most valuable contribution in aid of the faith. . .'"

of scientific controversy, mostly attacking the Darwinian theory, of which the best known are *Life and Habit* (1877), *Evolution Old and New* (1879), and *The Deadlock in Darwinism* (1890). He also wrote a travel book on the Alps, and some curious excursions into the authorship of the *Odyssey* and the origin of Shakespeare's sonnets.

For a man of such varied talents—besides his literature and science, he was also a musician and had paintings exhibited at the Royal Academy—his performance appears a little disappointing. No doubt this was due partly to the fact that he was out of sympathy with both the conventional religion and the conventional science of his time ; he had no assured public, so his natural protestant disposition led him in later years to something not far removed from eccentricity. His reaction to certain aspects of the Victorian age was as valuable as it was sincere, but unfortunately his satire was directed against nearly everything that seemed to him to be merely conventionally respected—including the plays of Shakespeare and the novels of Dickens. His love for Handel caused him to disparage other composers, as his contempt for the Pecksniffian and Podsnapian characteristics of Victorian family life caused him to belittle the institution of the family altogether. He is the chief Victorian satirist, but some of the writers he considered too highly esteemed—such as Shakespeare, Dickens, George Eliot—are greater than he, partly because they were too intelligent, in the highest sense, to remain content with the satirical.

Gissing, 1857-1903

There is a fiction concerning the life of George Gissing that is, unfortunately, far better known than his own novels. That he himself was largely responsible for it—according to his biographers—is perhaps poetic justice. He had several misfortunes in early life, but he appears to have continued to describe himself as a starving and unrecognised martyr of letters after his sending a copy of his first novel, *Workers of the Dawn* (1880), to Frederic Harrison had resulted in a successful recommendation to Lord Morley, editor of the *Pall Mall Gazette*, who also engaged Gissing as classical tutor to his sons. He refused to write more than a sketch or two for the *Pall Mall*, on the grounds that journalism was degrading work for a literary artist, and continued to live in comparative poverty because, as his friend H. G. Wells put it, "he grudged every moment taken by teaching from his literary purpose, and so taught as little as he could."

Ideally speaking, of course, Gissing was quite right; it is better for a novelist to devote the majority of his time to his novels, even if this means living in poverty, than for him to waste his genius on either journalism or teaching. But, considering the great number of previous distinguished novelists—Defoe, Fielding, Dickens, Thackeray, George Eliot, etc.—who had spent a considerable portion of their working lives in journalism of one sort or another, and considering the great number of writers who had combined professions of different sorts with distinguished achievement in literature—Shakespeare was an actor, Milton a civil servant, Blake an engraver, Arnold an Inspector of Schools—Gissing's claim to exceptional status cannot altogether be justified. Since Austin Harrison says that the novelist's account in later life of his "continued struggles with abject poverty" was "fiction", we are forced to conclude that Gissing needed that belief to support his self-esteem and that he was aware, like his character Reardon in *New Grub Street* (1892), that what he had written was mostly unworthy of his abilities.

This novel is perhaps his best—a convincing picture of the literary world in the late Victorian age. What makes it so remarkable is that the chief character, Edwin Reardon, with precisely Gissing's own attitude to literature, is presented as dispassionately as the journalistic social climber Jasper Milvain or the old-style heavy reviewer Alfred Yule. Gissing was particularly good in ironical treatment of women; his portrait of Amy in *New Grub Street*—"she smiled with a delicious shade of irony; her glance intimated that nothing could be too subtle for her understanding"—can be compared with the devastating portraits in *Isabel Clarendon* (1886) and with the portrait of Mrs Rossall in *A Life's Morning* (1888) :

> This lady had just completed her thirty-second year ; her girls were in their tenth. She was comely and knew it, but a constitutional indolence had preserved her from becoming a woman of fashion, and had nurtured in her a reflective mood, which, if it led to no marked originality of thought, at all events contributed to an appearance of culture. At the time of her husband's death, she was at the point where graceful inactivity so often degenerates into slovenliness . . . Her mourning was unaffected ; it led her to pietism ; she spent her days in religious observance, and her nights in the study of the gravest literature. She would have entered the Roman Church but for her brother's interposition. The end of this third year of discipline was bringing about another change, perhaps less obvious to herself than to those who marked her course with interest, as several people did. Her reading became less ascetic, she passed to George Herbert and the *Christian Year*, and by way of the decoration of altars proceeded to thought for her personal adornment.

In these matters Gissing owed something to Jane Austen and *Middlemarch*, and may have influenced, in his turn, some of the work of Somerset Maugham and L. H. Myers.*

His other novels include *The Unclassed* (1884), *Demos* (1886), *Thyrza* (1887), *The Emancipated* (1889), and *Born in Exile* (1891). They are mostly concerned with the sufferings of sensitive individuals in squalid surroundings. It has been said that the reason for the tragedy of such characters as Reardon in *New Grub Street* and Gordon Peak in *Born in Exile*, and thus for the partial tragedy of Gissing himself, was their choosing to abide by the standards of Dr Johnson in an age when Lord Northcliffe was just round the corner. The argument has a certain weight, but against it must be recorded

* Mr Maugham (born 1874) comes into nineteenth-century literature by virtue of his early success, *Liza of Lambeth* (1897). The picture of literary society in his *Cakes and Ale* (1930) can be profitably compared with *New Grub Street*. L. H. Myers, the son of George Eliot's Cambridge friend, was possibly influenced by the Gissing treatment of conventional women in his first novel *The Orissers* (1923).

the fact that Dr Johnson, for the first half of his career, turned his hand to whatever in the journalistic line he could possibly make an honest penny by, and that Gissing himself refused even to indulge in the higher journalism represented by such admirable papers as the *Pall Mall Gazette*. The literary standard of some of the late Victorian journals was at least as high as that of the *Gentleman's Magazine*, for which Dr Johnson wrote.

Gissing's volume of reminiscences, *The Private Papers of Henry Ryecroft* (1903), had a posthumous success; it led to a kind of fictionised biography by Morley Roberts entitled *The Private Papers of Henry Maitland* (1912). *Charles Dickens: A Critical Study* (1898) is probably the best short book on its subject. It is certainly an indication of Gissing's complete sincerity about literary art, however much this was combined in his life with less admirable qualities, that so great an admirer of Dickens should have been, in his attitude to journalism and popular fame, so very un-Dickensian. Gissing was also a shrewd observer of the contemporary social and political scene; his comment on the Boer War, to take but one example from his letters—"This reckless breaking with the fine English tradition is a sad proof of what evil can be wrought by inculcating the spirit of vulgar pride and savage defiance"—shows how well he could have fitted in, had he so chosen, with the true Victorian higher journalism that was almost completely shattered by the Northcliffe Revolution.

Stevenson and George Douglas

Like his fellow North Briton, Andrew Lang, Robert Louis Stevenson (1850-94) was a miscellaneous writer who attempted, mostly with success, a wide variety of literature. He is known to everyone by his fine boys' book *Treasure Island* (1883) and its successors, *Kidnapped* (1886) and *Catriona* (1893). He owed much to Scott in these books, as also in *The Black Arrow* (1888) and *The Master of Ballantrae* (1889). His originality is seen more in the fantastic tales of *The New Arabian Nights* (1882), in the famous mystery story *The*

Strange Case of Dr Jekyll and Mr Hyde (1886), in the farcical *The Wrong Box* (1889), and, above all, in the unfinished novel, *Weir of Hermiston* (1896), considered by many critics his finest achievement.

His personal history is well known ; almost as accurately as Pope he could have referred to "that long disease, my life." In search of health, he went first to Switzerland, then to the Pacific coast of America, finally to Samoa in the South Seas. His last years produced some of his best work : apart from *Weir of Hermiston* and some island sketches, he wrote, in collaboration with his step-son Lloyd Osbourne, two realistic novels of South Sea life, *The Wrecker* and *Ebb-Tide*, besides an unfinished novel, *St Ives*, later completed by Sir Arthur Quiller-Couch. Though the boys' romance *Treasure Island* may well outlast his more adult novels, Stevenson's development seems to have been away from Scott-ish fiction to Scottish realism. Whether the completed *Weir of Hermiston* would have lived up to the promise of the first chapters, no one can say with assurance ; he was working on it when he finally succumbed to the disease that had cut short the career of Keats and the Brontës.

His non-fiction work includes the books of travel, *An Inland Voyage* (1878) and *Travels with a Donkey in the Cevennes* (1879); *A Child's Garden of Verses* (1885); and numerous essays, collected in such volumes as *Virginibus Puerisque* (1881), *Familiar Studies of Men and Books* (1882), and *Memories and Portraits* (1887). His celebrated "exquisite style", like that of his admired Meredith, was sometimes something of a pose; and the essays do not appeal to all twentieth-century tastes. There is an interesting contrast between the plain style of Butler, which recalls Swift and Cobbett, and the rather precious style of Meredith and Stevenson ; there is not much doubt which is the traditional English style, though some of the "precious" effects have a certain value of their own, as future generations will probably find amusement in the clever fantasies of *The New Arabian Nights* and their Chestertonian successors.

George Douglas Brown (1869-1902), who wrote under the name of George Douglas, is chiefly famous for *The House with the Green Shutters* (1901), a masterpiece of Scottish fiction. It can be considered as bearing a similar relation to Hogg's *Justified Sinner* as Stevenson's romances to Scott's, and some modern Scots critics have deemed it superior to anything Stevenson wrote and to most of the *Waverley Novels*. An English reader will be likely to notice the general similarity between the tragedy of Gourlay in Douglas's novel and the tragedy of Henchard in *The Mayor of Casterbridge*; Douglas owes little or nothing to Hardy, but is able to achieve much the same sense of inevitable destiny.

Rutherford and Macdonald

Mark Rutherford, whose real name was William Hale White (1829-1913), was educated for the Congregationalist ministry, but abandoned his vocation on grounds of conscience, becoming for a time an agent for the agnostic publishing firm of Chapman, with which George Eliot was associated. His spiritual struggle is described in *The Autobiography of Mark Rutherford* (1881) and *Mark Rutherford's Deliverance* (1885). *The Revolution in Tanner's Lane* (1887) is his finest novel, dealing with the troubled times of the Regency with a deliberate moderation as admirable as that of the early Radicals depicted. *Miriam's Schooling, Catherine Furze, Clara Hopgood*, are interesting variations on a single theme : the isolation of an individual of some culture in the perishing but still active Puritanism of a village in the East Midlands about 1850. Rutherford also wrote an excellent small study of Bunyan, in whose Bedford he was born and some of whose virtues as a writer he possessed.

George Macdonald (1824-1905) had a career, but in Scotland, rather similar to Rutherford's. He, too, took to literature after giving up his Congregational ministry. He is best known by his novels *David Elginbrod* (1863) and *Robert Falconer* (1868), which portray the folk of his native Aberdeenshire, and by his famous fairy-tale *At the Back of the North Wind* (1871).

Other Late Victorian Novelists

The Victorian period as a whole, it is necessary to repeat, was a period of great development in the novel, both in quality and quantity. We have naturally taken, in this chapter and in Chapter VI, only the most important—either in literary importance or literary fame. The "minor" novels of the late Victorian age are very numerous; some of them may well be considered by some readers as more important than those we have treated in more detail.

A feature of the period was the number of exciting novels, not expressly written for boys and girls, but which boys and girls could enjoy at least as much as their elders. These include such famous things as R. D. Blackmore's *Lorna Doone* (1869), Rider Haggard's *King Solomon's Mines* (1885), *Dead Man's Rock* (1887) by "Q" (Arthur Quiller-Couch), Conan Doyle's *White Company* (1891) and his series of Sherlock Holmes adventures, beginning with *A Study in Scarlet* (1888), Stanley Weyman's *Gentleman of France* (1893), and Anthony Hope's *Prisoner of Zenda* (1894). The first novels of H. G. Wells, and some of the early work of Joseph Conrad and Rudyard Kipling, also come into this category. These writers, and others, will be discussed in our final chapter.

The intense popularity that we have remarked of Mrs Henry Wood and Miss Braddon was shared by some of their immediate successors, notably Rhoda Broughton, with *Cometh Up as a Flower* (1867), and "Ouida" (Louise de la Ramée), with *Under Two Flags* (1867); and by later "best-sellers", whose fame extended well into the twentieth century, such as Marie Corelli, author of *The Sorrows of Satan* (1895), and Hall Caine, who was a friend of Rossetti. Two other writers connected in different ways with the Pre-Raphaelite Movement won success as novelists: Maurice Hewlett, with *The Forest Lovers* (1898); and William De Morgan, who, at the close of a busy artistic life, produced the first of a long series of Dickensian novels, *Joseph Vance* (1906), in his sixty-seventh year.

Of the novels and stories in various fields, equally popular in some cases with those just mentioned, but mostly of greater literary worth, can be named, in conclusion, Olive Schreiner's *Story of an African Farm* (1883); the Australian tales of Henry Lawson; Walter Besant's *All Sorts and Conditions of Men* (1882), a novel attacking the social evils of the East End, with which can be compared Israel Zangwill's *Children of the Ghetto* (1892) and Arthur Morrison's *Tales of Mean Streets* (1894); George Du Maurier's *Trilby* (1894); "Q" 's *Astonishing History of Troy Town* (1888) and Eden Phillpotts's *Children of the Mist* (1898), concerning Cornwall and Devonshire respectively; and the deservedly popular humorous achievements of F. Anstey in *Vice Versa* (1882), Jerome K. Jerome in *Three Men in a Boat* (1889), George and Weedon Grossmith in *The Diary of a Nobody* (1892), and William Pett Ridge and W. W. Jacobs in their Cockney classics.

Mrs Humphry Ward, a niece of Matthew Arnold, wrote serious novels on various social problems, notably *Robert Elsmere* (1888), a study of religious doubt. It has been said that her novels contain every virtue save readability. More interesting is J. H. Shorthouse's *John Inglesant* (1880), a story of the spiritual struggles of the seventeenth century, which proved popular with High-Churchmen, has been successfully revived in our time, and is probably one of those minor novels of the period which are superior to some of the work of the great novelists.

CHAPTER XI

LATE VICTORIAN POETRY
1869-1898

> "So also I cut myself off from the use of *ere, o'er,
> wellnigh, what time, say not* (for *do not say*), because,
> though dignified, they neither belong to nor ever could
> arise from, or be the elevation of, ordinary modern
> speech. For it seems to me that the poetical language
> of the age should be the current language heightened,
> to any degree heightened and unlike it, but not (I mean
> normally : passing freaks and graces are another thing)
> an obsolete one."
>
> HOPKINS : Letter to Bridges.

Hopkins, 1844-89

Gerard Manley Hopkins, whom we have mentioned briefly
in Chapters VII and VIII, is considered by some modern
critics the greatest poet of the Victorian age. He is certainly
the greatest poet we shall be discussing in this chapter, for of
his contemporaries who may be considered by some readers
as superior, we have already treated of Swinburne among the
Pre-Raphaelites, Meredith and Hardy are probably greater as
novelists than poets, while Bridges belongs as much to
Edwardian poetry as to Victorian.

It might be objected that Hopkins, by reason of his posthumous publication, belongs to the twentieth century almost
entirely. But the fact remains that he was born in 1844, was
converted to Roman Catholicism in 1866, and from 1868 to
his early death from typhoid was a member of the Jesuit
Order, at first in Ireland, then in Lancashire.* He practised

---

* A somewhat similar instance is provided by the seventeenth-
century poet Thomas Traherne, whose works were not discovered till
about 1896 and not published till 1903. He is one of the best religious
poets of the seventeenth century, and no one would consider him,
because of his publication, as a poet of the Edwardian age ! Hopkins
is, of course, much less *of* his century than Traherne ; but, on the
other hand, we are not paying full tribute to his originality unless
we see him, as he actually was, as a contemporary of Swinburne and
Hardy who died young in the same year as Browning.

verse-writing from an early age, and wrote prize poems while
at school. Then, after his entry into the priesthood, he decided
to give up poetry for a time. What he had already written,
he records,

> I burnt before I became a Jesuit and resolved to
> write no more, as not belonging to my profession, unless
> it were by the wish of my superiors ; so for seven years
> I wrote nothing but two or three little presentation
> pieces which occasion called for. But when in the winter
> of '75 the *Deutschland* was wrecked in the mouth of the
> Thames and five Franciscan nuns, exiles from Germany
> by the Falck Laws, aboard of her were drowned I was
> affected by the account and happening to say so to my
> rector he said that he wished some one would write a
> poem on the subject. On this hint I set to work and
> though my hand was out at first, produced one.

When, however, he offered *The Wreck of the Deutschland* to
the Jesuit magazine, the *Month*, the poem was considered so
odd that (Hopkins records) "they dared not print it."

It is usual for non-Catholic critics to deplore, if not the
priest-poet himself, at any rate his obstinate seven years'
silence ; it is no less usual for Catholic critics to defend both
the sacrifice and the argument that the priest and the poet
were essentially one. The probability is that Hopkins would
have written much more poetry had he not become a priest,
but that he would not have achieved the particular poetry that
makes him so outstanding a figure in Victorian verse. The
poet of *Spring and Fall* would still have existed, and that is
certainly a very great poem :

> Margaret, are you grieving
> Over Goldengrove unleaving ?
> Leaves, like the things of man, you
> With your fresh thoughts care for, can you ?
> Ah ! as the heart grows older
> It will come to such sights colder
> By and by, nor spare a sigh
> Though worlds of wanwood leafmeal lie ;
> And yet you will weep and know why.
> Now no matter, child, the name :
> Sorrow's springs are the same.
> Nor mouth had, no nor mind, expressed

> What heart heard of, ghost guessed :
> It is the blight man was born for,
> It is Margaret you mourn for.

The poet of that, and *Binsey Poplars*, and a few other pieces, would still have existed ; there is no particular connection between the poet and the priest in such poems as these. But we should probably not have had *The Windhover* ("To Christ our Lord"), for example ; nor that astonishing early poem, *The Habit of Perfection*, which may owe something to Blake and Keats, but which plainly owes a great deal to the priest as well (or to the youth who was determined to become a priest):

> Elected Silence, sing to me
> And beat upon my whorlèd ear,
> Pipe me to pastures still and be
> The music that I care to hear.
>
> Shape nothing, lips ; be lovely-dumb :
> It is the shut, the curfew sent
> From there where all surrenders come
> Which only makes you eloquent.
>
> Be shellèd, eyes, with double dark
> And find the uncreated light :
> This ruck and reel which you remark
> Coils, keeps, and teases simple sight.
>
> Palate, the hutch of tasty lust,
> Desire not to be rinsed with wine :
> The can must be so sweet, the crust
> So fresh that come in fasts divine !
>
> Nostrils, your careless breath that spend
> Upon the stir and keep of pride,
> What relish shall the censers send
> Along the sanctuary side !
>
> O feel-of-primrose hands, O feet
> That want the yield of plushy sward,
> But you shall walk the golden street
> And you unhouse and house the Lord.
>
> And, Poverty, be thou the bride
> And now the marriage feast begun,
> And lily-coloured clothes provide
> Your spouse not laboured-at nor spun.

That poem can fairly be said to represent one side, the happier side, of Hopkins's religious dedication. The last "terrible sonnets", with the sonnet *Justus est*, can be taken as representing the inward struggle, the consciousness of sterility. *Justus est* is one of his finest achievements, to be compared with this passage from a letter to his friend Bridges : "If I could but get on, if I could but produce work, I should not mind its being buried, silenced, and going no farther ; but it kills me to be time's eunuch and never to beget":—

> Thou art indeed just, Lord, if I contend
> With thee ; but, sir, so what I plead is just,
> Why do sinners' ways prosper ? and why must
> Disappointment all I endeavour end ?
>   Wert thou my enemy, O thou my friend,
> How wouldst thou worse, I wonder, than thou dost
> Defeat, thwart me ? Oh, the sots and thralls of lust
> Do in spare hours more thrive than I that spend,
> Sir, life upon thy cause. See, banks and brakes
> Now, leavèd how thick ! lacèd they are again
> With fretty chervil, look, and fresh wind shakes
> Them ; birds build—but not I build ; no, but strain,
> Time's eunuch, and not breed one work that wakes.
> Mine, O thou lord of life, send my roots rain.

If *The Habit of Perfection* is remarkable for the sensuous vigour with which it treats the theme of renunciation, *Justus est* is no less remarkable—and no less paradoxical—for the Shakespearean dramatic strength with which Hopkins confesses his sense of weakness. Neither poem could have been written, evidently, without the combination of literary and Christian feeling that is also so obvious in the religious poets of the early seventeenth century. *Justus est* and the "terrible sonnets" can profitably be compared with many of the poems of spiritual conflict to be found in the *Temple* of George Herbert.

Hopkins and Bridges

When Hopkins resumed writing verse, after the *Month* had refused to print *The Wreck of the Deutschland*, he proceeded with his technical experiments*, sending his poems

---

* Where successful, it should be added, these "experiments" were mainly traditional—bringing back that Shakespearean vigour to which Keats was referring, when he wrote "English must be kept up."

for criticism to his friends Robert Bridges and Canon Dixon. They were both poets themselves, and we have indicated briefly in Chapter VIII the interesting nature of Dixon's limited talent ; but, though he gave Hopkins generous praise and the more intimate friend Bridges tried his best to understand the poems sent, it seems that Hopkins was destined, by the sheer originality of his genius in the age he was living in, to pursue a lonely path. It is the correspondence to Bridges, in particular, that reveals this. What Hopkins wanted was correspondence in the other sense, the sort of literary affinity which Wordsworth bore to Coleridge and Coleridge to Wordsworth. What he mostly got was friendly incomprehension which led, on his side, to greater singularity. The two poets of the *Lyrical Ballads* did not mind their contemporary isolation ; for Wordsworth had Coleridge and Coleridge Wordsworth ; a thousand misapprehending friends could not have made up for that happy affinity. A good part of the reason for Hopkins's later dejection can be traced to that poetic isolation which made the asceticism of the Jesuit Order, so happily embraced at first, so much harder to bear.

Bridges was a distinguished man, but he had essentially an academic, not an original, mind. (His relation to Hopkins can be compared with the Regency reviewers' to Wordsworth or the attitude of A. W. Ward, the *Globe* editor, to Pope.) He found most of his friend's poems distasteful, and there are few more interesting things in English literature than the letters of Hopkins to Bridges, some of them including criticisms of Bridges's poems by Hopkins, more including the criticisms of Hopkins upon Bridges's criticism of Hopkins's poems. Occasionally, of course, Bridges was quite right in his objections ; some of Hopkins's rhyming, for example, is as unjustifiable as some of Browning's.*

---

* He was fond of "ear-rhymes", for instance in *The Loss of the Eurydice* :

> But what black Boreas wrecked her? he
> Came equipped, deadly electric. . .

where, incredible as it may seem, "wrecked her he", with the hard "C" of the first word in the next line, makes a rhyme with "electric." An even more audacious instance is to be found in a verse from another poem :

It is difficult to say whether Bridges was to blame for not publishing a collection of his friend's poems till 1918. (A few items he had printed in his war-time anthology, *The Spirit of Man*, two years before.) That he was not unconscious of Hopkins's powerful originality—however much he disagreed with many of its manifestations—can be seen from the introductory sonnet to his dead friend which he printed at the beginning of his collection. It ends with these lines :

> Go forth : amidst our chaffinch flock display
>   Thy plumage of far wonder and heavenward flight !

But, in the prose introduction, he was inclined to stress the "Oddity and Obscurity", whereas Hopkins is surely at his best, like every other poet, when he is being least odd and least obscure. The poems we have quoted (and there are a good many similar) are obviously superior to such a thing as *The Leaden Echo and the Golden Echo*, which opens :

> How to keep—is there any any, is there none such, nowhere
>   known some, bow or brooch or braid or brace, lace,
>   latch or catch or key to keep
> Back beauty, keep it, beauty, beauty, beauty, . . . from
>   vanishing away ?
> O is there no frowning of these wrinkles, rankèd wrinkles
>   deep,
> Down ? no waving off of these most mournful messengers,
>   still messengers, sad and stealing messengers of grey ?

There is a fair amount of such experimenting in Hopkins (like much modern poetry, more interesting typographically than poetically); it spoils to a certain extent even such fine poems as *The Wreck of the Deutschland* and *Spelt from Sibyl's Leaves*. But the final stress should be laid, in Hopkins, on the achievement of such poems as we have quoted,

> A bugler boy from barrack (it is over the hill
> There)—boy bugler, born, he tells me, of Irish
>   Mother to an English sire (he
>   Shares their best gifts surely, fall how things will)

where "sire he" with the "sh" of "shares" in the next line makes a somewhat blarneyish rhyme with "Irish." In the next verse of this poem Hopkins rhymes "boon he on" with "Communion", which out-Brownings Browning, and is not, as so many of Browning's ingenious rhymes are, intended to be read whimsically.

as the final stress, in regard to Bridges's relationship with Hopkins, should be laid, not on the excessive caution which made him wait thirty years before publishing his collection, but on his introductory sonnet, his determination to emphasise his friend's seriousness, and on the fact that he kept for eventual publication, not simply the poems of Hopkins, but the entire correspondence he had received from him. He played a part, in other words, in the production of two of the classics of nineteenth-century literature ; and this was the utmost a friend could do who was not qualified by nature or training to be to Hopkins what Coleridge was to Wordsworth or what Wordsworth to Coleridge.

Bridges's Early Work

Born in the same year as Hopkihs, Robert Bridges long outlived his friend, dying in 1930. He is as much a twentieth-century poet as a nineteenth ; he published his most ambitious poem, *The Testament of Beauty*, in 1929.

He was educated at Eton and Oxford, qualified as a doctor at St Bartholomew's, but abandoned medicine for literature in 1882. His first volume of poems in 1873 was followed by the sonnet-sequence, *The Growth of Love* (1876), and *Eros and Psyche* (1885), a narrative from the famous prose story of Apuleius. It was not until the first four books of *Shorter Poems* appeared in 1890 that Bridges became at all widely known, though even as late as 1913, when he succeeded Alfred Austin as Poet Laureate, he was so unknown to the general public that popular newspapers complained that the title had been given to a man whom nobody had ever heard of. A fifth book was added in 1894, and the whole collection was republished as *Shorter Poems* in 1896. Various others were included in a collected edition that began to appear in 1898. He had also written several pieces in dramatic form, such as *Prometheus the Firegiver* (1883) and *The Feast of Bacchus* (1889).

The preference of the contemporary poetry-reading public for his short lyrics was sound judgment, though when a recent biographer speaks of "poems entirely flawless" he is not so much praising his subject as revealing his own incapacity for critical expression. His last, ambitious poem, *The Testament of Beauty*, which had a certain popular success, has been described by a critical admirer as "the table-talk of a scholar expressed in conventional poetic diction, though in an unconventional metre. In vital poetic value it cannot for a moment be placed on the level of such a poem as *The Prelude*." Similarly, Bridges's dramatic works are unlikely to be read with profit by those who appreciate lyrics like *After the Gale*, a poem in the third volume of 1890 which is sufficiently representative of the poet's attractive talent in this field that its last few verses can be quoted not unfairly in conclusion :

> The snow-white clouds he northward chased
> Break into phalanx, line, and band :
> All one way to the south they haste,
> The south, their pleasant fatherland.

> From distant hills their shadows creep,
> Arrive in turn and mount the lea,
> And flit across the downs, and leap
> Sheer off the cliff upon the sea ;

> And sail and sail far out of sight.
> But still I watch their fleecy trains,
> That piling all the south with light,
> Dapple in France the fertile plains.

The Verse of Meredith

George Meredith had an even longer career as poet than as novelist. He published his first poem, in *Chambers's Journal*, as early as 1849. It was followed, among others, by *Poems* (1851); the series of fifty sixteen-line "sonnets", *Modern Love* (1862); *Poems and Lyrics of the Joy of Earth* (1883); *Ballads and Poems of Tragic Life* (1887); *A Reading of Earth* (1888); *A Reading of Life* (1901); and *Last Poems* (1909).

Modern Love has been compared with some of Browning's work, and in general Meredith has greater affinity with Browning and Landor than with Rossetti, whose house he shared for a time. He is hardly to be called a "Pre-Raphaelite poet", even in the extended meaning we gave to that designation in Chapter VIII. Probably the best-known piece in *Modern Love* is the following :

> Thus piteously Love closed what he begat :
> The union of this ever-diverse pair !
> These two were rapid falcons in a snare,
> Condemned to do the flitting of the bat.
> Lovers beneath the singing sky of May,
> They wandered once ; clear as the dew on flowers :
> But they fed not on the advancing hours :
> Their hearts held cravings for the buried day.
> Then each applied to each that fatal knife,
> Deep questioning, which probes to endless dole.
> Ah, what a dusty answer gets the soul
> When hot for certainties in this our life !—
> In tragic hints here see what evermore,
> Moves dark as yonder midnight ocean's force,
> Thundering like rampant hosts of warrior horse,
> To throw that faint thin line upon the shore !

The most divergent estimates have been made, both of *Modern Love* and of Meredith's verse in general. A recent critic has claimed (like Browning of the *Sonnets from the Portuguese*) that there are single "sonnets" in Meredith's sequence "that vie with any of Shakespeare's." Tennyson was so impressed by the lyric *Love in the Valley* that he declared that, having once read it, he could not get the music out of his head. While *The Times*, in its obituary notice in 1909, estimating his work as a whole, both in fiction and poetry, placed him only a little below Shakespeare in English literature. Against these high estimates, we have the words of a critic in the *Athenaeum*, that "Meredith had the ear of an organ-grinder and the vision of a chorus-fancier", and a more recent criticism that *Modern Love* is "the flashy product of unusual but vulgar cleverness working upon cheap emotion."

The contemporary test is, of course, to what extent Meredith is actually read. Most of his novels have not retained the public interest of Hardy's, nor have they received the respectful attention paid in recent years to those of Henry James ; while his verse, if highly esteemed in some academic quarters, seems to have suffered much the same fate, in contrast to Hopkins, as that of Bridges. Perhaps the truth can be summed up by saying that, to those readers who prefer Hopkins to Bridges and Browning, Meredith appears an interesting but minor poet ; while to those who prefer Browning and Bridges to Hopkins, or who can see little difference between them, Meredith can be compared with Shakespeare without the least sense of absurdity.

We are on less controversial ground when we turn to consider Meredith's un-Tennysonian attitude to the doctrine of Evolution, which he embraced with eagerness. This is apparent particularly in *Poems and Lyrics of the Joy of Earth*, in *A Reading of Earth*, and in *Last Poems*. Meredith had the kind of pantheist religion whose God is Mother Earth ; in these poems he urged that Man must understand the Spirit of the Earth which gave him birth :

> For love we earth, then serve we all,
> Her mystic secret then is ours.
> We fall, or view our treasures fall
> Unclouded, as beholds her flowers.

> Earth, from a night of frosty wreck
> Enrobed in morning's mounted fire
> When lowly, with a broken neck,
> The crocus lays her cheek to mire.

Hardy's Early Poems

Hardy, like Bridges, wrote his most ambitious poem in the twentieth century—the blank-verse epic-drama of the Napoleonic Wars called *The Dynasts* (1904-8). Throughout his long life he was writing those short poems which represent his most popular, and perhaps his most enduring, achievement. Only one volume—*Wessex Poems* (1898)—comes within our period ; it was followed by *Poems of the Past and Present* (1902).

Some of the *Wessex Poems* had been written much earlier than the 'nineties. But dates are not very important, in Hardy's case, for it is difficult to trace any development from his early verse of the 'sixties and 'seventies to the verse of

the 1917 collection ; and his best poems, it is generally agreed,
come indifferently from earlier work and late. His poetry has
obvious affinities with his novels ; personal memory and
experience of the countryside play a large part in the greatest
achievements of both.   One of his finest poems of personal
memory is one of his earliest—*Neutral Tones*, written in 1867,
published in 1898 :

> We stood by a pond that winter day,
> And the sun was white, as though chidden of God,
> And a few leaves lay on the starving sod,
>   —They had fallen from an ash, and were gray.
>
> Your eyes on me were as eyes that rove
> Over tedious riddles solved years ago ;
> And words played between us to and fro—
>   On which lost the more by our love.
>
> The smile on your mouth was the deadest thing
> Alive enough to have strength to die ;
> And a grin of bitterness swept thereby
>   Like an ominous bird a-wing . . .
>
> Since then, keen lessons that love deceives,
> And wrings with wrong, have shaped to me
> Your face, and the God-curst sun, and a tree,
>   And a pond edged with grayish leaves.

That is typical of Hardy in one mood ; such poems have
the beauty which comes from economy of words, a quiet
rhythm, a choice of direct and vigorous phrase, a frequent
irony. A mental process of the kind evoked in the last stanza
quoted is familiar to most people. At an emotional crisis
some part of our material surroundings seems to be strangely
appropriate to our stress of mind, so that for ever after similar
surroundings have the power of recreating the emotion and
giving it a precision which it would otherwise have lacked.

Although such poems as this represent a considerable
achievement in themselves, Hardy's principal strength was
his variety, his ability to turn from the mood of these poems
to the attractive sentiment of, for instance, *The Darkling
Thrush*, and from that to such a combination of shrewdness
and eccentricity as *Friends Beyond*. This poem is too long
to quote entire, but we can catch the spirit of it if we give,

first of all, the opening verses and then some of the middle
dialogue and then the conclusion ; it opens :

> William Dewy, Tranter Reuben, Farmer Ledlow late
> at plough,
> Robert's kin, and John's, and Ned's,
> And the Squire, and Lady Susan, lie in Mellstock
> churchyard now !
>
> "Gone," I call them, gone for good, that group of
> local hearts and heads ;
> Yet at mothy curfew-tide,
> And at midnight when the noon-heat breathes it back
> from walls and leads,
>
> They've a way of whispering to me—fellow-wight who
> yet abide—
> In the muted, measured note
> Of a ripple under archways, or a lone cave's stillicide.

Later comes the finely rendered dialect of the farmer and his
wife :

> "Ye mid zell my favourite heifer, ye mid let the
> charlock grow,
> Foul the grinterns, give up thrift."
> "If ye break my best blue china, children, I shan't
> care or ho."

Then, all speak as follows :

> "We've no wish to hear the tidings, how the people's
> fortunes shift ;
> What your daily doings are ;
> Who are wedded, born, divided ; if your lives beat
> slow or swift.
>
> Curious not the least are we if our intents you make
> or mar,
> If you quire to our old tune,
> If the city stage still passes, if the weirs still roar
> afar."

The poem ends on Hardy's usual philosophical note :

> Thus, with very gods' composure, freed those crosses
> late and soon
> Which, in life, the Trine allow
> (Why, none witteth), and ignoring all that haps
> beneath the moon,

> William Dewy, Tranter Reuben, Farmer Ledlow late
>   at plough,
> Robert's kin, and John's, and Ned's,
> And the Squire, and Lady Susan, murmur mildly to
>   me now.

We have most of the distinguishing traits of Hardy's poetry in this fine poem : the rural scene, of course ; the habit of contemplation ; the frequently strange, sometimes archaic, turns of speech ; and the ironic, faintly pessimistic philosophy to round them off. The result is as attractive, in much the same way, as the novels. It is not surprising that Hardy's work appeals to many readers who have no taste for Meredith's more self-conscious "earthiness" or for the too archaic language of Hardy's old friend and neighbour, William Barnes. The best poetry of Hardy is likely to live as long as that of Burns.

Thomson and Henley

James Thomson (1834-82) is usually distinguished from his eighteenth-century namesake, the poet of *The Seasons* and *Rule, Britannia*, by the initials "B.V.", representing "Bysshe Vanolis", a name under which he wrote. He comes into this chapter, rather than an earlier, because the majority of his verse was published in book form just before his death, in the two volumes *The City of Dreadful Night and Other Poems* (1880) and *Vane's Story and Other Poems* (1881).

He was born in Scotland, the son of a sailor, and became an army schoolmaster. Adopting atheistic and republican views, in company with his friend Charles Bradlaugh, he was relieved of his post in 1862, and afterwards tried various occupations—lawyer's clerk, mining agent, etc.—besides writing for the press. He might have made a comfortable living out of journalism, but both his intemperate habits and his political and religious convictions worked against him, and his later life was darkened by poverty and ill-health. In 1882 he became seriously ill while visiting his friend, the blind poet Philip Marston, and died soon afterwards in University College Hospital.

He began writing verse early in life, and from 1860 his work appeared chiefly in Bradlaugh's *National Reformer*, under the signature "B.V.", some of it attracting the favourable attention of Kingsley and Froude. *The City of Dreadful Night* was published originally in the *Reformer* in 1874, and, when the author's melancholy death eight years later drew fresh notice to him, this poem and a few others in the 1880 and 1881 volumes attained a considerable reputation.

It is difficult to see a great deal of value in them now ; they have been called, indeed, "near-poetry" and "journalism in verse." *The City* has a certain historical importance, as illustrating a reaction to nineteenth-century science that is equally distinct from Tennyson's and Meredith's. Tennyson expressed a Christian perplexity, Meredith a pantheist optimism ; Thomson seems at once atheistic and pessimistic, getting a sort of gloomy relish, however, out of the miseries he describes. There is little of Hardy's wisdom in this long poem, and nothing of the vitality of Hopkins.

In the 'nineties, W. E. Henley (1849-1903) became widely known, both for his patriotic pieces, such as *Pro rege nostro* ("What have I done for you, England, my England ?"), and for the poem first published in *A Book of Verses* (1888) which ends :

> It matters not how strait the gate,
>   How charged with punishments the scroll,
> I am the master of my fate,
>   I am the captain of my soul.

But Henley's verse is not all of this kind. He was a student of French verse, and also of French art, and he has been called "the first French impressionist in English poetry." Probably his most enduring things are his *vers libre* experiments in the set of poems called *In Hospital*, which owes something to the American poet Whitman, and perhaps also to Browning, as well as to the contemporary French poets. He tried other French verse-forms in *Hawthorn and Lavender* and *London Voluntaries*.

He was early crippled by the amputation of one foot, owing to tuberculosis. Like Andrew Lang, he became journalist, reviewer, essayist, editor, as well as poet. His critical opinions were received with respect in the 'seventies and 'eighties, but he survives to-day rather by his experiments in verse, by the memory of a remarkable courage in the midst of illness, and by some interesting plays which he wrote in collaboration with his friend Stevenson. *Admiral Guinea* and *Deacon Brodie* are the best known of the plays, and they are still performed from time to time.

Thompson and Alice Meynell

Associated by some with "the aesthetic school" of the 'nineties, as Henley with the contemporary "Imperialist school", Francis Thompson (1859-1907) is better treated in this chapter than with the *Yellow Book* and the Rhymers' Club. A "born Catholic", not an aesthete converted to Catholicism for *Epicurean* reasons, he wrote both mystical verse and songs in praise of the cricket of his native Lancashire. Settling in London, he suffered from poverty and ill-health for many years, but in the early 'nineties he became known to Wilfred and Alice Meynell, who secured the publication of his poems in 1893. Later works were *Sister Poems* and *New Poems* (1897).

His reputation rests upon a few short poems, notably *In No Strange Land*, and on the long "Pindaric" poem, *The Hound of Heaven*, which formed one of the 1893 collection. He has little connection with his Catholic contemporary Hopkins, in either style or feeling, and the relevance of his poetry to that of the early seventeenth-century religious poets—insisted on by some critics—does not appear very profound. He is perhaps rather to be associated with Coventry Patmore. The opening of *The Hound of Heaven* is a good example of his manner :

> I fled Him, down the nights and down the days ;
> I fled Him, down the arches of the years ;
> I fled Him, down the labyrinthine ways
>   Of my own mind ; and in the mist of tears
> I hid from Him, and under running laughter.
>   Up vistaed hopes I sped ;
>   And shot, precipitated,

Adown Titanic glooms of chasmèd fears,
From those strong Feet that followed, followed after.
But with unhurrying chase,
And unperturbèd pace,
Deliberate speed, majestic instancy,
They beat—and a Voice beat
More instant than the Feet—
"All things betray thee, who betrayest Me."

Alice Meynell (1847-1922) was a friend of Ruskin and Henley; she published her first book of poems, *Preludes*, in 1875, and her essays include *Rhythm of Life* (1893). Two of her most popular poems are *Christ in the Universe* and *The Wind is Blind*.

Housman, 1859-1936

Both Francis Thompson and A. E. Housman had a great influence on the "Georgian poets" of 1912 and after. Housman belongs partly to nineteenth-century poetry because his most famous work, the series of poems called *A Shropshire Lad*, was published in 1896. His two other volumes of verse came out in 1922 and 1936, but some of the poems in these later collections were written at the same time as the *Shropshire Lad*.

He has been compared with his near-contemporary Hardy, and also with the ex-collier poet Joseph Skipsey; but the other comparisons that have been made—with FitzGerald and with Bridges—are probably sounder. The attractive fatalism of the 1896 volume has affinities with *Omar*, and the scholarly public who appreciated the *Shorter Poems* of Bridges admired Housman's pieces also. Few poets since Gray have gained such a reputation on so small a body of work. He wrote most of the poems of the *Shropshire Lad* while working as a clerk in the Patent Office. Later he became professor of Latin at University College, London, and afterwards at Cambridge. His brother Laurence Housman (*b.* 1865) wrote novels and verse, but became best known to the twentieth-century public by his plays.

The opening poem of *A Shropshire Lad* celebrates Queen Victoria's Jubilee, and several others commemorate the British army in Africa and India ; but most treat of the English countryside and the loves and deaths of country-dwellers in much the same spirit as some of Hardy, but not with the intimate experience and originality of expression of the Wessex poet's best work. The attractive nostalgia of Housman's verse can be seen from one of the shorter lyrics of this 1896 volume ; its relation to a good deal of the "Georgian Poetry" of 1912-22 is plain enough :

> Loveliest of trees, the cherry now
> Is hung with bloom along the bough,
> And stands about the woodland ride
> Wearing white for Eastertide.
>
> Now, of my threescore years and ten
> Twenty will not come again ;
> And take from seventy springs a score,
> It only leaves me fifty more.
>
> And since to look at things in bloom
> Fifty springs are little room,
> About the woodlands I will go
> To see the cherry hung with snow.

Other Late Victorian Poets

Some poets who wrote or started writing in the period covered by our chapter—in particular, those belonging to the "Aesthetic School" and the "Celtic Revival"—will be discussed in our consideration of the 'nineties. We can close this chapter by mentioning briefly some of the minor poets who were writing at the same time as Swinburne, Hopkins, and the early Hardy.

It is customary in literary history of any period to find minor poets—poets whom only scholars have read—who were nevertheless widely known in their time. The stock example is Martin Tupper, whose *Proverbial Philosophy* has been mentioned. Philip James Bailey (1816-1909) was a poet of a similar sort. His *Festus*, first published in 1839 and steadily enlarged till the "jubilee" edition of 1889, was a long verse-drama written in imitation of Goethe's *Faust*. What was considered to be its profundity was much admired in its day.

Superior to Tupper and Bailey, but not likely to be read again with the respect of our grandfathers, were two poets of the same name as their greater contemporaries: Sir Edwin Arnold (1832-1904) and Sir Lewis Morris (1833-1907). Arnold was a member of the staff of the *Daily Telegraph*, the paper whose "Corinthian style" was the target of Matthew's irony; he became famous for *The Light of Asia* (1879), a rendering in blank verse of the life and teaching of the Buddha. Morris was a Welsh poet who shared Arnold's fluency; *Songs of Two Worlds* and the ambitious *Epic of Hades* were his most widely-read works.

Sir William Watson (1858-1925) was once a poet so esteemed as to be considered a possible successor to Tennyson as Poet Laureate; he received a knighthood for his literary eminence. The choice for the Laureateship eventually fell on Alfred Austin (1835-1913), who had made his name by a satirical poem, *The Season*, published as early as 1861. Watson, like T. E. Brown, survives in lyric anthologies, while his more ambitious work is forgotten. Austin survives in literary history as the editor of the *National Review* and as the most cynical choice for Laureate since Pye received the crown in 1790.

W. S. Blunt (1840-1922) was a satirical poet who in 1869 married Lady Anne Noel, Byron's granddaughter, with whom he travelled in the East. He became a supporter of Arab aspirations and the Egyptian nationalist movement, tried to enter Parliament as an advocate of Irish Home Rule, and wrote many anti-Imperialist books. Individual in his verse as in his life, he first became known by the *Love Sonnets of Proteus* (1880).

Sir Henry Newbolt (1862-1938) was a poet more in the patriotic tradition of Macaulay and the later Tennyson, and if his *Admirals All* (1897) had come out a few years before, he would perhaps have succeeded the latter as Poet Laureate. From one point of view, he would have been a very good choice, for his public-school, mildly imperialist, intensely patriotic view of life was the kind of thing sought for at the time, and he could write of such matters with almost the ease

and skill of Macaulay. *Drake's Drum* is his most famous
piece, too well known to be quoted here ; it compares well, as
a patriotic poem, with Macaulay's *Armada*, and, when set to
music, many a baritone must have been grateful for it, as
many a tenor for the songs of Moore.

Among the women poets of the period, Mary Coleridge
and Emily Lawless deserve mention. The two ladies Katherine Bradley and Edith Cooper, who wrote together under the
name of "Michael Field", produced many poetic dramas
which are never likely to reach the stage. More successful in this line, but still too "literary", were the plays of
Fiona Macleod (William Sharp) and the popular *Paolo and
Francesca* (1899) by the poet and actor Stephen Phillips.

CHAPTER XII

THE END OF AN ERA

1888-1902

"God of our fathers, known of old,
　　Lord of our far-flung battle-line,
　　Beneath whose awful Hand we hold
　　　Dominion over palm and pine—
　　Lord God of Hosts, be with us yet,
　　Lest we forget—lest we forget !"
　　　　　　　　　　　　KIPLING : *Recessional.*

"I have forgot much, Cynara ! gone with the wind,
　Flung roses, roses riotously with the throng,
　Dancing, to put thy pale, lost lilies out of mind ;
　But I was desolate and sick of an old passion,
　　Yea, all the time, because the dance was long :
　I have been faithful to thee, Cynara ! in my fashion."
　　　DOWSON : *Non sum qualis eram bonae sub regno Cynarae.*

"What we want is not music for the people, but
bread for the people, rest for the people, immunity from
robbery and scorn for the people, hope for them, enjoyment, equal respect and consideration, life and aspira-
tion, instead of drudgery and despair. When we get
that I imagine the people will make tolerable music for
themselves, even if all Beethoven's scores perish in the
interim."　　　　　　　　SHAW : *Music in London.*

Importance of the 'Nineties

We observed in an earlier chapter how "early Victorian"
in literary history comes to mean usually the period from
about the late 'twenties to the late 'sixties, and an historian
has remarked that "Victorian" and "nineteenth century" in
general history "become for many of us almost interchangeable
terms."

The importance of the 'nineties is that this decade seems
to represent, in more than dating, the end of the nineteenth
century and the beginning of the twentieth. So many things

in Victorian life either declined or came to an end during
this short period, and so many other things, most of which we
associate with the twentieth century, began their career. The
'nineties saw the recession of the Gladstonian, Liberal peace,
and the rise of the new, commercial Imperialism; the decline
of the old journalism, and the beginning of the new; the end
of the Aesthetic Movement, and the rapid rise, from small
beginnings in the late 'eighties, of the Fabian Movement of
informed social criticism; the decline of Victorian melodrama, and the gaining popularity of the problem play; the
passing of Victorian insularity, and the rising influence of
Continental ideas; the decline in orthodox religion and
morality, and the increasing prevalence of that less Puritan
way of life which had previously been the vogue only among
isolated individuals and coteries.

All these things, and their related literature, concern the
'nineties, either in particular or in culmination. It is a con-
fusing decade, partly because movements fundamentally hostile to one another—for instance, the new Imperialism and
the new Socialism—gained ground at the same time; partly
because writers usually connected with one movement had
contacts with another—as Oscar Wilde, the Aesthete *par
excellence*, held Socialist views, as Rudyard Kipling, the voice
of Imperialism, had family connections with the Pre-Raphaelites, the fathers of the Aesthetes, and as the Fabians, Shaw and
the Webbs, supported the imperial wing of the Liberal party.

In social and political history, and in the literature related
to them, the decade of the 'nineties, then, was the time of
definite change. No such change is observable in some important aspects of literature proper. In poetry, for instance, the
"Victorian era" extended to the early Georgians, and twentieth-century poetry can be said to have begun only with the
publication of Eliot and Pound, aided by Hopkins and the
later Yeats, in the decade 1916-25. In fiction, too, no great
change is noticeable between the last novels of George Eliot
and such varied early twentieth-century novels as Bennett's
Old Wives Tale, Forster's *Where Angels Fear to Tread*, and
Lawrence's *Sons and Lovers*, while the work of James and

Conrad spans together almost the entire half-century from 1875.

That is why, in this book, we have devoted the two preceding chapters to late Victorian literature proper, keeping this concluding chapter mainly for the literature connected with the social and political changes of the 'nineties. It it not possible, of course, to draw any definite line between "literature proper" and "literature connected with social and political changes", but it will be granted that such writers as Shaw, Wells, Kipling, even the Aesthetes themselves, have political or social connotations that are not particularly noticeable in contemporaries like Bridges, Hardy, Gissing, James, Conrad, or Housman. When we think of Imperialism, we immediately think of Kipling, too ; Fabian Socialism conjures up the vision of a red-bearded Irishman ; Science and H. G. Wells became almost synonymous terms for thousands of readers from 1895 onwards ; while the still favoured designation, "the naughty 'nineties", brings in, amidst much else, such things as the *Yellow Book* and the peculiar tastes of some of the followers of that harmless Oxford don who wrote *Marius the Epicurean*.

We are probably justified, then, in devoting this concluding chapter mainly to a number of movements of equal importance in social and in literary history. With much of literature proper, it needs to be repeated, there is no definite dividing line between nineteenth century and twentieth—unless we take the period 1910-20 as the nearest we can get to a division. But with social-literary history the nineteenth century ends as accurately in the 'nineties as it began almost exactly a hundred years before. And the decade is exceeded in complexity only by the period of the Industrial Revolution.

The New Imperialism

What is surprising about the majority of early Victorian literature, when considered alongside the contemporary expansion of British rule, is its lack of interest in the Empire. Dickens, the most popular writer of all, hardly mentions the subject ; the nearest he gets to it is in the treatment of the military family, the Bagnets, in *Bleak House*. His attitude was typical of the ordinary, Gladstonian Englishman of the middle classes and the Trade Unions. In 1860 most people were convinced that, with the granting of self-government to the colonies, the Empire was dead. It was not until Disraeli's Crystal Palace speech of 1872 that the imperial movement began in earnest; and even then it was abhorred by many typical Victorians.

Economics, politics, technical invention—all played their part in the change from the earlier modest or indifferent attitude to the normal attitude of the 'nineties. Victorian pacifism and the cult of "little England" gave way to bellicose imperialism by a succession of events which included developments of steam transport, foreign competition, and the rise of the German Empire, as well as those events—the speeches of Disraeli, the Suez Canal shares, the Imperial Crown of India, the Zulu and Afghan Wars, etc.—more usually associated with it. The very term "jingo", normally connected with the 'nineties, goes back to 1878, when the supporters of Disraeli's pro-Turkish policy against Russia adopted as their war-song a music-hall ditty containing the line, "We don't want to fight, but by jingo if we do . . ."

So the "new imperialism" of the late 'eighties and 'nineties, culminating in the rather sordid commercial adventure of the Boer War, was itself a culmination of a changed attitude towards the Empire that had begun in the early 'seventies. It was, very largely, a break in English tradition, and it is not an accident that it was connected in the 'nineties with the Northcliffe revolution in journalism.

Kipling, 1865-1936

The greatest exponent of the new imperialism was not Disraeli, nor even Rhodes or Chamberlain or the future Lord Northcliffe, but the author of a book called *Plain Tales from the Hills*, which, published in its collected form in 1888, immediately won enormous popularity. The young author, Rudyard Kipling, who was a journalist in India 1882-9, followed this success by *Soldiers Three* (1888), *The Light that Failed* (1890), *Barrack Room Ballads* (1892), *Many*

Inventions (1893), the two *Jungle Books* (1894-5), *The Seven Seas* (1896), *Captains Courageous* (1897), *Stalky and Co.* (1899), and *Kim* (1901)—to mention the chief that come within the period covered by this chapter. Between the ending of the Boer War and 1914, the popularity of Kipling declined, then renewed itself for a short time during the Great War, and afterwards fell away almost completely. His greatest popularity, and his most characteristic achievement, belong, quite naturally, to the period 1888-1902 of which he was the imperial voice.

It is fairly easy, at this distance of time, to separate the good from the bad in Kipling. It is generally recognised, for instance, that his best service to the Empire was rendered, not by his crude politics and his hymns of hate, but by his pictures of the British people at their work in all the regions of the world —as the celebrated poem *Recessional*, which *The Times* published in 1897 on the morrow of the Diamond Jubilee, expresses, for all its consciously humble manner, the better side of the imperial mind. The Biblical phraseology in this poem clearly indicates that, for Kipling and a good many of his contemporaries, the British were God's chosen people, chosen not so much for privilege as for service. This may be a sentimental, bumptious, half-baked idea, but it is, at any rate, preferable to the other side of Kipling—the side that gave us the stories of revenge, the notorious line, "Good killing at Paardeburg, the first good killing of the war", and this astonishing conversation from *Stalky and Co.*: "'Just imagine Stalky let loose on the south side of Europe, with a sufficiency of Sikhs and a reasonable prospect of loot!'—'You're too much of an optimist, Beetle.'" The "loot", the economic motive, doesn't predominate in Kipling, and it would be unjust to say that his talk of service and "burdens" was consciously designed to cover it up.

His chief literary merit is in the early short stories, in his *Jungle* books, meant principally for children, in *Kim*, and in the *Barrack Room Ballads*. This last may possibly be his most enduring work, though such a piece as *Tommy*, for instance, good though it is, was a piece designed to meet a particular need, defending with dignity and humour—if a trifle condescendingly in its studied dialect—"the common soldier" against that mixture of abstract enthusiasm and personal disdain which was so prevalent among the late Victorians. The defence is sound enough :

> We aren't no thin red 'eroes, nor we aren't no blackguards too,
> But single men in barricks, most remarkable like you. . .

Kipling and Conrad

Although some of Conrad's early works—*Almayer's Folly* (1895), *An Outcast of the Islands* (1896), *Tales of Unrest* (1898)—earned him the title of the "Kipling of the South Seas", there is an interesting contrast between the two writers, put at its most obvious by a recent biographer of Kipling, who writes : "Conrad holds delicate balances and weighs motives and worth as grimly as Justice herself; Kipling is a partisan who backs his heroes to the last." In other words, Conrad at his best is comparable with such great novelists as Jane Austen and George Eliot, while Kipling is superior to, but fundamentally on the same level as, such rightly popular magazine writers as Conan Doyle or Rider Haggard. Kipling is responsible, not only for a good deal of rather shoddy "patriotism", but for much of the subsequent developments in journalism and advertising. (He is one of the writers always recommended by advertising teachers.) Conrad, though influenced in his early life by Marryat and truly regarded as the Laureate of the British Merchant Service, was a student of the French masters and was intimately connected with the civilisation of the Continent. Kipling, despite his family connections with the Pre-Raphaelites, was essentially the genius of rawer, colonial civilisations; his advocacy of the supremacy of the White Race was very popular in America, where he lived from 1892 to 1896, and he was the acknowledged hero and model of Jack London.*

* Also of the early Edgar Wallace, who was a war correspondent in South Africa from 1899, and who frankly imitated Kipling in both his short stories of army life and in his novel *Sanders of the River*.

Conrad himself hardly comes into nineteenth-century literary history, because his greatest novels and *nouvelles*—for instance, *Typhoon, Nostromo, The Secret Agent*—were written in the Edwardian age. But *The Nigger of the 'Narcissus'* (1897) and *Lord Jim* (1900) belong to our period, and to the most attractive side of his work, and, more important still, his early life at sea and elsewhere formed the experiences which he often drew on in later life. His command of a river steamer in the Belgian Congo in 1890 was the genesis of perhaps his greatest *nouvelle, Heart of Darkness*. This, after appearing in *Blackwood's Magazine*, was published in 1902 as part of *Youth—A Narrative; and Two Other Stories*. The epigraph from *Grimm's Tales* which Conrad placed at the beginning of this collection is a good illustration of his philosophy :—". . . but the Dwarf answered : 'No, something human is dearer to me than the wealth of the world.' "

The Newspaper Revolution

Kipling was the Voice of Empire, in the sense thÀt he was its poet and novelist ; other influential Imperial voices in the 'nineties were the politicians Rhodes, Rosebery, and Chamberlain, and the newspaper proprietor Alfred Harmsworth, who became Lord Northcliffe in 1905.

Northcliffe—as it is convenient to call him, to distinguish him from his younger brother Harold Harmsworth, who became Lord Rothermere in 1914—was the chief instrument in the newspaper revolution that occurred in the 'nineties. He was an Irishman who apparently knew little or nothing about the literary tradition of the English people, and his *Daily Mail*, founded in 1896, was—despite some better points —remarkably like the sort of American journalism that Dickens had satirised in *Martin Chuzzlewit*. It was considered to be appropriate to the new reading public that had been formed by the Education Act of 1870 ; but this was a misapprehension, in view of the popularity of such excellent papers as Cobbett's and his successors right through the nineteenth century. It is important to keep entirely distinct the Liberal measure of 1870 and the Northcliffe revolution of 1896, because the former was a sincere effort towards public education, while the latter was a vigorous attempt, sponsored by the Conservative party, to substitute for public education national and imperial propaganda.

The revolution in journalism and advertising was not, then, a genuinely popular or democratic movement. It had no connection with the increasingly democratic Liberal party, no connection with such popular movements as the trade-union or the co-operative ; it was part of a general scheme by the Conservative party to take a greater hold upon London newspapers for propaganda purposes. Immediately *before* the revolution, as no less an authority than Mr Winston Churchill has pointed out, "The newspapers catered obediently for what was at once an educated and a popular taste."

What were the consequences of the Northcliffe revolution ? —which, to do Northcliffe justice, had been partly prepared for by a decline in the level of the old journalism in the 'eighties. The first consequence is obvious enough : instead of the newspapers "catering obediently for what was at once an educated and a popular taste", there began the twentieth-century distinction between "educated" public and "popular." The second chief consequence was hardly less serious : Northcliffe and his colleagues and commercial rivals had their virtues and their valuable qualities, and some parts of their revolution were necessary and praiseworthy, but the inevitable result of their methods of "big business" was either to drive more old-fashioned competitors from the field or to take them over, so creating a near monopoly. This is particularly apparent in the evening press : there are now (1950) only three London evening papers, the *Evening News*, the *Evening Standard*, and the *Star* ; how many there were before the newspaper "revolution" led inevitably to the newspaper "guillotine" can be seen from a passage in one of the Sherlock Holmes stories :—"Run to the advertising agency," says Holmes, "and have this put in the evening papers." "In which, sir ?" asks the commissionaire. "Oh," replies Holmes carelessly, "in the *Globe, Star, Pall Mall, St James's Gazette,*

Evening News, Standard, Echo, and any others that occur to you." *

We mentioned the decline in the level of the old journalism. This, of course, is a development difficult to trace briefly, but we can mention one instance—which has, significantly, a connection with the growth of imperial sentiment. In 1883 W. T. Stead took over the editorship of the *Pall Mall Gazette* from John Morley, and made the Expansion of Empire one of the planks in a policy that increased the paper's circulation but turned it from a sober literary organ, for which Matthew Arnold had written, into a newspaper almost of the type later made famous by Northcliffe. Stead's biographer says, indeed, that Northcliffe was "in his younger days much indebted to Stead for valuable help and counsel." That the *Pall Mall* under Stead sometimes did good work in the social field—particularly in showing up juvenile prostitution—must be mentioned in fairness.

So the situation in regard to the newspaper revolution is similar to that of the new imperialism, which was connected with it: both were culminations in the 'nineties of developments which were taking place in the 'seventies and 'eighties. All the blame cannot be laid at the door of the Imperial parties, nor, indeed, at the door of the new journalism, for it is a melancholy fact that *The Times* itself—as a recent volume of its *History* frankly admits—must bear a good deal of responsibility for provoking the Boer War.

The Fabians

The complications of the 'nineties are nowhere seen more plainly than in the imperial and undemocratic tastes of some

---

* A literary historian, in an authoritative work, writes: "At the end of the nineteenth century, the Londoner had nine evening papers to choose from; now he has three. No one will have the hardihood to assert that these survive through any special fitness: they are in every respect inferior to their vanished rivals. The *Echo*, the *St James's Gazette*, the *Pall Mall Gazette*, the *Globe*, and the *Westminster Gazette* had qualities to which the existing evening papers of London can make no pretence; and they were crushed out of existence by brute forces that have nothing whatever to do with journalism."

prominent members of the Fabian Society—a Socialist propagandist and research organisation which had been founded in 1884.* The Fabians split on the imperialist issue, some being strong opponents of the policy that led to the Boer War (and perhaps to the Great War), while others, notably Bernard Shaw and Sidney Webb, were supporters of Rosebery and Chamberlain. Webb wrote an article in the *Nineteenth Century* in which he congratulated Rosebery on having forsaken the pacifist tradition of the old Liberal party ; and Shaw made speeches protesting against the doctrine that small nations had the right to determine their own government.

A feature of the Liberal party during this period was its increasing democracy : most of the local Liberal organisations were controlled by artisans and trade unionists. But the Fabians were sometimes as undemocratic as their rivals, the Marxist "Social Democratic Federation", founded about the same time by Karl Marx's disciple H. M. Hyndman. Shaw's notorious phrase—"I have never had any feelings about the English working classes except a desire to abolish them and replace them by sensible people"—is not only proof of an astonishing ignorance about the development of English culture and democracy, but can be fairly compared with Marx's phrase about "the reactionary lusts and prejudices of the workers."

This, with the Webbs' attempt to introduce into English life the Bismarckian State Socialism of Prussia, represents the worse side of the Fabian Movement. The better side was, of course, the labours they undertook in the fields of local government and historical research. The leading figures were Sidney

---

* Its name was derived from Fabius *Cunctator*, a Roman general who earned that nickname, meaning "delayer", for his cautious tactics against Hannibal ; and it referred to the hope of the Society to bring about Socialism by a succession of gradual reforms. Among the early members were the psychologist Havelock Ellis, the Anglican clergyman Stewart Headlam, the future theosophist Mrs Besant, the civil servant Sidney Webb, the professor Graham Wallas, the journalist Bernard Shaw, besides such ardent reformers as Edward Carpenter and Henry Salt. Newspapers influenced by Fabian or similar ideas in the 'nineties included the Liberal *Daily Chronicle*, edited by H. W. Massingham, and the Socialist *Clarion*, edited by Robert Blatchford.

Webb and his wife Beatrice, *née* Potter, who had served her apprenticeship in the great social survey undertaken by Charles Booth. Their books included a *History of Trade Unionism* (1894), and their influence on actual practice in the twentieth century was nearly as great as the influence on early Victorian legislation of Bentham and the Benthamites.

Shaw's Journalism

Bernard Shaw was the most famous member of the Fabian Society, which he joined soon after its foundation. He was born in Dublin in 1856, and came to London when he was twenty; he died in 1950.

His early drama will concern us later on; here we must notice his early work in journalism. He is one of the greatest journalists and pamphleteers in English literature, a writer worthy of comparison in this field with Swift and Cobbett. That he was also one of the greatest of even Irish-born orators —and the Irish are as prominent in this line as in journalism and the drama—is the unanimous opinion of all those old enough to have heard him in his prime.

His first literary efforts were five novels, written between 1879 and 1883; they constitute his only real failure, and their titles need not concern us. He first attracted general attention by his articles on music, contributed to the *Star* during 1888-9 under the signature "Corno di Bassetto." Next came the music articles in the *World* (1890-4) and the dramatic criticisms in the *Saturday Review* (1895-8). In 1889 he had edited, and contributed to, *Fabian Essays in Socialism*, and in 1891 he published the essays called *The Quintessence of Ibsenism*.

His music and dramatic criticisms are among the best in English; he wrote as he spoke—bold, witty, full of enthusiasm and prejudice. His exposure of the conventional values of his time was as relentless here as in the early plays and prefaces. Against the typical undemocratic assertion quoted in the last section may be fairly contrasted the no less typical passage of eloquence—from one of his music criticisms— quoted in the epigraph to this chapter.

The Early Wells

The connection with the Fabian Movement of H. G. Wells (1866-1946) was less important, both in his and their early careers. In the last five or six years of the Victorian age, Wells was connected, above all, with the achievements of science. The success of his early scientific romances—*The Time Machine* (1895), *The War of the Worlds* (1898), *When the Sleeper Wakes* (1899), *The First Men in the Moon* (1901), to name some of the chief—was as tremendous as the themes ; no writer since Dickens had so great a success so early in life. And it was not simply an English or an Anglo-American success ; Wells gained almost from the first a European reputation. It was on the huge sales of translations of his early scientific novels and stories that the prosperity of a distinguished French publishing house was mainly founded ; and this was a pleasing return, in the relationship of Anglo-French popular fiction, for the earlier scientific romances of Jules Verne, which from the 'seventies onwards were so great an attraction to British youth.

The main literary importance of Wells belongs to the series of Dickensian novels which he wrote in the Edwardian age. These achievements were foreshadowed by *The Wheels of Chance* (1896) and *Love and Mr Lewisham* (1900). Wells resembles Dickens, not only in his early gigantic success, but in his lower-middle-class origin and in his treatment of London and suburban characters. He wrote many books throughout a long working life, much of his later production being frankly propagandist. He is likely to be known to future ages by his Edwardian novels and the best of his scientific romances—each of which is supreme in its class and period.

The Revival of the Drama

In a recent short history of English drama, out of more than a hundred and fifty pages only six are given to the pre-1892 nineteenth century. We discussed some of the implications of this barren stretch of dramatic time in an earlier chapter, and, whatever individual criticisms we may make of the plays of Shaw, Wilde, and their contemporaries, our gratitude to these men should never be lost sight of. The stress must always lie on their initial achievement, their break away from an enfeebled melodramatic tradition.

The outstanding figure is Shaw, whose own dramas were an extension of his dramatic (and social) criticism.* His entire *théâtre* belongs to "comedy"—in the old, almost Jonsonian sense—whether he is writing about prostitution or a modern Pygmalion. His dramatic career extends from 1892 to 1947, and only the first half-dozen or so of his fifty plays belong to the nineteenth century.

Some of these are among his finest achievements. His taste for empty paradox—the very thing, by the way, he had criticised in W. S. Gilbert—grew as he became world-famous, and these comparatively unpopular first plays are relatively free from this rather irritating brilliance. In *Widowers' Houses* (1892) he dealt with slum landlordism, and in *Mrs Warren's Profession* (1894) with prostitution, in a style at once witty and profound. In *Arms and the Man* (1894) he suggested that the romantic heroism of the soldier was a mere invention of civilians; in *The Philanderer, You Never Can Tell*, and *Candida*, he dramatised respectively the "new woman" of the pseudo-Ibsenites, the "new parent" and the old, and the marriage of a Socialist parson. All these plays can be fairly criticised for some defect or another—in *Candida*, for instance, there is the perfectly serious portrait of an incredible poetaster—but they were so very much superior to the average "commercial play" of the period that it seems fantastic that they gained their first real fame, not on the boards (*Mrs Warren* was actually banned by the censor), but by the publication in 1898 of the two volumes of *Plays Pleasant and Unpleasant*. Shaw is probably the only dramatist who has become famous in print first, then in the theatre afterwards.

Before each volume of his plays, from now onwards, he wrote a long, witty preface, the best of which can be

* The dramatic criticism of such writers as William Archer, A. B. Walkley, Edmund Gosse, and George Moore was also important at the time. The influence of European dramatists, particularly Ibsen, whom Archer translated, can be seen in much of the early Shaw and in Archer's book *The Old Drama and the New*.

compared, for journalistic brilliance, with the best of his earlier
criticism.   His philosophy of life, outlined in these prefaces
and then dramatised, is too big a subject for any brief
treatment here; it mainly belongs in history, like his overwhelming theatrical success, to the twentieth century.   The
achievement of Shaw has been the subject of numerous books
and articles, by Shaw and other admirers; his limitations can
perhaps best be seen in the comparison with his fellow-Irish-
man J. M. Synge, whose plays were written from 1903 to
1909.

Shaw and Oscar Wilde are the chief figures in this late
Victorian dramatic revival, but we can mention briefly here,
before going on to consider the career of Wilde, which is
connected with the Aesthetic Movement, several other dramatists who reacted, in their different ways, against the stock
Victorian tradition.

Henry Arthur Jones, whose early work we mentioned in
Chapter V, wrote in the 'nineties and after many problem
plays, notably *The Liars* (1896).   Sir Arthur Pinero (1855-
1934) was the most popular exponent of this kind of drama;
among his successes were *The Second Mrs Tanqueray* (1893)
and *Trelawny of the Wells* (1898).   Most of the dramatic
work of Sir James Barrie lies outside our period; already a
popular novelist, mainly by his *Little Minister* (1891), he
turned to the stage about the same time as Shaw, scoring
a success with his farcical comedy *Walker, London* (1892).
Of the comic operas of W. S. Gilbert (1836-1911), it will be
sufficient to remark on his successful partnership with Sullivan,
and their continued—and deserved—popularity.

Wilde, 1856-1900

Of Oscar Wilde's four comedies—*Lady Windermere's
Fan* (1892), *A Woman of No Importance* (1893), *An Ideal
Husband* (1894), *The Importance of Being Earnest* (1895)—
the last-named is by far the most important.   It is accepted
now as a classic comedy in the artificial "drawing-room"
style, much the wittiest play produced in Britain since the
time of Sheridan.

It is not full of talk, as most of Shaw's plays are ; it is full of conversation. Wilde himself, it is generally agreed, was one of the most eloquent and witty conversationalists in English—even Irish—history ; he has often been compared with Sydney Smith and Disraeli. Born in Dublin, he became at Oxford and afterwards a leader of the aesthetic circle burlesqued in Gilbert's *Patience* and in Robert Hichens's novel *The Green Carnation*. His *Poems* appeared in 1881, and the macabre *nouvelle, The Portrait of Dorian Gray*, ten years later. In 1891 also appeared his critical essays *Intentions* and his pamphlet, *The Soul of Man Under Socialism*, written after hearing a lecture by Shaw.

For Wilde the whole purpose of life lay in artistic creation ; but he had been a disciple of Ruskin as well as of Pater at Oxford, so he became a Socialist for much the same reasons as Morris earlier, because he felt that a change of economic and social system would cause art to be more widely spread.

Like the Fabians, he combined a tenderness for the lower classes with a certain cheerful contempt for them. This superior attitude changed, however, in his last troubled years, after his two years' imprisonment for homosexual offences 1895-7. The Wilde of *De Profundis* and *The Ballad of Reading Gaol* (1898) was "a sadder and a wiser man" than the early Aesthete. The reference to the *Ancient Mariner* is quite appropriate, for there is clearly some influence of Coleridge—whom Wilde also resembles in his power of conversation and in the rather unsatisfactory nature of his achievement—in *The Ballad of Reading Gaol*.

The End of the Aesthetic Movement

The career of Wilde is partly symbolic of the career of the Aesthetic Movement in its culminating period in the late 'eighties and 'nineties. He spent his last years in Paris ; and the Aesthetic Movement was as much a Parisian product as an Oxonian. He was converted to Roman Catholicism ; so were Henry Harland, editor of the *Yellow Book*, the poets Dowson and Lionel Johnson, the novelist Frederick Rolfe

("Baron Corvo"), and others. He had perverted sexual tendencies; and these are apparent in several others of the *fin de siècle* or decadent school, most obviously in Rolfe.

But there is more to the Aesthetic Movement, even in its last phase, than just French influence, Papist tendencies, and addiction to drink, women, drugs, etc. Behind it stand Pater and the Pre-Raphaelites, and with it are connected the artists Whistler and Beardsley, and also to a certain extent "the Celtic Revival", associated with the novelist George Moore, the journalist Frank Harris, and the poets W. B. Yeats and "A.E." (G. W. Russell).* Posterity may see the Aesthetic Movement as an early item in the career of Yeats. The opening poem of his *Responsibilies* (1914) refers to

> Poets with whom I learned my trade,
> Companions of the Cheshire Cheese . . .

The "Cheshire Cheese" was the meeting-place of the Rhymers' Club, who produced two volumes of verse: *The Book of the Rhymers' Club* (1892) and *The Second Book of the Rhymers' Club* (1894). Yeats's companions included Ernest Dowson, Lionel Johnson, Arthur Symons, Richard Le Gallienne, and Ernest Rhys; and among the poems printed were such well-known pieces as Yeats's *Lake Isle of Innisfree*, Johnson's *By the Statue of King Charles at Charing Cross*, and Dowson's *Cynara*. John Davidson's *Fleet Street Eclogues* (1893) was also a collection much admired at the time, but it hardly contains anything equal to the best verse of the Rhymers.

* It should be added that "the Celtic Revival" in its full sense was a more important thing than a mere appendage of the Anglo-French aesthetic movement. In a lengthy history of English literature in the late nineteenth century, "Anglo-Irish" poetry and prose (*i.e.* work done by Irishmen in English) would need a separate chapter. We have considered some of the more important figures, and we can mention here the poet Aubrey de Vere and the historian and romancer Standish O'Grady. The influence of O'Grady's work was tremendous; if any single writer can be said to have initiated the Celtic Revival in its full sense—intimately connected with the political movement for independence—it is he. From the point of view of literature alone, the Revival reached its zenith with the founding in 1904 of the Abbey Theatre, Dublin, and the plays of Synge.

The main influence of the Aesthetes was through two short-lived periodicals, the *Yellow Book* (1894-7) and the *Savoy* (1896). The former was the real organ of the Movement, though it also printed such writers as Henry James, Arnold Bennett, Charlotte Mew, Kenneth Grahame, John Buchan, and Canon Beeching; the latter, which opened with an article by Bernard Shaw, was edited by Arthur Symons, who wrote *The Symbolist Movement in Literature* (1899). The tone of the *Yellow Book* was set by the illustrations of Aubrey Beardsley; and in general the literary contents lived up or down to that curious mixture of Pre-Raphaelitism and precocity. It aroused a storm of protest, but now seems almost innocuous and completely unexciting; whether that change itself represents its influence is uncertain.

In fiction, the work of that rather spurious genius George Moore (1852-1933) must be mentioned. Born in Ireland, he was educated in the cafés and studios of Paris, and tried to paint before turning to literature in London. His *Confessions of a Young Man* (1888) was the first of his autobiographical fantasias; his first novel, *A Modern Lover* (1883), was followed, among others, by *A Mummer's Wife* (1885), *Esther Waters* (1894), and *Evelyn Innes* (1898). Probably the best of these is the popular *Esther Waters*, though *A Mummer's Wife*, inspired by Flaubert's *Madame Bovary*, has been much praised. Moore was an aesthetic dilettante, but deserves respect for making better known in England some of the contemporary French poets and artists.

Short stories and *nouvelles* naturally flourished in this Gallophil atmosphere. We can mention in conclusion the work in this field of Max Beerbohm, M. P. Shiel, Arthur Machen, Frank Harris, "Baron Corvo", Henry Harland, and Hubert Crackanthorpe. Of the various controversies concerning the 'nineties, and Oscar Wilde in particular, that went on after they had both died—and which are associated with the rather curious figures of Lord Alfred Douglas, T. W. H. Crosland, and Frank Harris—all that needs to be said here is that they belong, like George Moore's autobiographies, to the history of self-advertisement rather than literature.

The Early Poetry of Yeats

We began this book with a great nineteenth-century poet, Wordsworth, who wrote his early poetry in the eighteenth century ; we end it with a great twentieth-century poet who wrote his early poetry in the nineteenth. Wordsworth is probably the greatest poet of the one century, Yeats is likely to be considered the greatest poet of the other.

W. B. Yeats (1865-1939) was the son of a well-known Irish artist. His early narrative poems and lyrics often remind us of the Pre-Raphaelites—Morris rather than Rossetti—but they are undoubtedly the early works of original genius, probably the best verse produced in their time. His poetic dramas are comparatively unimportant ; they include *The Countess Kathleen* (1892) and *The Land of Heart's Desire* (1894). During this period he was also writing prose, notably the collection of Irish sketches *The Celtic Twilight* (1893), and was absorbed in problems of mysticism.

In the collected edition of the lyrics, containing some three hundred pages, the nineteenth-century part occupies only about seventy-five. So we must not claim too much for the young Yeats, in view of the astonishing achievement, both in quality and quantity, of the older poet. His best work, in general, dates from 1914 to 1933. But there are some fine things in each of the early volumes. *Crossways* (1889) contains, for instance, *The Sad Shepherd, Down by the Salley Gardens, The Ballad of Moll Magee*, and *The Falling of the Leaves. The Rose* (1893), dedicated to Lionel Johnson, contains, besides the famous *Innisfree*, such notable poems as *To the Rose upon the Rood of Time, The Rose of the World, A Dream of Death, The Ballad of Father Gilligan*, and *To Ireland in the Coming Times.* And some of the vigour that makes him, even thus early, not merely a charming Pre-Raphaelite dreamer, can be seen in a short poem, *He thinks of his Past Greatness when a Part of the Constellations of Heaven*, in the 1899 collection, *The Wind Among the Reeds* :

> I have drunk ale from the Country of the Young
> And weep because I know all things now :
> I have been a hazel-tree, and they hung

The Pilot Star and the Crooked Plough
Among my leaves in times out of mind :
I became a rush that horses tread :
I became a man, a hater of the wind,
Knowing one, out of all things, alone, that his head
May not lie on the breast nor his lips on the hair
Of the woman that he loves, until he dies.
O beast of the wilderness, bird of the air,
Must I endure your amorous cries ?

The End of the Victorian Age

We have seen that, so far as social history is concerned, the Victorian era and the nineteenth century truly came to an end during the 'nineties. The Queen herself did not long outlive the century more than half of which bears her name ; and the Boer War, virtually over at the time of her death, came to an end early in 1902. The Liberal party, which had been dominant so long during her reign and then had suffered the recession of the late 'nineties and early twentieth century, was returned to power in 1906 with a huge majority.

The Edwardian age is, of course, outside the limits of this book, but we have rightly considered a few of the more important Edwardian writers who did their early work under Victoria. Conrad, Wells, James, Bridges, Housman, Bennett, Binyon, Sturge Moore . . . these writers, of varying ages and in various fields, became more widely known in the early twentieth century. Yeats encouraged Synge to write those dramatic masterpieces, which, together with the work of Yeats himself, Shaw, Galsworthy, Barrie, Maugham, Granville-Barker, and other playwrights, make the Edwardian drama so superior to the Victorian. Religious, historical, and political controversy remained a feature of literature : Belloc and Chesterton, McCabe and Coulton, Shaw and the Webbs . . . such writers had their influence and their enemies. A disturbing aspect of journalism was the increasing power over the press of a few "newspaper barons", with the tendency, already noted, of newspapers to deteriorate in quality and decrease in number.

Looking back now, after this brief glance forward, what is the most distinctive feature of Victorian and nineteenth-century literature ? Compared with the literature of more modern times, we can fairly lay the stress on its seriousness, combined with its popularity ; compared with the literature of the eighteenth century, we can lay the stress on its variety. It is one of the most interesting centuries in English literature, in all but the drama ; and it is the century which we to-day have rightly come back to, for more mature consideration, after the inevitable denigration of our twentieth-century adolescence.

BIBLIOGRAPHY

(a) MAIN SOURCES OF THE PRESENT WORK

Where the author desires to express his special indebtedness to particular parts or chapters, the detailed references will be found in parentheses, following the main reference.

(i) History

DAWSON, Christopher. *The Spirit of the Oxford Movement.* 1933. A brilliant and original book, written from the Roman Catholic point of view.

GRISEWOOD, Harman (foreword to). *Ideas and Beliefs of the Victorians: An Historic Revaluation of the Victorian Age.* 1949. Talks by fifty authorities, originally broadcast on the B.B.C. Third Programme. (The contributions by Noel Annan, Alfred Cobban, J. W. Davidson, Christopher Dawson, R. C. K. Ensor, Humphry House, Bertrand Russell, F. Sherwood Taylor, G. M. Trevelyan, and G. M. Young.)

HALÉVY, Élie. *The Growth of Philosophical Radicalism.* Translated 1928, new edition 1949, from the French, 1900. The authoritative work on Bentham and the Utilitarians. *A History of the English People in the Nineteenth Century.* Translated 1924 from the French, first volume 1913. Five volumes, corresponding to two of the original, in the *Pelican* series, first volume 1938. The outstanding work on the subject.

HAMMOND, J. L. and Barbara. *The Age of the Chartists.* 1930. Reconstructed and revised in a more general form for the non-specialist reader as *The Bleak Age*, 1934. New edition of this in the *Pelican* series, 1946, enlarged and revised.

KEIR, David. *Newspapers.* 1948. A brief general account in the *Merlin* series. For a more critical account of the developments of the 'nineties and after, see *The Press and the Organisation of Society*, by Norman Angell, 1933.

SAINTSBURY, George. *A History of Nineteenth Century Literature:* 1780-1900. Third edition, revised, 1901.

SAMPSON, George. *The Concise Cambridge History of English Literature.* 1941. An authoritative academic work, based in detail on the fourteen volumes of *The Cambridge History of English Literature,* edited by A. W. Ward and A. R. Waller, 1907-16. (Part of Chapter XI, Chapters XII-XIII, part of Chapter XIV.)

SOMERVELL, D. C. *English Thought in the Nineteenth Century.* 1929. An excellent general work. (Material on Scott, the Evangelicals, Malthus, the Utilitarians, Tennyson, the Oxford Movement, Science and Religion, and Imperialism.)

STRONG, L. A. G., and REDLICH, Monica. *Life in English Literature.* 1932. New edition, 1949. A simple introduction, with examples. (Part III: Goldsmith to Browning.)

WYATT, A. J., and CLAY, Henry. *Modern English Literature: 1798-1935.* Second edition, enlarged, 1936. (Chapters I-XII.)

(ii) Criticism

AVELING, Edward and Eleanor Marx. *Shelley's Socialism.* First printing 1948 of lectures delivered 1888.

CHURCHILL, R. C. *Disagreements: A Polemic on Culture in the English Democracy.* 1950.

COLE, G. D. H. *Persons and Periods.* 1938. Reprint in the *Pelican* series, 1945. (The chapter on Cobbett.)

ELIOT, T. S. *Selected Essays.* Second edition, revised and enlarged, 1934. (Essays in Section VII on Arnold and Pater, Francis Herbert Bradley, Wilkie Collins and Dickens.)

JACKSON, Holbrook. *Dreamers of Dreams: The Rise and Fall of Nineteenth-Century Idealism.* 1948. (The chapters on Carlyle, Ruskin, and Morris.)

LEAVIS, F. R. *New Bearings in English Poetry.* 1932. (Chapter V: the first detailed study of Hopkins.) *Revaluation: Tradition and Development in English Poetry.* 1936. (The chapters on Wordsworth and Keats.)

The Great Tradition: George Eliot, Henry James, Joseph Conrad. 1948. (The chapter on George Eliot and the note on Dickens's *Hard Times.*)

(editor). *Scrutiny: A Quarterly Review.* 1932-date. Original critical work on past and present literature. (Essays on Jane Austen by Q. D. Leavis and D. W. Harding, on the Great Reviews by R. G. Cox, on nineteenth-century journalism by Denys Thompson, on Hopkins and on Bentham and Mill by F. R. Leavis, on Hardy by Frank Chapman, on Gissing and on Jefferies by Q. D. Leavis, on Dickens and the dramatic tradition by R. C. Churchill.)

LEAVIS, Q. D. *Fiction and the Reading Public.* 1934.

ORWELL, George. *Critical Essays.* 1946. Essays on literature and society, from a Socialist viewpoint. (The essays on Dickens and Kipling.)

ROBERTS, Michael. *The Modern Mind.* 1937. (Chapters VI and VIII.)

SANTAYANA, George. *Interpretations of Poetry and Religion.* 1900. (The essay on Browning and Whitman.)
Soliloquies in England and Later Soliloquies. 1922. (The essay on Dickens.)

STEPHEN, Leslie. *Hours in a Library.* Three series, various dates.

SWINNERTON, Frank. *George Gissing: A Critical Study.* 1912.

THOMPSON, Denys. *Reading and Discrimination.* 1934. (Material on Lamb and Hardy.)

WOOLF, Virginia. *The Common Reader.* 1925. Reprint in the *Pelican* series, 1938. (The chapters on Jane Austen, the Brontës, George Eliot.)

Articles: in the *Adelphi* by John Middleton Murry; in the *Literary Guide* by Marjorie Bowen and A. D. Cohen; in the *New Statesman and Nation* by Noel Annan, Raymond Mortimer, V. S. Pritchett, and R. A. L. Smith; in the *Spectator* by W. J. Turner; and in the *Contemporary Review*, the *Criterion, John o'London's Weekly*, the *New English Review, Politics and Letters*, and *Tribune* by R. C. Churchill.

(iii) Biography

ACLAND, Alice. *Caroline Norton.* 1948. (Material on the Regency background.)

BULLETT, Gerald. *George Eliot.* 1947.

BURDETT, Osbert. *The Brownings.* 1928.

COLE, G. D. H. *William Cobbett.* 1925. An outstanding biography.

CROFT-COOKE, Rupert. *Rudyard Kipling.* 1948.

CROSS, J. W. (editor). *George Eliot's Life, as related in her Letters and Journals.* New edition: no date.

FORSTER, John. *The Life of Charles Dickens.* 1874.

MEYNELL, Esther. *Portrait of William Morris.* 1947.

MILLMORE, Royston. *Brief Life of the Brontës.* 1947.

MORLEY, John (first editor). *English Men of Letters.* Various dates. (The volumes on Thackeray by Anthony Trollope, on Wordsworth by F. W. H. Myers, on Tennyson by Alfred Lyall, on Browning by G. K. Chesterton, on Rossetti by A. C. Benson.)

MORPURGO, J. E. (editor). *Charles Lamb and Elia.* In the *Penguin* series, 1948.

PEARSON, Hesketh. *Dickens: His Character, Comedy, and Career.* 1949.

REITZEL, William (editor). *The Autobiography of William Cobbett.* 1947. New edition of *The Progress of a Plough-Boy to a Seat in Parliament*, first compiled 1933.

SHARP, William. *Dante Gabriel Rossetti: A Record and a Study.* 1882.

STEPHEN, Leslie. *Some Early Impressions.* 1903. Interesting observations of Mill, Maurice, Kingsley, Newman, Carlyle, Ruskin, Tennyson, Darwin, Huxley, Spencer, Stevenson, etc., of the University reforms of the 'fifties and 'sixties, and of the "higher journalism" of the pre-Northcliffe era.

THOMAS, Edward. *Richard Jefferies: His Life and Work.* 1909. An excellent biography.

THOMPSON, Edward. *Robert Bridges:* 1844-1930. 1944. The centenary portrait.

(iv) Editions and Anthologies

Edited by:—

AITKEN, James. *English Letters of the Nineteenth Century.* In the *Pelican* series, 1946.

BAX, Clifford. *The Poetry of the Brownings.* 1948. An anthology, with commentary.

EVANS, Marjorie R. (with introduction by B. Ifor Evans). *An Anthology of Victorian Verse.* 1949. A much smaller anthology than the *Oxford*, q.v., but more representative, partly owing to the greater space given to Hopkins since the collected edition.

FISHER, James. *The Natural History of Selborne,* by Gilbert White. 1947. With White's poems.

FORMAN, Maurice Buxton. *The Letters of John Keats.* 1935.

FURLONG, Norman. *English Satire.* 1946.

GORE, John. *Creevey.* 1948.

JACKSON, Holbrook. *On Art and Socialism: Lectures and Essays by William Morris.* 1947.

MILFORD, H. S. *The Oxford Book of Regency Verse.* 1928. Reissued 1935 as *The Oxford Book of English Verse of the Romantic Period:* 1798-1837.

QUILLER-COUCH, Arthur. *The Oxford Book of Victorian Verse.* 1912. Comprehensive, if rather erratic: "Q" included Ezra Pound and others among "the Victorian poets", on the analogy of the Jacobean dramatists being often comprehended in "the Elizabethans."

RAY, Cyril. *Scenes and Characters from Surtees.* In the *Falcon Classics* series, 1948.

READ, Herbert, and DOBRÉE, Bonamy. *The London Book of English Prose.* Second, revised edition, 1949.

The London Book of English Verse. Second edition, 1949.

RHYS, Ernest. *The Prelude to Poetry. Everyman* edition, 1927. Essays on poetry by Scott, Wordsworth, Coleridge, Byron, etc. A useful collection.

RUBINSTEIN, Stanley. *The Street Trader's Lot: London* 1851. 1947. Selections from Henry Mayhew's *London Labour and the London Poor.*

SAMPSON, George. *Selected Essays of Hazlitt.* 1917. Useful Introduction and detailed Notes on Hazlitt, Lamb, and their contemporaries.

(b) FURTHER READING

The material on nineteenth-century literature is as proportionally voluminous as the work itself. In addition to those mentioned above, the following brief list of books notable in their several fields may be useful recommendation for some readers.

(i) History

COLLET, C. D. *History of the Taxes on Knowledge: Their Origin and Repeal.* 1899. Reprint in the *Thinker's Library* series, 1933. An authoritative work on the struggle for liberty of the press.

DOBRÉE, Bonamy. *The Victorians and After. Introduction to English Literature* series. 1938. Covers the period 1837-1914.

GAUNT, William. *The Aesthetic Adventure.* 1945. A useful introduction to the period of Swinburne and Pater, George Moore and Oscar Wilde.

HOUSE, Humphry. *The Dickens World.* 1942.

JACKSON, Holbrook. *The Eighteen Nineties.* 1913. Reprint available in the *Pelican* series: new issue, 1950.

LASKI, Harold. *Political Thought in England from Locke to Bentham. Home University Library.* 1920. An excellent general study of the eighteenth-century background of the Utilitarians.

MORGAN, Charles. *The House of Macmillan* (1843-1943). 1943. The centenary portrait of one of the most distinguished of Victorian publishing foundations. Compare, for Regency book-selling and publishing, the memoirs of Constable and Murray.

(ii) Criticism

BRADBROOK, M. C. *Joseph Conrad: Poland's English Genius.* 1941.

BROOKS, Cleanth. *The Well-Wrought Urn: Studies in the Structure of Poetry.* 1949.

FORSTER, E. M. *Aspects of the Novel.* 1927.

GARDNER, W. H. *Gerard Manley Hopkins:* 1844-1889. A detailed centenary study: first volume, 1944; second, 1949.

MURRY, John Middleton. *Aspects of Literature.* 1920.
The Problem of Style. 1922.
Studies in Keats. Second, revised edition, 1939.

SHAW, Bernard. *Dramatic Opinions and Essays.* 1907.
Back to Methuselah: A Metabiological Pentateuch. 1921. Reprint in the *Penguin* series. The Preface: on Darwin and Lamarck.
Our Theatres in the 'Nineties. Three volumes, 1931. Collected from articles in the *Saturday Review*, 1895-8.

SPEIRS, John. *The Scots Literary Tradition.* 1940. The chapter on George Douglas.

STEPHEN, Leslie. *An Agnostic's Apology.* 1893. Reprint in the *Thinker's Library*, 1931. The essay on Newman.

VERSCHOYLE, Derek (editor). *The English Novelists.* 1936. The essays by Edwin Muir on Scott, by Sean O'Faolain on Dickens and Thackeray, by Catherine Carswell on Butler, by Graham Greene on Henry James.

WILLEY, Basil. *Nineteenth-Century Studies.* 1949.

WILSON, Edmund. *The Wound and the Bow.* 1941. The essays on Dickens and Kipling.

WOOLF, Virginia. *The Common Reader: Second Series.* 1932. The essay on Hardy.

(iii) Biography

BRAILSFORD, H. N. *Shelley, Godwin, and their Circle.* *Home University Library.* 1913.

FORD, Ford Madox. *Return to Yesterday.* Reminiscences of Henry James, Conrad, and their contemporaries.
Mightier than the Sword. 1938. Memories and criticisms of Swinburne, Hardy, Hudson, James, Conrad, and other writers.

GILCHRIST, Alexander. *Life of William Blake.* 1863. Reprint in the *Everyman* series.

GODWIN, George. *The Great Mystics. Thinker's Library,* 1945. The chapter on Blake.

GOSSE, Edmund. *Father and Son: A Study of Two Temperaments.* 1928. Reprint in the *Penguin* series.

HOBSON, J. A. *John Ruskin, Social Reformer.* 1898.

HONE, Joseph. *W. B. Yeats:* 1865-1939. 1943.

JOAD, C. E. M. *Samuel Butler.* 1924.

LEGOUIS, Emile. *The Early Life of William Wordsworth,* 1770-1798. *A Study of "The Prelude."* English translation from the French.

MATHEW, David. *Acton, the Formative Years.* 1946. The first part of a detailed biography and study of the great Victorian historian, by a distinguished modern historian.

MOTTRAM, R. H. *Buxton the Liberator.* 1946. Early chapters useful for cultural background of the late eighteenth century and early nineteenth.

PEARSON, Hesketh. *The Smith of Smiths.* 1934. Reprint in the *Penguin* series. On Sydney Smith of the *Edinburgh Review.*

The Life of Oscar Wilde. 1946.

SADLEIR, Michael. *Trollope: A Commentary.* 1927.

TENNYSON, Charles. *Alfred Tennyson.* 1949. A detailed biography by the poet's grandson.

INDEX